D1736161

# ONLY THE LIGHT MOVES

"We went down into the silent garden,
Dawn is the time where nothing breathes,
The hour of silence. Everything is transfixed; only the light moves."

Leonora Carrington

# ONLY THE LIGHT MOVES

## ★ ★ ★

FLYING COVERT RECONNAISSANCE MISSIONS IN
THE VIETNAM WAR

## FRANCIS DOHERTY

AIR WORLD

AIR WORLD

## ONLY THE LIGHT MOVES
### Flying Covert Reconnaissance Missions in the Vietnam War

First published in Great Britain in 2023 by
Airworld
*An imprint of*
Pen & Sword Books Ltd
Yorkshire – Philadelphia

Copyright © Francis Doherty, 2023

ISBN 978 1 39905 701 1

Typeset by SJmagic DESIGN SERVICES, India.

Printed and bound in the UK by CPI Group (UK) Ltd.

Pen & Sword Books Ltd includes the Imprints of Atlas, Archaeology, Aviation, Discovery, Family History, Fiction, History, Maritime, Military, Military Classics, Politics, Select, Airworld, Frontline Publishing, Leo Cooper, Remember When, Seaforth Publishing, The Praetorian Press, Wharncliffe Local History, Wharncliffe Transport, Wharncliffe True Crime and White Owl.

For a complete list of Pen & Sword titles please contact

PEN & SWORD BOOKS LTD
George House, Units 12 & 13, Beevor Street, Off Pontefract Road,
Barnsley, South Yorkshire, S71 1HN, England
E-mail: enquiries@pen-and-sword.co.uk
Website: www.pen-and-sword.co.uk

or
PEN AND SWORD BOOKS
1950 Lawrence Rd, Havertown, PA 19083, USA
E-mail: uspen-and-sword@casematepublishers.com
Website: www,penandswordbooks.com

# Contents

First Words About Years Ago: Do I Die Today? ........................................vi

Chapter 1    Dawn..............................................................................1

Chapter 2    *Nha Trang's* Mosquitos........................................7

Chapter 3    O-1 Bird Dog ..........................................................20

Chapter 4    Be Like Dad............................................................36

Chapter 5    MACVSOG .............................................................56

Chapter 6    Celestina .................................................................68

Chapter 7    The Central Highlands..........................................72

Chapter 8    Our Bloody Spring ................................................98

Chapter 9    Arlie Deaton .........................................................113

Chapter 10   John Glimis Pappas ............................................133

Chapter 11   Lloyd Harbor ........................................................144

Chapter 12   The Top of Richard Lane.....................................149

Chapter 13   Alabama Sweet Tea..............................................153

Chapter 14   Just Like Dad.......................................................157

Chapter 15   Ask Me No Secrets..............................................168

Chapter 16   Now Dad Knows .................................................175

Chapter 17   Ashes....................................................................182

Chapter 18   My Old Heart.......................................................188

Last Words .........................................................................................197

Acknowledgements............................................................................201

References...........................................................................................204

Index ..................................................................................................206

# First Words About Years Ago

# Do I Die Today?

**FOB2, *Kontum*, 1970**

The colors of back then, the sounds from that time, the smells from those days, they hang not on the edges of memory. No. They live in the center of moments ago. Unchanging over years, constant in their content, unrelenting in their persistence. Refusing to submit to the eraser of the past. The colors of me are brown. I am brown. My skin is brown. From the sun and from the earth in this compound that is powdery, dry, and lifeless. It clogs the pores of my face and my scalp, clings to the backs of my hands, my neck, and my ears. I wonder if I will ever be clean again.

The *Dak Bla* is brown, sluggish, silted, and thick. I can almost hold its water in my cupped hands, so full of other things that it barely oozes between my fingers or slips by the grassy banks that contain it.

The clothes I wear are brown. The trucks and jeeps and tents and sandbags around me are brown. Even my Bird Dog, my airplane. Brown. A brown that makes no statement. It is not supposed to. Because this drab hue is meant to be nondescript. To not call attention to itself, but rather to lose itself in everything around it. A brown that isn't seen, a brown that is just there.

Animal sounds are alarms. When they are quiet, I listen harder. In the mornings before dawn, the chatter of monkeys and birds announce normalcy, no predators, all is well. The absence of their singing, howling, squealing, means that something is hunting. Something may move on four legs. Something may move on two. This is a part of the day that is fraught with fear. No noise. The reassuring song of my Bird Dog's engine fades into the background. I know it is there, but its consistent melody is predictable, which makes it reassuring. I don't listen to its monotonous throb; I listen for its missed beat. My engine's missed beat is as frightening as quiet monkeys.

A siren's pre-dawn wail is surprising when it goes off, but my response is automatic. Incoming! Get to the floor, flak jacket and helmet on, my hand strangling the sling of my AR15. Crawl for the bunker and listen to the whumps or cracks. Whumps mean mortars, cracks mean small arms, and small arms mean the compound is being assaulted. Whumps scare me but not as much as cracks, because cracks mean that I might see someone, and have to fire this rifle at someone. And someone might fire back, or fire first.

Even now, when I hear rotor blades shredding the air, I look up. Helicopters. The sound is unmistakable, a memory inescapable. Whupwhupwhupwhupwhup, a rhythmic percussion of metal and air. To a team in contact, the sound of our F-4s' whining turbines with tongues of flame flashing from their exhausts, or the chugging throb of the A-1s' big radial engines, shouts safety. Under the umbrella of the attack aircraft, the whupwhupwhup of a Huey means survival. The rapid staccato of the door gunners' .30 caliber machine guns means protection as the team climbs on board. The roar of the Huey's engine as it climbs away means life.

Vietnam is a cacophony of smells. The sour smell of rotting vegetation mingles with the sweetness of jasmine vines. A sauce of fermented fish heads mingles with the sharp nasal pinch of ground chili stirred into a sesame oil. Livestock feces fertilizes rice paddies, and the air is fouled with diesel fuel fires disposing of the contents of our latrines.

What is remembered so profoundly is the smell of myself. Of the brown flight suit that has soaked up the smell of me. A brown cocoon of sweat-drenched Nomex, which is not supposed to burn, so rigid from salt that it could walk to the airplane without me in it. The blanket of humidity that keeps me wet, but never cool. The moisture that soaks the stiffness out of the Nomex but makes its smell worse. A smell of humid damp and sweaty rivers of fear, stains from my churning stomach splashed on me, which made me almost ill. If the water is turned on at our compound, I try to stand under it for as long as I can. And scrub my body without taking my flight suit off, then scrub my naked self. Scrub until I scrub myself raw. Then go after my flight suit again. I rinse it, I rinse myself, but both still assault my nose. Someday, I mutter, I will get clean.

Fear smells. Its odor is stirred into the other smells, leaks out from my armpits, it runs down my back, and drips into my eyes. It rides on bullets that race toward the Bird Dog. It reminds me of my mortality. It demands that I pay attention. Fear tests my reaction time, strains the relationship between reason and response. It shouts at me to move without thinking.

It whispers to me that I would be better off if I don't listen to what panic is demanding that I *do*. That I just *do*, that I should trust the *do*. And if I trust it, *do* will guide my hands and feet, direct my ears and eyes. It will keep my heart from exploding.

An Air Force F-4 swoops down in a roar of twin turbines, filling my cockpit with the howl of its engines. A big fighter-bomber, it dwarfs my Bird Dog. It launches a series of rockets that slam into a huge compound we have found. Flame and dirt and leaves splash upward out in front of it, and the F-4 continues down. Straight, unswerving, descending. I look for muzzle-flashes from anti-aircraft guns but don't see any. The F-4 continues. Down. The words begin to form. My voice starts to say, "pull up." But the F-4 can't hear me. Before the words take shape a flash of orange. The F-4 skips off one ridgeline like a flat rock flung across glassy water. A napalm canister ignites behind it. I see the airplane's nose drop. It bores into the jungle and explodes in a fireball of napalm and rockets and high explosives. I close my eyes for only a moment. I cannot spare another.

Compassion ceases to exist. It has no foothold in combat. It cannot. If I see a face attached to a body, if a voice shouts to me, if eyes find mine, I will have to make the target human. My Bird Dog shields my conscience from the carnage around me, even though it is so close. I can almost touch my enemy. Their faces unclear, their voices unheard, their eyes indiscernible. But they move, they run, they shoot or shoot back. I point at them with marking rockets; the F-4s kill them.

I think my airplane protects me from accountability. I don't have to hold myself responsible. Because I don't shoot to kill. I only identify targets. But I am wrong. Because there is a day when I fire a flechette rocket at close range. Little darts called nails. This rocket hits a man and turns his midsection into a burst of red. I cannot claim that I am one step removed this time. I fired the rocket. I see him die. And in my dreams, I will replay all of this. Over and over, again in the dark, where Vietnam rages, where nightmares drench my bedsheets. Nightmares enough to last a lifetime.

I know my flying-partners in the present tense. They have little past and no future tense. If you asked me about Phil Phillips, I could tell you that he grew up in Knoxville, didn't go to college, was at Fort Knox when I was there, and plays a very good guitar. I know that Phil is married, and that his wife has an unbelievable body, no sharp angles anywhere on it. I know this because Phil has a poster-sized photo of her tacked on the wall of our hooch. Her name is Sandy; Phil's given name is Claude. He doesn't talk about what will come after all this. Doug Krout is from Colorado and can sleep through anything. He is married, and his wife's name is Jeanie. I could be wrong though. Not once did Doug speculate about his future. John Meyers is mostly American Indian. He is married to a woman named Alvilda, is only in the here and now, and is convinced that he is bulletproof. This is as close as I get to the personal lives of the pilots with whom I fly. Sometimes we share a beer and maybe eat dinner together at night. We almost never eat in the mess hall on this Special Forces compound, Forward Observation Base Two. It is usually closed by the time we get back from flying all day. Dinner is up to us. Boiling water cooks little bags of rice and dehydrated vegetables and shrimp. With a hot chili oil that our hooch-maid, the young woman who cleans our hooch, a room not much bigger than a sandbagged hut, gave me. I am the only one who likes it. If we talk at all we usually talk about what we saw that day, where we saw it, and what we might do about what we saw. We don't say anything about surviving. We're here, drinking beer. We survived. Today.

We like each other, but we pretend that we are not close. Acknowledgement of how much we cared about one another happens only years later, at a reunion at the Vietnam Veterans Memorial. For now, we act as if we are keeping one another at arm's length, in a parade, marching distance apart, looking straight ahead. I know what these boys look like, and they in turn know what I look like, but our straight-ahead eyes cannot acknowledge that we have memorized every detail of each other's faces. We act as if we won't risk closeness, because maybe tomorrow a face might be missing. If I stop to really consider this, I know that it's a lot of baloney, a fake steeliness. Should something happen to any of them I would be devastated. I say I don't know them. And yet I have come to love them.

The people who ride with me on reconnaissance flights, the Special Forces recon men, the SOG team members? I know their names and faces. Nothing more. I doubt if they know my name because they never refer to me by it. They simply call me SPAF, my radio call-sign when I'm flying. It stands for Sneaky Pete Air Force. That's who I am. To them that is my name. They fly with me once, or maybe twice. And then, in the bloody spring of 1970, the mission changes. I seldom fly with a recon man after late winter bumps into spring. I get photo missions. If I fly a photo mission, a second airplane is flown by another SPAF pilot, usually Phil. Another boy, like me, who volunteered to be here. One of us is about 500 ft off the ground, the high ship, the cover ship. The other Bird Dog, the low ship, has the photographer in the backseat, and is flying with the airplane's wheels almost touching the treetops.

The photographer, using a huge lens on his Pentax, takes hundreds of pictures of what we find along and near the Ho Chi Minh Trail. These supplement and sometimes take the place of recon teams on the ground, inserted by Hueys into landing zones near the Trail. There are usually eight to ten men to a recon team: two or three Americans, the rest *Montagnards*, indigenous people recruited by our Special Forces. In the bloody spring of 1970 these teams suffered dead and wounded on every mission. Too many troopers are dying, the Special Forces command decides. Our photo missions replace some of the teams on the ground. Ten men on a team; one pilot in an old airplane. My Bird Dog and I mitigate the body count.

I don't wonder if I'm going to be shot at. There is a better than fifty-fifty chance that I am going to fly into AK-47 hell. When I know that I have to fly one of these missions I ask myself the same question each time. Do I die today?

Brown? Today I own nothing that is brown. Especially not a brown that disappears into leaves and vines and canopy. My eyes refuse to acknowledge that color which once covered me, the everywhere and the not-there color.

Rotor blades that slash the air? They are not benign. That sound can't be. It never blends into the background music of everyday life. A helicopter will always bring the memory of tracer rounds, bullets streaking red, ours. Or green. Theirs. Intersecting bullet-arcs of combat. Of rescue. Of death.

And sweat? I still sweat rivers. But not like I once did, when the rivers that ran down my back soaked my flight suit with fear. When I reeked of fear. When I tried to scrub and scrub and scrub. Tried to peel the fear-soaked skin from me.

Someday I will get clean.

*First printed in the Journal of Creative Nonfiction, issue 77, spring 2022*

# Chapter 1

# Dawn

**June 1970, Tenth Month**

It's so dark in the early morning. No ambient light, so the cloudless sky is a kaleidoscope of stars. The air is still, filled with night sounds. Birds, crickets, monkeys. Night sounds are good. If there's movement in the dark the crickets and birds shut right up. They're noisy now. I taxi with all the outside lights turned off and the instrument lights as dim as I can make them. No point in illuminating my silhouette. I'll turn them up just before getting on the runway and check the engine indications while lining up in the middle. I hope.

There are no runway lights at *Kontum*'s airfield. I can't really see the centerline. If one was ever painted on the metal mats that pretend to be a runway, it is long gone. But I can see the edges of this metal strip so guessing where the middle is should work. I ease the throttle up and feed in a little right rudder to counteract the torque. The control stick is full back to keep the tail wheel on the ground. I snap on the landing light to be sure I'm not going off into a rice paddy, then snap it off again. I am too good a target. The Bird Dog is sort of centered, going straight. The engine gauges check. As I ease the throttle up to take-off power and as the speed comes up, the control stick moves forward to neutral as if it knows what to do. The tail wheel comes up off the ground. And then so do I.

I sneak the Bird Dog up to about 50 ft heading west and then start S-turning, climbing to about 3,000 ft above the ground. I'll have to climb higher as I get closer to Laos, lots of mountains. But for now, 3,000 ft will work. Out of small arms range, it's time to turn on the red rotating beacon and wing-tip lights. I'm probably the only airplane awake at this hour, but maybe not. Could be somebody else up here on dawn patrol. There's nobody in the back seat again. Flying alone before sunrise is quiet, and beautiful.

1

This is when flying can be like slow dancing. Romantic. Sensual. No noise except for the song the engine sings. The sun slowly lights the sky behind me. No sun in my eyes. The mountains below are magical, especially in this early morning light. I think that in another lifetime it would be neat to wander around down there. Maybe with a fly rod. But not now.

Not now, not solo over the border. A little more than scary. If I need to put the airplane down, I'll be on my own because nobody will know exactly where I am.

Often there are two of me up here. One of me recognizes the possibility of dying. Because somebody almost always dies in combat. That one of me becomes focused on doing what I'm supposed to do. And not dying in the process. Not dying totally engages my brain. There's a little time yet before I get to the place where death, maybe my death, is waiting. "In transit" is a time when the other of me can look out the window at the beauty of this place. Appreciating the beautiful reinforces my humanity. It helps me keep in touch with the good in me. The world below me is such a visual feast. Mountainy jungle, waterfalls. Light playing with the colors of the earth, so many shades of green competing for my attention. I can love this time, if only for a little while. So, I always look because I need to feel the joy of it. The joy of it keeps my heart from hardening.

I cross over *Dak To*, *Ben Het* and then *Dak Seang*. Now above Laos I turn off all the lights. No point in making it easy for Charlie. I'm looking for a section of the Ho Chi Minh trail that just disappears. It must be down there somewhere. I can track it just so far and then it vanishes. I think the North Vietnamese Army (NVA) have made bamboo lattice panels that they camouflage with foliage to hide stuff. Maybe they're using them to disguise this trail.

I check in with Studies and Observation Group (SOG) operations at Leghorn, a radio relay station perched on a pinnacle to the north of me. I use my call-sign, SPAF Two, plainly in my transmission. But when I tell them where I am going it's all in code. Funny thing is the NVA knows exactly who I am. I don't know if they've broken our codes, but they know the pilots. They've called me on other mornings. Using my call sign. One time they said my name.

"Good mo-ning *Dai uy* [Captain] Doh-ty."

It took a while before my hands stopped shaking. But they're not talking today. Could be they're still asleep. Probably not.

Time to get down closer to the trees. I could just throttle back and fly gliding S-turns down. But there are more fun ways to get out of altitude. I put the Bird Dog into a left steep turn, a turn that uses almost a ninety-degree bank angle, and add a little bit of climbing elevator to keep the nose from dropping. As soon as I feel the lower wing begin to stall, to lose lift and stop flying, I push top, or right, rudder as far as the pedal will go, and the left wing comes up and continues over as the Bird Dog flips upside down and starts to spin to the right. I let the airplane make three revolutions, then let go of the stick, push a little left rudder to stop the spin, and gently pull the nose up to level. Bingo. Treetops.

It's cool this morning. The cockpit side windows are open, latched up to the underside of their respective wings. I roll up my sleeves because the cool feels good and raise the visor on my flight helmet. I don't need sunglasses until I start working the visible trail to the point at which it disappears. Then I'll be flying north and south, S-turning and circling, searching for tracks, always listening for the snap of a bullet as it goes by, looking for the green streak it makes if it's a tracer round. Nobody is shooting at me yet.

I follow the road south until it disappears into heavy jungle. All I can see are mountains cloaked in too many variations of green to count. I fly up a gorge so narrow that the Bird Dog can't be turned if I get too low. So, I fly a slow *Dutch roll*. The airplane drifts down one side of the gorge as low as I can go and still climb up the other side, then I do the same thing again, rocking my wings in long, lazy arcs.

I'm hanging out the window looking hard for a hint. I think I see something. Maybe. But I continue sliding from side to side through this long skinny slit between ridgelines without tipping my hand. I register a landmark in my head. I'll come back to that place if it stays quiet. It stays quiet, so after a while I come back.

Throughout all this I keep a constant scan going on the engine instruments. Everything is normal. Good, because there's nowhere to go if the engine quits. Except straight ahead, hoping for softer bamboo. I need to switch from my left fuel tank to my right. Pretty simple. A round plate with a selector switch shaped like an arrow. Move the arrow from the Capital L to the Capital R. High tech, this Bird Dog.

I plan my recon route so that the sun is to my left and at my back as I head south through the gorge. This way the sun's angle at this early hour will shine sideways through the leafy canopy, exposing the road that I hope is there. That makes two of us flying sideways this morning, me and the sunshine.

There! Got it! The first bridge! The road is a series of bridges that crisscross the entire length of this tiny valley. By the time I reach the end of the gorge I count forty-seven bamboo bridges. "Leghorn, Leghorn, this is SPAF-Two. Any TACAIR [tactical air fighter-bombers] on station?" I get two flights of two F4s, four Phantoms in total, coming from one of our air bases in Thailand. I run the first pair of Phantoms in from south to north with a break to the west, back towards the Thai border in case we start taking fire. They have 250 lb. bombs. On my mark the first Phantom drops his load which is set to detonate on impact; the second Phantom delays detonation so that the bomb burrows into the ground. I'm trying to take out the bridges and their footings. As soon as the second F4 breaks off and turns west I mark the target further into the gorge. The second flight starts their run, but north to south, the opposite direction, with the same set-up on the bombs and the same westerly climb out. We receive moderate ground fire, but we take out three bridges. The F-4s report no damage. The Bird Dog shakes when bullets hit it. I see two holes in the underside of my right wing.

I return the following morning, by myself again. This time I let the Bird Dog glide down to about 1,200 ft, cross-controlling as always. The throttle has the engine quietly at idle. If I listen past the sound of the engine, I can hear the wind sigh as it flows over the airplane's wings. Adding power now and pulling the nose up, making a big right turn as I do. Then right rudder, and the Bird Dog is upside down again, just not spinning. Pulling out of the dive just above the trees and aiming for the opening in the gorge. Nobody is shooting at me yet.

The bridges, destroyed yesterday, have been rebuilt overnight. The new spans of green bamboo are like neon signs, the same gestures of nose-thumbing defiance the Vietnamese have been making for a thousand years. I curse and laugh at the same time. I laugh because these new bridges don't surprise me at all. In fact, I would expect no less from these tenacious people. I curse at our *beau geste*, at our stupidity for not heeding history, at our callous waste of life. That my friends, Bird Dog pilots Bessor and Weisner and Cozart and Aiken and Ridgeway and Pisacreta and Wood, Special Forces troopers Krupa and Poole and Armstrong, will never grow up, never grow old. Commemorated memories of young men on black granite. Much too soon.

In Vietnam my feelings grew calluses, like the ones from the saltwater-coated clam rake that hardened the skin on the palms of my hands, in the summer between my junior and senior year at Chaminade High School. The calluses got thicker the following summer, the summer before the University of San Francisco. That summer I was digging graves instead of clams. In Queens, with my friend Bunky Egan, at Cypress Hills Cemetery. I wondered about what I felt then, on the clam boat or at the cemetery, but I wondered with the perspective of a teenaged boy. What I wondered, about almost everything, was uninformed, immature, self-centered, convinced I knew everything. My insecurity was disguised as conviction. Now, when I'm old and looking in the rearview mirror, I realize that my feelings reflected what I was sure of. And that, no matter what I thought, was not much. Not in the cemetery, the clam boat, or the Central Highlands.

Looking down from my Bird Dog's window at the moonscape we had created in Laos, I realized that my feelings about this war, feelings I thought I was once so certain about, were not so certain anymore. Had they become as callused as my hands once were? I think they had.

When I arrived in Vietnam I started out as a skeptic, full of doubt about our purpose here, but I was willing to give the jumble in my heart and head time to coalesce, to become something I could count on to give me direction, to help me survive. I needed time to digest this place. Because I didn't know what to think about the right or wrong of it, and nothing I saw prompted anything definitive. Until an early June morning when I flew into a very skinny Laotian gorge and found the hidden part of the Trail that we had been looking for. And then I blew it up in several places. The North Vietnamese fixed it overnight, and I was greeted by green bamboo construction the next morning. I looked at what had been done in the dark and was a skeptic no more. I became a believer that morning. The rebuilt bridges said:

"We live here, not you."

My feelings were a stew of deep sorrow and frustration.

I traded skepticism for cynicism, an open mind for an angry, narrow field of vision. I saw the new green bamboo bridges and became incensed. Not because they were there and the craters in the ground that I had orchestrated had been repaired. Oh no. I was furious because Don Armstrong's head had been splattered all over the back of Phil Phillips's airplane. In a few months

Fritz Krupa would lay sprawled face down on matted elephant grass and bleed out. And Roger Pisacreta would be blown out of the sky.

Now, whenever I try to understand this whole war, I always wind up in the same place. In *Nha Trang*, on my first full day in Vietnam. In a chubby major's office, where the only thing in that room bigger than the major was his indifference. The major who was so smothered by boredom that he could hardly move his mouth, let alone the rest of him. I stood in front of his desk, sort of at parade rest, attention, and at ease all at the same time, while he, still seated, barely gestured at the big wall-mounted map behind him. All those blue pins in clusters around places most of which I had just heard of today, like *Dong Ha* and *Chu Lai* and *Qui Nhon* and *Quang Ngai*. These little cities, the ones I had never heard of until just now, and the big cities like *Da Nang* and *Saigon* and *Hue Citadel*, the ones I already knew about? That's where the blue pins clustered. Around these cities. We were the blue pins. The red ones? The Viet Cong and the North Vietnamese? They were everywhere else. And yes, the chubby major did say with no hint of sarcasm that we were winning. I waited until that morning, months later, when I saw the green bamboo, to laugh and cry and feel sick to my stomach. Then asked the empty backseat of my Bird Dog, "We're winning? What? Jesus, Mary, and Holy Saint Joseph! Why are we here?"

I believed in God then. I still do. But I also knew that fate was what I made it. Nobody else. And, like coloring within the lines, I had to play this game by the rules. Because there were consequences to the choices, and the promises, I made. My parents hated that I was in Vietnam. But I put on a uniform. My father did too. I had Army Aviator wings pinned over my heart by my mother. My father's mother pinned Army Air Corps wings over his heart too. He kept his word. He would know if I didn't keep mine. More importantly, so would I. So, there was no hiding in the closet or under the bed. No shortcut to getting out of harm's way. I prayed to God – *now I lay me down to sleep, I pray the Lord my soul to keep* – to help me be safe, but I was responsible for dodging the bullet that might have said my name. The bullet that could have ended my life. Nobody else. I promised to do what I was doing. I volunteered. I also promised my mother, Celestina, over the phone from Fort Knox, when I told her that I was going to flight school and then had to tell her that I was going to Vietnam, that I would come home in one piece. The hard part was figuring out how to keep those promises.

# Chapter 2

# *Nha Trang's* Mosquitos

"For the people who live it, history is personal. And if you live it intensely, you feel you own it, or it owns you."

Hodding Carter, *New York Times,* 18 October 2018

**September 1969, First Month**

I couldn't open my eyes all the way. It was dark and I couldn't see very much. It's not that I couldn't see because it was night. This place was lit up like Times Square. I couldn't see because my eyes were swollen shut; they felt like they were glued together. I think my face was swollen too. Mosquitos. My first night in Vietnam. I was eaten alive by mosquitos.

Stumbling out of this screenless hovel where I was unable to sleep, I decided that the only way I was able to navigate was to hold my right eye open. Blurs began to find definition, objects became distinct. A soldier who sounded very young took my arm. I couldn't exactly see him to tell if he was very young or not. And if he was young, what did that make me? An antique at 24?

"Are you alright, lieutenant? What happened to your face?"

He guided me to a medical hut.

"The *'Bac Si'* can check you out, sir."

My first words in Vietnamese. "*Bac Si.*" I had been in Vietnam for less than twelve hours and the first words I learned were Vietnamese for medic. Hell of a start, lieutenant. The *Bac Si* gave me a shot of cortisone and smeared my bites with cortisone cream. My whole head was one big bite. He invited me to sleep on one of the gurneys. There were screens on the windows and fans whirring at takeoff power overhead. If they were attached to the gurney I would have been hovering like a helicopter.

This building had a bathroom and a shower, so I retrieved my duffle bag from the screenless hut and got cleaned up. The shower had hot water, which in a few months would become a very big deal for me. Hot water became all that stood between me and the apocalypse. I stayed in there so long my skin looked like a wrinkly peanut shell. Between the hot shower and the mosquito bites my face resembled an English Muffin, with nooks and crannies everywhere, which made shaving in the morning very iffy.

The medic informed me that I was to report to the MACV Replacement Office. MACV, another Army acronym. It meant Military Advisory Command, Vietnam. Major Somebody had my orders, unit assignment, and travel instructions ready. I got another cortisone shot and headed off to look for the Replacement Office.

The chubby major, sprawled at his desk, in front of his giant map, cluttered with all those blue and red push-pins, informed me that there would be a C-130 going to *Qui Nhon* in forty-five minutes.

"Be on that airplane, lieutenant. When you get to Qui Nhon, report to the 18th Aviation Company. Their orderly room is right on the airfield. Make sure you have all your paperwork. Goodbye." He was becoming impatient to be rid of me, and I believe I was just told not to let the door hit me in the ass on my way out of his office.

I thanked him, gathered up my documents, and saluted. Saluting is required. Major Somebody could barely lift his arm to salute back. Being that encumbered by ennui must have been overwhelming. Better get out of here before he got angry. And then I slowed down and just left. The major wasn't going to get angry. That would have required too much effort. So much for *Nha Trang*.

*Qui Nhon* was a city right on the South China Sea. The water was pale emerald-green this morning. I imagined I could smell the ocean, a smell that found its way to me despite all the other smells that Vietnam tried to overwhelm me with. Maybe I thought I could smell the ocean because I could always smell it growing up on Lloyd Neck. Maybe I just wanted something familiar to grab on to. The 18th's orderly room was right on the airfield, exactly where Major Somebody said it would be. I put my duffle bag on the floor as the clerk got to his feet and saluted. I returned it, then shook his hand and introduced myself.

"Frank Doherty." I said not very militarily.

He smiled, and I reminded myself that,

"I need to be a lieutenant, lieutenant."

The door behind the clerk's desk opened and my commanding officer, another major, was giving me a thorough eyeballing. My salute was more formal, snappier, more military. He didn't smile or laugh, and it felt like he didn't even see me.

"Welcome to the 18th."

"Thank you, sir."

"You understand the mission, lieutenant?"

"Yes, sir."

"Very good. There's an airplane leaving for *Da Nang* in twenty minutes. Climb in the right [copilot] seat and get the feel of things. Captain Barber knows you're on your way. He'll explain the mission in detail when you arrive. And lieutenant, don't bend one of my airplanes."

"No, sir.

I believed that my C.O. had a stick permanently implanted up his butt. So much for *Qui Nhon*.

The mission was uncomplicated. I was assigned to the second platoon, located up the coast, at Marble Mountain, just below *Da Nang*. The Army and Marines shared this airfield. We were right on the beach, a short walk from the South China Sea. I looked out the window on landing and spotted a sandbar jutting into the water at the south end of the airfield. The sandbar created some decent waves. I thought I could body-surf there. How great was this?

Captain Barber turned out to be a very easy-going guy. The beauty of being here at Marble Mountain, aside from the beach and the sandbar waves, was that Major Company-Commander was far to the south of us. The airplane, a *De Havilland* Otter, was a small passenger or cargo hauler. One big, round engine, a tail wheel, and a chunky, fat wing that was engineered for lift, not speed, and went across the top of the fuselage, right over the cockpit. It held ten passengers, two pilots up front, and a crew chief in the back. During the week we flew up and down the coast, from *Dong Ha* to the north of us right on the Demilitarized Zone (DMZ) to *Quang Ngai*, down south. *Quang Ngai*, the *Batangan Peninsula*, *My Lai*, all that. Nobody smiled in *Quang Ngai*. And sometimes we flew into *Qui Nhon*, to where Major Company-Commander, with the stick permanently implanted up his butt, ruled his little sandcastle.

On Saturdays we flew the Viet Cong (VC) shuttle from Marble Mountain to *Hue Citadel*, then back to Marble. And from Marble to *Quang Ngai*, then back again. Up the coast, then down the coast. Then down the coast, then up the coast. Ten Viet Cong prisoners each way, blindfolded and hands tied in front, but no crew chief in the back. Instead, a guard wearing a flak vest and carrying a loaded M-16. Forty prisoners every Saturday morning, and no one was happy. About the third Saturday I flew this I happened to turn around; I watched as the prisoner in the right-side front seat, blindfolded and hands tied, reached up and adjusted the overhead air vent. From the look of his blindfold, I didn't think he could see the vent. He just knew where it was. It occurred to me that this guy had been here before.

We parked the Otter on the ramp adjacent to the runway in Hue. It was late September. I had been in Vietnam for three weeks. This was my first trip into the Citadel as Aircraft Commander. The Citadel, the old Imperial City of *Hue*, nestled close to the Perfume River. It was once an elegant palace, home to the *Nguyen* dynasty. The last *Nguyen* emperor had been gone since 1945, when the French reoccupied their old colony after the Second World War. The airfield, *Tay Loc*, had one runway which pointed northwest and southeast, and was within *Hue Citadel*'s walls. A postage stamp of an airfield. All the buildings and walls that I was able to see from the cockpit were pockmarked from bullets that struck them during the previous winter's *Tet* offensive. Reminders of so many deaths. The copilot and I watched as a crowd gathered around the passenger door at the rear of the Otter, our ten-seat airliner, waving *piasters* at the Vietnamese guard who stood there. They were all talking at the same time, gesturing at and pleading with the guard. Because there were empty seats on the airplane, and we were going back to *Da Nang*. It appeared that the guard was selling them. I asked our crew chief, Joe Calabrese, how often this happened. He laughed.

"All the time, *Trung uy*" (lieutenant).

His hands were jammed into his pants pockets, observing the whole operation. I smiled and wondered if Joe was doing more than observing. Maybe he was in on this deal. War or no war, making a buck, or a *piaster*, would always win out. It looked like we were running an airline and I (and my flying partner) didn't even know it. Did we get a percentage of the proceeds?

A Vietnamese Air Force (VNAF) Huey hovered and then landed alongside us, on my side of the Otter, away from the gaggle of people by our door. A VNAF major climbed down from the pilot's seat and walked to the other side of his helicopter, reached in through the big side door, and lifted out a Honda scooter. He opened the copilot's door and helped a woman in a pale green *Ao Dai* and black silk pants out of the cockpit. She was small, lithe but delicate, her black hair a startling contrast to her pale skin. Her *Ao Dai*, a traditional Vietnamese dress, was as delicate as she was. And this woman was far more beautiful than my copilot. I didn't think Major Company-Commander would consider a trade.

The gaggle trying to buy seats on our airplane along with the Vietnamese major and the woman in the pale green *Ao Dai* made me wonder if what I saw on *Hue Citadel*'s ramp was part of the normal commerce of this war. It must have been. I began to pay attention to the people that I saw. Not just to the little kids standing by the sides of roads, or the ubiquity of bullet-scarred buildings. I started really looking at people. The streets of every Vietnamese city were teeming with people. The old *Hue Citadel* was no exception. I studied their physical features of course, and the expressions on their faces. Did these faces look weary or angry? Were they weather-beaten? In any case, they were always interesting. The young women, like the girl who climbed out of the major's Huey, seemed so beautiful. Small, silken, graceful, demure, and poised. City girls, shop girls, secretaries, in pastel *Ao Dais* of every color, carried umbrellas to shade them. Some in black silk pants and white blouses. Many wore conical hats, which like the umbrellas, protected their skin from the sun.

There were farmers from villages here too. Peasant men and women, their skin burnished a brownish bronze, their reddish-black teeth stained by chewing *Betel nut*, a mild high. Their clothes hung off them. Their bodies had no excess baggage. Skin-shrouded bones, with ropey muscles and gnarled hands. Among the knots of people, paths opened on the streets for the elderly, usually bent and hunched from working the rice farms, using water buffalo as tractors, and their hands for everything else. They almost scuttled as they moved through the crowds. And the crowds deferred to them, and revered them, and honored them because they were old.

I studied the young men I saw, at what they were doing and what they were wearing. I saw a lot of boys who didn't appear to be in the Army of the Republic of Vietnam. Most of them had their eyes almost hidden behind dark-tinted, gold-rimmed sunglasses. Ray-Ban Aviators. The eyes that I was able to see were filled with disdain for me. Not for me in particular. I guess I was the day's generic G.I. so I got all their undisguised loathing. Why? What was I missing? I hadn't been here long enough to figure this out yet. The Vietnamese have been fighting off one invader after another for centuries. The Chinese, the Japanese, the French, and now us. We were invaders. I didn't know this yet. But I would. Eventually I would.

These young men, almost all in light slacks and white short-sleeved shirts, walked in pairs, their pinky fingers linked with their companion. A common custom in this country. An expression of friendship. Were they students? VC? Draft dodgers? Secret agents? Street hustlers? Probably one and maybe more than one of these "occupations." A few were wearing all or part of a uniform. No insignia or indication of rank on any of these guys. The major in the Huey was the real deal, but I sensed that these boys were just hanging out. Pretend gunslingers. Some were carrying weapons. M-16s, or pistols in gun belts strapped around their skinny waists. Some had bandoliers of bullets crisscrossing their narrow shoulders. Saigon Cowboys, Joe Calabrese called all of them, then laughed derisively. The streets seemed clogged with Calabrese's Saigon Cowboys. They were everywhere.

Back at Marble Mountain a Green Beret captain was sitting at our officers' club bar, working on a seriously full tumbler of scotch. I met him when I first got to Marble; he was attached to the 5th Special Forces here. I didn't know what he did, and I had the feeling that if I asked him, he probably wouldn't tell me anyway. I had landed earlier in the evening, showered the day's dried sweat off me and made my way here. The captain looked very tired. He'd been "in country" for a while, and whatever he was doing was kicking his ass.

I said hi to Ben the bartender, then asked, "Can I get a gigantic beer, and would you bring Captain LaRue an extremely large glass of whatever he's drinking?"

I thanked Ben, then turned to the captain.

"Dick, I've been thinking about some things that puzzle me and would it be okay if I ask you a question or twenty?"

I had my very earnest face on. I hated being unsure of anything. I related the day's events to him. The Vietnamese major using an Air Force Huey as his personal station wagon and letting his girlfriend fly as his co-pilot, the airfield guards selling seats on our airplane, aimlessly meandering Saigon Cowboys crowding doorways and street corners. Images that provoked my question, "Are we fighting this war all by ourselves?"

Dick pointed to his empty glass and held up two fingers. Ben the bartender nodded and put two tumblers of scotch in front of us. I guessed that the answer to my question was going to take a while, and maybe that's why Dick had decided I wasn't drinking beer anymore. My questions weren't simple even if they sounded that way, and his answers weren't going to be simple no matter how they sounded.

"Everybody kicks back money. From the bottom up."

Dick was smiling, gentling me along.

"So, the South Vietnamese Army company commander takes a cut from the pay of every man in his company and passes a portion of that cut upstream. It goes from one commander to the next higher to the next higher until the money gets to the top of the command structure. The more names on the duty roster of a company, the more money is collected. Dead guys don't get paid. If nobody fights, nobody dies, everybody gets paid, and more money flows uphill. That's why Vietnamese commanders are reluctant to engage the NVA. And those who do, don't last very long. Essentially, go along to get along."

"If nobody fights, nobody dies."

That's what Dick said. Nobody? Really? Well, maybe not South Vietnamese soldiers, whose commanders maintain their headcounts to keep the money coming in. But our guys were dying. Friends of mine from college, from flight school. They were dying. I studied the almost-gone ice in my glass of almost-gone scotch and asked, "What about the major in the Huey with the green *Ao Dai* co-pilot?"

"Who knows? Maybe the major has connections. Maybe he's a squadron commander and that's his command helicopter. Maybe it's just a bigger version of the Honda scooter. Sometimes I think that the Vietnamese are in this to grab what they can. Don't mean to sound so cynical, but it's hard not to, Frank."

"Okay, then. What about the Cowboys in the Ray-Bans?"

Dick looked at me, took a gulp of scotch, and laughed.

"We have those guys at home too."

He finished his scotch, picked up his beret from the bar, and slid off his stool.

"Time to go. Early morning tomorrow."

I decided that it was my "big picture" that was too big. And I thought that maybe Dick was too cynical. At least for right now he was too cynical for me. I didn't know anything about this war because I didn't know anything about this country, about its people, or about its history. I was assuming, and assumptions were seldom sure things. From now on I was going to look at the people but not judge. I was going to take in as much as I could, observe all that I could, learn as much as I could.

Except that I didn't exactly do any of that. Because eventually I discovered that Dick's cynicism wasn't dishonest. I discovered that it was easy to become angry with Vietnamese soldiers who wouldn't fight for their own country. If they wouldn't fight, why should I?

But none of this really hit home until I was face to face with combat. When bullets snapped by my cockpit window, screamed under my airplane's wings or off my airplane's nose, or along the side of my head. Combat was waiting for me. It was just a few months away. Waiting for me in the mountains of the Central Highlands. Waiting until I climbed into a Bird Dog. In November. Over Cambodia.

Right then, at the end of September, in Marble Mountain, flying an Otter, a little cargo plane, the war, such as it was, was benign. I didn't think anyone had ever taken a shot at me. I could keep an open mind. Cynicism and anger couldn't suck me in or harden my heart. Not yet. I was able to ask a lot of questions of people who had been here a while. And some of the answers I got, like the ones given by Captain LaRue, were earnest and thoughtful. Other answers were a lot of baloney that I discarded right away. Like the first time I heard somebody refer to an Asian mindset. What kind of garbage was that? How could someone who had been in Southeast Asia for a few months, or even a few years, have a handle on what these people thought? That it was any different than what a white boy like me would think? Asian mindset? That conjured up visions of inscrutable Mandarins wearing wispy mustaches and brocade jackets with gaping sleeves that hid their hands when they crossed their arms, because that was where Mandarins concealed their daggers.

But I didn't ask any more questions, or search for answers in the faces I saw. Because at the end of September, toward the end of my short time flying Otters at Marble, I was assigned an extra duty. Captain Barber asked me to look in on an orphanage, where its children and their protector, Sister Angela, crowded the conversation that I had in the bar with Dick out of my mind.

"Believe in Angels, then return the favor."

Anonymous

**October 1969, Second Month**

The first time I visited the orphanage the rain felt almost sticky because it was so warm. I was soaked from the sweat inside of my poncho as well as from the thunderstorm that had dumped gallons of water on me. I pulled my jeep into the courtyard of a shabby complex of buildings and was met by a tiny Vietnamese woman in a nun's habit and wimple (head-covering), and an umbrella bigger than she was. The orphanage was run-down, but not bleak in the least. The soaking-wet kids, except for a teeny boy she held in her arms, an infant with a giant head (hydrocephalus), danced in the rain around me, my jeep, and Sister Angela. They danced, their feet splashing in puddles, because of her. Because she loved them. That was all it took. It was impossible not to embrace these kids, most of them half Vietnamese and half American. The Vietnamese called them *Bu Doi* – which meant dust of life – and hated them, and hoped the streets and alleys would consume them. As I looked around the complex, I realized that my first impression was wrong. At first glance I thought that these children had nothing. But they were dancing in the rain. They were protected, and safe, and loved. They had everything.

I never knew anything about Sister Angela. She spoke no English, and my few words of Vietnamese were phonetic nonsense. We communicated with gestures, smiles, bows and her hands held in mine. Was there a school? I saw an empty room. No desks. No chairs. I also don't ever remember seeing another nun at the compound. There were other women, but they were dressed in black silk pants, white blouses, and those conical straw hats that peasant women wore. And sometimes rubber flip-flops on their feet. Not always flip-flops. Lots of times barefoot. Were they nuns? I didn't think so, but there was no one I could ask, so I never did find out. Sister Angela was always dressed in her veil and white habit, with black rosary beads looped through the sash around her waist. Only once or twice did I see her face without a smile.

We had cases of Combat-rations, sometimes called C-Rats or C-Rations, in the little supply closet behind the 18th's ready room. C-Rations were boxes that contained cans of food. An entree of something edible, like franks and beans or meatballs and spaghetti, or something dreadful, like pork loaf and lima beans. There might be a can of fruit. There could also be something pretending to be peanut butter. A packet of cocoa maybe. And totally dried out cigarettes, four in the package. The C-Rations were just stacked in our supply closet because we had a mess hall at our compound. So, I usually brought a case or two of them with me. Whether or not the kids ever ate them didn't matter, the canned food was there just in case. I never opened the cases to see what meals the individual boxes contained. I just hoped they weren't all pork loaf in aspic and lima beans.

The orphanage compound had a small chapel. A bare room really, adorned by a crucifix above a wooden table that served as the altar, and off to one side of the altar, a statue of Mary in her obligatory blue robe. That was it. No long wooden pews or benches. No chairs here either. Just a bare room. Screenless windows allowed in a lot of light which prevented the tiny space from closing in on me, because Catholic churches had a way of closing in on me.

Occasionally, when the children were napping, and when it was empty, I went into the chapel, sitting on the ground against the back wall, my elbows resting on my bent knees. I didn't exactly pray. Not an Our Father or a Hail Mary. I was just thinking about where I was and why I was doing what I was doing in this country, and in this place. It seemed to me that the more I tried to make sense of what I was doing, the more my questions multiplied. I did pray once.

My taking on the orphanage project was a giant irony. I had been absent from my faith since the seventh grade. You've read, no doubt, about the abuse of children by members of the clergy? About thousands of priests as sexual predators molesting all those young boys? I was an altar boy in the seventh grade, in 1958, at St. Patrick's School. I was one of those young boys.

Sister Angela came into the orphanage's little chapel and reached out her hand to me as I stood up. She faced the altar and made the Sign of the Cross. As her right hand moved toward her forehead, so did mine. She placed her palms together and so did I. Then I closed my eyes just like always. I don't remember what my prayer was about. In another place and time different nuns with thick Irish brogues told us never to ask God for something just for ourselves. I almost never did. On this day I probably asked God to keep these people safe.

I wrote letters to local newspapers back home, to my high school, to my college, to my parish church, to Boy Scouts and Girl Scouts and Cub Scouts and Brownies. I begged for food, for clothes, for money. They didn't contact me in return. They were much smarter than that. They contacted my mother. And Celestina Doherty, whose son was in Vietnam and was sponsoring an orphanage in *Da Nang*, took over. She organized a food and clothes drop-off site, several bake sales, and a bank account to deposit donations of money. She was interviewed by *The Long Islander*, the local newspaper, where her picture was shown surrounded by packages. I just wrote the letters. My mother did everything else. She made my letters a success.

For the first time in a long time a spotlight shone on my mother. Celestina graduated from high school but did not attend college even though she was very smart. She begged my grandfather Antonio, who was Mom's champion in all ways but this, to let her stay in school. His opinion on advanced education for women remained prehistoric. Celestina became a secretary. Once married she stood in my father's shadow. He was the war-hero airline pilot, and she was the mom. Now she had something to grab on to, interviews to give, and attention to enjoy. A chance to be recognized without having to share the applause with anyone else. My letters home told her how proud I was of her; how thankful I was for her help. Her letters to me let me know how proud Celestina was of herself.

I was flying when the lieutenant in charge of mail distribution showed up at our operations office demanding to know who I was, how come he had enough packages to fill a Deuce-and-a-half (a two-and-a-half-ton truck), with the overflow jamming a smaller three-quarter-ton truck to the brim, and a stack of envelopes addressed to me, taking up all the space at his mail room? Had I been there I would have told him, "Talk to my mom."

Lieutenant Mailman let me borrow the Deuce-and-a-half, so he must not have been too upset.

I flew a mission to *Hue Citadel* and *Dong Ha* the next morning, then drove our three-quarter-ton truck over to the mailroom. Lieutenant Mailman was waiting for me. We loaded the extras into my truck; the Deuce-and-a-half was already loaded with so many boxes that the mail clerks tied a tarp over the top to keep the top boxes from falling out. And the lieutenant drove.

As we pulled into the orphanage compound Sister Angela came out from one of the buildings. When she looked at our overflowing trucks, I thought I saw her knees buckle. When I handed her an envelope containing the money that had been donated, Sister Angela began to cry. It took only a half a minute before Lieutenant Mailman and I had kids in our arms, and we all became a teary tangle of hugs.

When I wasn't in the airplane I was at the orphanage. I only saw these kids, the nun, and nothing else. Even when I was not there, I was. I daydreamed about the food and clothes that I hoped my mother would be able to send to them. I tried to come up with ways to expand Mom's reach so that we were able to collect as much of everything as we could. If I saw another beautiful girl in a green *Ao Dai* climb out of a Huey, or a line of people trying to buy tickets on an airplane I was flying, or Saigon

Cowboys in Ray-Bans wandering aimlessly through the streets, maybe I would see them. But maybe I wouldn't. Maybe I was too busy to notice the things I promised myself I would notice, things I thought that mattered. I didn't bother with these things anymore. What mattered to me now? The orphanage mattered. And the airplane. And surviving that year. Only the orphanage, the airplane, and surviving the year.

Since then, I have often thought about a bare chapel in Vietnam, and a dim broom closet in St. Patrick's elementary school. The darkness of this broom closet, next to the boys' bathroom, in sharp contrast to the light streaming through open windows in the chapel. But the stifling broom closet has always remained connected to the bare chapel. The dark masked everything but Reemy's face. I could see his eyes wide and glowing through the thick lenses of his glasses. I could see the sweat beading across his upper lip. I could feel the priest's hand slide under the waistband of my jockey shorts. I could hear the rasp of the zipper on his black trousers as they were being opened. I could feel him touch me and knew he was touching himself. Then I ran, and I never went into St. Pat's alone again.

Two very different places defined by two people, a nun, and a priest, with a religion common to them in name only. The chapel of Sister Angela was daylight-bright, airy, and open. Reemy's broom closet was cloying, closed, and dark. Was Reemy so full of self-loathing that he had to hurt children? I don't know. I do know that his hands were wet-warm. Slippery almost, they sought to defile me.

Sister Angela's fingertips, cool and soft, touched my face. Her eyes, full of tears, thanked mine.

At Mass, before communion, we Catholics prayed:

> "Lord I am not worthy that thou shalt come under my roof.
> Say but the words and my soul shall be healed."

On this day, the day that Lieutenant Mailman and I delivered the donations Celestina sent to Angela, two women, Heaven, and Angel, gave those words life.

Almost thirty years later, on a midnight Delta flight from Los Angeles to Cincinnati, one of our flight attendants on the airplane was Vietnamese American. After the cabin service was completed, I left the cockpit, walked back to the aft galley, and introduced myself to the beautiful young woman. I told her I served in Vietnam during the war and asked about her family. She was the only survivor; her parents and sisters were killed during the Viet Cong attacks that took place during *Tet*, a big Vietnamese celebration, in 1968. She lived in a Catholic orphanage in *Da Nang* until she was adopted by a sergeant, who in 1971, brought her back to Detroit. She remembered the tiny woman who rescued her, an abandoned baby, an abandoned *Bu Doi*, left by the orphanage's doorway. Left for Sister Angela. Sometimes our world is so small.

# Chapter 3

# O-1 Bird Dog

At the end of October, I'd been at Marble for two months and the suffocating boredom that was this mission was turning me into a grouchy, nasty, miserable jerk. The Otter was fun to fly; any airplane was fun to fly. But what I was doing was not fun. It was mind-numbingly dull. The last straw came the day I had to fly the maintenance officer back to *Qui Nhon*. He was a lieutenant, a pilot just like me; he had been checking our logbooks and maintenance records, and now he was sitting in the copilot's seat. We had a few of our guys in the back, plus the crew chief. The weather at Marble was partly cloudy, but it was supposed to rain later farther south. After takeoff Lieutenant Maintenance-Officer removed his headset so the radio didn't disturb him, pulled out a book and started to read.

By the time we got south of *Chu Lai* it was drizzling, the sky solid gray. Wisps of cloud, called virga, hung below the overcast and announced that the weather was going to get worse. I asked my not-much-help helper to radio *Qui Nhon* to check the wind and visibility. He looked out ahead of us, told me he was able to see just fine and went back to his book, so I made the radio call. I talked to *Qui Nhon*. It was raining, it was pouring, the old man was snoring. The closer we got to *Qui Nhon* the louder the old man's snoring got.

I couldn't see anything but rain. Up and down had disappeared along with straight ahead. I hadn't flown on instruments since I left Fort Rucker. But I was flying them now: artificial horizon, air speed, heading, turn and bank. I needed to descend so that I could get beneath this overcast, so that I could see in front of me. Except that there were low coastal mountains all around *Qui Nhon*, so no descent yet. Our best bet was to turn east, to get out over the water, and that's what I did. When I thought I was far enough away from the coast, just as I decided to start down, a hole in the clouds opened. Not a big hole, but big enough. I was able to see the water, so I pushed the

Otter down as fast as I could make it go. The altimeter, the instrument that told us how high we were, scared the daylight out of me. We were so low that we were skimming the bottom of the clouds with the top of the airplane and if I wasn't careful the wheels were going to be skimming the water where the sharks lived. The beach was visible through the rain, and we turned north, back to Marble Mountain.

Lieutenant Maintenance-Officer had been babbling since we turned out over the water, babbling faster as we descended through the hole in the clouds, and now he babbled about wanting to know where we were going. Once we were safe, I turned to him with undisguised anger, told him we were going back to where we started, and told him to stop talking. Now it was quiet. I was able to see out in front of me, and blue sky started to break through the clouds. Working together should have been a simple thing. Except when Lieutenant Maintenance-Officer panicked and let the rain splattering on the windshield obscure the job, when he needed to help me inside the cockpit. Who needs this?

It was sunny in *Da Nang* and in *Qui Nhon* the following day. The crew chief sat next to me in the cockpit on the way down. Lieutenant Maintenance-Officer was exiled to the back, no pleasantries exchanged. We parked on the 18th's ramp, and I asked the crew chief to look after our airplane, thanked him for his help this morning, and told him that the beers were on me when we got back north. My company commander was in his office. The major returned my salute, and I announced my desire to get a transfer to a Bird Dog unit. I didn't tell him that the maintenance officer was an awful pilot. I thought the major probably knew that. Instead, I told him that I loved the airplane, hated the mission, was bored out of my mind, and didn't want to do this anymore. I made it all about me. Then I asked the major to please get me out of here.

His whole face turned into a frown. He looked up at me, looked at me for the first time since I arrived at the 18th. Judging by the way he scrutinized the name tag stitched on my flight suit, I wondered if he was trying to figure out who the hell I was. After a long minute he picked up his phone and asked to be connected to Major David Naumann, CO of the 219th Reconnaissance Airplane Company. After a short conversation – an unhappy lieutenant, maybe a malcontent, possibly a troublemaker – the major hung up and told me to fly the Otter back north (no Lieutenant Maintenance-Officer this time), get packed, and to be ready to leave Marble that afternoon. My copilot north would be the pilot who would fly me to my new unit. Someplace called Camp Holloway, in the Central Highlands. Where the O-1 Bird Dogs lived.

"You're dismissed, lieutenant. Get out of my office."

He didn't stand or return my salute. I got the feeling that I was almost in a lot of trouble; maybe the major decided I just wasn't worth the bother. Did I care? Not one little bit.

Late that same day I dumped my duffle bag on the floor of the 219th's orderly room. It was heavy with everything the Army issued me along with a few things I owned. Next came my helmet bag, and then my rifle. I was at Camp Holloway in the Central Highlands, close to the Cambodian border. No South China Sea, no beach, no Lieutenant Maintenance-Officer. Just tree-covered mountains everywhere. The day was drippy humid, and I was already pitted out. What else was new? It was humid. Of course, it was because it was Southeast Asia. The equator was just down the street.

I looked around this plywood office, then at the map of mostly *Binh Dinh*, *Pleiku*, and *Kontum* provinces. And at the big plaque hanging on the wall. It showed my new unit's mascot. In the middle of the plaque was a painted figure of a Headhunter. A brown man with blubbery lips in a grass skirt, a necklace of teeth, and a bone in his topknot. This caricature was confusing to say the least. With all the racial stuff going on back home how could this make sense? And I wondered how the African Americans in this unit felt about it. I decided that since I had to be here for at least ten more months, and I had other battles to fight, I was going to take a pass on this one.

A bleached human skull with some missing teeth sat on the company clerk's desk, which added to the already skewed ambiance of this place. When I asked to transfer out of the 18th, a transport, cargo, and liaison airplane company, I asked to go to a Bird Dog outfit that was seeing a lot of action. The skull told me that maybe I should have been careful what I had wished. That's what I got to be now. A Headhunter.

A door behind the clerk's desk opened and now there was this giant guy standing in front of me. Captain Don Shipp was one of the biggest men I had ever seen. Once an offensive tackle for the University of Texas-Arlington, he was now the executive officer of the 219th. I wondered how he could fit in a Bird Dog's tiny cockpit. His Jack-O-Lantern smile was wrapped around a "Hello lieutenant." Followed by, "Two job openings out there so you have a choice. You can go to work for the 4th platoon, which means you'll be here at Holloway. You'll fly in support of the 4th Infantry

Division, adjusting artillery, doing convoy cover and route reconnaissance. You'll also fly mortar-watch and stand as officer of the guard several nights a month."

Captain Shipp then listed about five too many extra duties I'd have. I say nothing and wait to hear the other option.

"Or you can head up to *Kontum* and join the 2nd platoon. You'll replace Captain John Meyers and work for the Special Forces operation up there."

I was waiting for the recitation of extra duties. Shipp just looked at me and smiled, the Jack-O-Lantern now a Cheshire Cat grin. No extra duties? Special Forces? The 2nd platoon worked for me.

I would have to remain at Holloway for what I thought was going to be only a week before going to *Kontum*. I had to get some refresher training, called an in-country check-out, in the O-1. I hadn't flown a Bird Dog since last June. I needed to get the feel of the airplane again. It was so much smaller and nimbler than the lumbering U-1 Otter, and just great fun to fly. An MG roadster instead of a big Ford station wagon. The landscape in the Central Highlands was jungle-covered mountains instead of the sandy coastal plain where the cities of *Da Nang, Qui Nhon, Hue, Quang Ngai* and *Dong Ha* were situated. The mountain cities of *Pleiku* and *Kontum* were mere hamlets in comparison.

I flew with the 219th's instructor pilot every day for a week, learning the terrain, landing on dirt strips and sometimes on dirt roads alongside Special Forces camps. I adjusted artillery, flew convoy cover for the 4th Infantry Division, learned how to make a grease-pencil gunsight for aiming the Bird Dog's four marking rockets, and orbited over Camp Holloway at night on a four-hour mortar watch. When I was by myself, I looped it, flipped it upside down into a spin, split-essed and steep-turned it until I made myself dizzy. This little airplane was so much fun! Then Don Shipp asked me if I would volunteer to fly a mission that required me to get a special briefing and to swear to keep the mission secret. No more all-night mortar watch, and I would have to remain at Holloway a few weeks longer. Immediately I said yes. I didn't know who I would be working for or what I would be doing or for how long I would be doing whatever this mission was until I landed at *Du Co*, a Special Forces camp, to get a mission briefing. I didn't care. I was excited. I was on the verge of combat. The adrenaline was just blasting through me. An Air Force major who didn't introduce himself and didn't want to know my name either told me that his call sign was Covey, that I was to stay in loose formation with his Bird Dog, orbit over a point he would designate, at about 10,000 ft, and wait for a whispered "Team Okay." That was my special briefing. No further information, no questions, and no talking about any of what I saw or did.

A ten-man Special Forces team was being inserted along the Ho Chi Minh Trail. I saw them, all camouflaged, wearing nondescript uniforms, and carrying unrecognizable weapons as they boarded Huey helicopters at *Du Co*. These guys had to be recon. I didn't know where they came from or who they were working for. I didn't know who I was working for either. The major, with me tagging along, flew in loose formation but well above the gaggle of Hueys, the two troop carriers, and four stubby Hueys that were set up as flying arsenals. Charlie-model gunships. Miniguns, rockets, and machine guns galore. We were going west. Toward the Cambodian border. Toward the Trail. The Ho Chi Minh Trail.

The insertion appeared to go off without a hitch, but what did I know? I'd never done this before. The Hueys left, the Air Force major left. And I was all by myself, waiting to hear a whispered "Team Okay" over a radio frequency that only the team and I knew. Except that I was sweating, squirming, and gritting my teeth, trying to focus, trying to stay calm. This was about more than jungle heat. I had to pee so bad my stomach hurt. I was more than desperate. I was in agony. None of my instructors, for the whole time I was in flight school, ever even hinted at what to do in a situation like this.

I didn't have a lot of options, and I had important business to look after. I mean, I wasn't up here for fun. We had inserted the Spike (recon) team into a landing zone that was surprisingly cold, and I was told by Major No Name that Cambodian landing zones were seldom cold. Except that this one was. The team was not taking any small arms fire. No North Vietnamese ambush. No bad stuff. Good, because now all I had to do was wait for them to call me. But not so good because my bladder was trying to ambush my brain.

I flew in circles at about 10,000 ft over Cambodia, while waiting for the recon team to please for God's sake check in. Small arms fire couldn't reach me up here. And I couldn't give the team's location away because I was too high for the NVA to try to use me to get a fix on our guys. But now it was too late, even if the team checked in right this instant. I couldn't make it back to the airfield at *Du Co* in time. It wasn't a long flight to *Du Co*, but I was too far from *Du Co* for my bladder and me.

It was my own fault. This "whoever these guys were" mission got delayed and delayed and delayed. I drank several cups of coffee while waiting for clearance to launch. About four cups, which was three too many.

I wasn't surprised that nobody explained to me why I was only supposed to hang around, waiting. I was a lieutenant; I didn't need to know why. Maybe Major No Name, the Air Force commander running this insertion, figured that the less we low-ranking officers knew the less we could screw things up. And to be honest, I really didn't care. My only concern was the "Team Okay." Until my bladder said "Hello" that is. I really needed to pee.

Okay, time to decide. Out the window? Out the door? In my boot? On the floor? Well, the boot and the floor were out. If I peed in my boot, it was sure to smell, and these were the only boots I had. If I peed on the floor, I would have to pay the crew chief fifty bucks to clean it up, and he'd surely tell his buddies that I wet my pants. I didn't think the door was an option because it would be hard to hold open and would act like a rudder, making the Bird Dog turn. The side window appeared to be my only hope. It latched up onto the underside of the wing, and I wouldn't have to hold it.

I unbuckled my shoulder harness and my lap belt, aimed the Bird Dog straight ahead, and then knelt up on my seat. Please God, don't let the team check in now. This was not a good time to be fooling around with a radio I was not quite able to reach from this position.

My right hand gripped the V strut that went from the glare shield up to the ceiling. The glare shield shaded the few flight and engine instruments this airplane had. After I got myself unzipped and freed up, my left hand held on to the bulkhead just aft of the big side window. Everything else was ad-libbed and hopeful. I tried to angle my hips far enough out the window so that I didn't spray the back seat. But the airplane started tilting in the direction I was leaning, and it occurred to me that the next thing that was going to happen was that I was going to fall out. I sat back down, got the airplane upright again, and thought that I was going to have to sacrifice my boot.

Wait a minute! What about my helmet bag? It was full of spare clips of ammo for my AR-15 (an M-16 with a collapsible stock that I had bungeed to the door). I could dump the clips on the back seat for now, pee into the helmet bag, then throw it out the window. It would flutter into the jungle like a soggy little parachute.

It was on the floor behind my seat. I unbuckled my harnesses for the second time, knelt on my seat again but backwards this time, and leaned over the seat back to get the bag. And that's when I saw the cotter pin that held the rear seat's control stick in place. A cotter pin! Kind of like a bobby pin for boys. It went through the stick! On both sides! The cotter pin connected the stick to the little box where all the cables were that went to the elevator and ailerons! And that meant the stick was hollow. Thank you, Jesus!

I pulled the cotter pin out and got the control stick up front and into position between my knees. I could pee into the stick and then hold it out the window with my palm over the open end. When I removed my hand, the pee would be sucked out downwind. So that's what I did.

All this fooling around couldn't have taken more than a few minutes. But now that my brain was re-engaged, I focused on the radio and the call I hadn't gotten. I checked in with the commander running this operation.

"This is Headhunter Four-Five. No joy."

That meant no one had come up on the frequency. All the while I was hanging out of the window, looking for something, anything. I asked to descend to about 1,500 ft above the jungle.

"Roger Headhunter, take a look, but not too close."

Power idling, my Bird Dog glided in big lazy turns, hopefully disguising my objective, focused on a tiny open spot in the green, and on the larger swatch of green all around. At 1,500 ft I saw the bullets, the tracer rounds. Ours red, theirs green. Then the radio came alive. No one raised their voice. They still whispered, but with desperation,

"Prairie fire! Prairie fire!"

That meant combat hand to hand. Prairie fire! Recon-ese for "the end of the world." The Charlie-model gunships raced back, the troop-carrying Hueys, called slicks, raced back, and Covey raced back. The gunships pounded the recon team's perimeter, keeping the North Vietnamese from overrunning the team. Covey directed them, and then brought in the slicks to extract the team, their wounded, and their dead. Despite shooting that never seemed to stop.

And I watched. Like the second-string quarterback, while Covey directed the show, listening and thinking about how I would have handled something like this. Eventually I did, but not until I joined the second platoon in *Kontum*. Here, with whomever these guys were, I was the back-up. I was new. I had so much to learn.

Please God, tell me that my ears didn't miss the whisper, that my bladder didn't drown my brain. Tell me that I didn't screw this up. Maybe the longest half-hour I'd ever flown up until then was the flight back across the border into Vietnam, back to *Du Co*. Agonizing over a few words I thought I should have heard. I kept telling myself that I didn't miss hearing them. I kept trying to convince myself that I didn't miss hearing them.

I didn't. In the mission debriefing I was told that the team had been in contact with the NVA since shortly after being inserted. That's why the radio call, the "Team O.K." was never transmitted. The team couldn't use the radio. They couldn't risk making a sound. Until the shooting started. I should have felt better, but I didn't.

This covert operation put recon teams on the ground along the Ho Chi Minh Trail almost weekly. Insertions, and then extractions. Sometimes a team was able to complete a mission. Often, they didn't. They almost always needed to be taken out by helicopter before they could complete a mission. These extractions were "hot." The team was in contact with the enemy, the North Vietnamese, soon after being inserted into the landing zone (LZ). AK-47s, rocket-propelled grenades, mortars, and machine guns were all being fired at a small group of Green Berets. And almost always someone was wounded. Or killed. From mid-February through June of 1970, someone would always be killed.

I had been in country (in Vietnam) since September 1969. It was now late November, and I now knew how to pee while airborne. That was big! Still, ten months remained on my tour in Vietnam. Ten months remained on my promise to fly an unnamed mission for some people I didn't know. Ten months of a secret war in Cambodia now and later Laos, along the Trail. Ten months of inventing ways to survive. Of staying alive for ten more months.

I flew out from Holloway and landed the Bird Dog at *Du Co*. I had been flying over the border every day for almost three weeks. On this morning three body bags lay along the edge of the runway. Two U.S. and one *Montagnard* were dead. The other four team members, a U.S. and three *Montagnards,* were wounded. I stood a short distance away, looking for the first time at what I hoped I'd never see. Wondering how many more times I would. As it turned out, I saw too many zippered black coffins. Way too many. For so many years after I returned home my dreams were populated by body bags, the people in them, and how they got there.

But this night, back at my unit's headquarters at Camp Holloway, I sat in the Doghouse, our little bar, staring into a glass of Scotch, asking myself a lot of questions. What magic trick could I use to make the bullets miss? How far would I go to do what I said I would do? How much was enough?

I had to figure out a way to make the bullets miss, because bullets were an everyday occurrence. Sometimes just a couple of pot shots by some farmer who took an old rifle with him to his paddy. Other times an entire arsenal of bullets from newer guns; big bullets or bigger bullets, some coming one at a time and some coming so fast they sounded like a chainsaw.

John Meyers, the pilot I would be replacing when I finally reported to the second platoon, wandered into the Doghouse just as I was about to leave. Captain Meyers was still assigned to the Special Forces compound in *Kontum* but was at Holloway for the night. I didn't bother with asking him why he was here. I just wanted John to tell me the magic trick of how to make the bullets miss. First, Crown Royal on the rocks, and then two words:

"Fly sideways."

John smiled his giant smart-ass smile, but the strain of flying these Sneaky Pete missions was evident in his eyes. He gave me the magic trick that could make the bullets miss. Fly sideways. His words probably saved my life.

An airplane really can be flown sideways. It's called cross-controlling, flying in a crab. The rice farmers with their antique rifles, and the NVA gun crews, always aim off the nose. Always. If I am going sideways, they are going to miss. Except every now and then when they don't. Then the Bird Dog takes bullets meant for me.

What about "Enough?" Enough? How much was enough? That was the other question I wondered about. It turned out I was never able to find an answer to that question because I really didn't need to ask. Fire fights happened, and I had to respond. I stopped thinking and simply trusted my instinct. Trust the "*do.*" How to do what was needed couldn't really be quantified, parsed, dissected, or measured. Stuff was exploding. Guns were banging away. I had to do everything I could possibly do to save as many lives as I could. And the rule I learned as a brand-new second lieutenant, the one about my men coming first? Well, here was the rule in real life. These guys down there on the ground came first. Before me. Always before me.

And my question: how much was enough? Enough was when those of us who flew in support of these men got them all out. All of them. The F-4 Phantoms or the A-1 Skyraiders in flights of two dropped napalm where they were directed. Helicopter gunships hammered the perimeter of the landing zone with rockets and mini guns. Then some of the bravest boys I have ever known swooped in and hovered their Hueys a few feet off the ground, holding steady while the living, the wounded and the dead were loaded on board. Because the gunship and slick drivers (pilots) believed that since they put a team on the ground it was their solemn duty to get them out. We all felt that way.

Since the NVA knew we would try not to leave anyone behind they threw everything they had at the Hueys as they came in to pick up the team. If the North Vietnamese shot down a slick (troop carrier) he knew we'd come back again and again and again. Until we recovered everyone. And sometimes my job was to direct the fighters and gunships so that the NVA had to burrow into the ground. So that they couldn't bring down a Huey. So that everyone was able to get out. The living, the wounded, and the dead.

Enough? There was no answer to enough. To how much was enough. It was a question that fear made me consider but was eventually dismissed as unnecessary. Enough? Enough was so much more than simply doing my job. Enough was doing everything I could. I volunteered to fly this mission. I said I would. I gave my word. That was enough.

### December 1969, Fourth Month

I charged up the stairs to *Pleiku* Air Force Base's tower control room. All windows, radios and radars. I'd never been in a tower before, so this was all new, and very cool. Just two days ago I was told that my father would be passing over *Pleiku*, the big Air Force base just north of Camp Holloway. My company commander, Major David Naumann, allowed me to take Bird Dog to *Pleiku* so that I could talk to Dad on *Pleiku* tower's radio. The tower chief introduced himself and the rest of his crew, then showed me where to sit and which radio I'd use to talk to TWA, to my father, who in a few minutes would be flying overhead. And then, there he was.

I have often thought about this overflight and how magical it was. There were ways to communicate with family, the normal ways almost everyone used. Cassettes and letters that were sent to and from Vietnam by mail. Occasionally a phone call via a radio relay could be made if you happened to be near a MARS (Military Auxiliary Radio Station) and got on the waiting list. It occurred to me then that I might have been the only G.I. who, during the war, talked to a family member who flew a commercial airliner over his head.

In early December, Dad had a MAC charter (Military Airlift Command) flight from John F. Kennedy to Hong Kong. TWA was contracted by the

Pentagon to fly troops to destinations close to Southeast Asia, and Hong Kong was essentially just around the corner. His route took his 747 right over *Pleiku* Air Force Base, in Vietnam's Central Highlands. Camp Holloway, my company's headquarters, was just down the block.

I told my parents about Camp Holloway and my new assignment as a pilot with the 219th Reconnaissance Airplane Company when I wangled my transfer out of flying Otters with the 18th Aviation Company. Celestina, and Francis, did need to know where I was after all, but that was pretty much all I could tell them about what I was doing. The truth was that for the next eight months I had to flat-out lie about what I was doing, not talking about Laos or Cambodia because the Studies and Observations Group (SOG) mission was highly classified. Had my mother found out about any of this, she would have come over and dragged me home by my ear.

On the day Dad passed over *Pleiku* eastbound, our company clerk at Holloway received a phone call from *Pleiku's* tower chief.

"Do you have a Lieutenant Doherty in your unit? You do? Well, tell him his father just flew over on his way to Hong Kong, and he checked in on our frequency. He'll be overhead again in two days flying back to the States. Ask the lieutenant to be in our tower at three pm so he can talk to his father on the tower radio."

I was just floored by this. It took me a few minutes to comprehend what was going to happen. Here I was in the middle of nowhere, and I was going to be able to talk to my dad. I was going to hear his voice. I was going to be looking up at his 747 as he flew over. Looking up at an airplane Dad was flying, hoping to see four water-vapor contrails streaming from the 747's big engines. And he would be looking down at me, or at *Pleiku* Air Force Base, where I would be holding a microphone in a hand that I was sure would be shaking as soon as I heard him check on the tower frequency. I had to get a "Hall Pass" from Major Naumann and an airplane from maintenance to do all this. But I did! I took a deep breath and smiled. Dad!

I remembered another time, when he pointed up at a 707 flying over our house in Fiddlers Green.

"You see that airplane?"

He told me that he could see the house on Fiddlers Green Drive from the cockpit of his 707 and could tell when I hadn't raked the leaves from the lawn or hadn't taken the garbage pails out to the end of the driveway. I probably should remind him that the garbage pails here at the *Pleiku* are, unlike Fiddlers Green, not my responsibility, and that the airfield's garbage pails couldn't be seen from his cockpit window anyway, no matter what fib he told. He was too high, the sky was too hazy, and the garbage pails too small. I wanted to make my father laugh. I wanted him to know that I hadn't forgotten his old joke.

Something else made me smile. My dad, realizing that he was going to overfly *Pleiku*, and remembering that Holloway was just a few rice paddies south, checked his low-altitude chart for *Pleiku* Tower's frequency, called the airfield, and gave the tower his approximate return time two days later. All this from a guy who never really got all his ducks in a row by himself. He was the "Captain," and he usually got somebody else to arrange them for him. Like me. I was always required to get all the information, to know all the facts, to have everything completely organized with no "maybes" or "not sures." School, homework, parties, dates, track meets. You name it, he wanted to know everything about whatever it was that I was doing, even if he ignored a few of the things I was doing. No detail was too insignificant for Dad. Especially now. Because his oldest boy was talking to him from a sand-bagged control tower protected by gun emplacements in the Central Highlands of Vietnam.

Looking back on this now I realize that there were times when it would have been so easy for one, the other, or maybe even the both of us, to say the magic words that boys, or men, or fathers, or sons, find so hard to say. I know that there was an effort made by my father to figure out a way to contact me. Low altitude charts, obscure military radio frequencies, guesstimating a return time, all of that said "I love you" without having to say the words And I in turn arranged an airplane, got excused from having to fly a mission on the afternoon of his return trip, made a takeoff and landing at a nearby air force base, and then sprinted up several flights of stairs to get in front of a radio and a microphone. So that I would be able to hear Dad's voice. Like father, like son, I didn't say the words either.

On the day of my father's return trip from Hong Kong I was in a meeting. The TWA overflight was supposed to happen at about 1500 hours. It was now 1415 and Major Naumann, our company commander, was still talking about "hooch maids." For as long as I was at Holloway, I was responsible for hiring, firing, and collecting money to pay the women who cleaned rooms, washed clothes, stole cigarettes, and occasionally slept with their employers. I only paid the ladies for cleaning and washing. The young men who slept in the cleaned rooms and wore the washed clothes made their own private "I don't want to know about it because I don't care" side-deals with the cleaning ladies, the mama-sans, the hooch-maids. Organizing hooch-maids was one of the extra duties I would be able to get rid of when I finally got to *Kontum*. Sitting in that meeting meant not flying. I thought to myself that I really need to get to the second platoon full-time, as soon as possible. I'm a shit-hot, bullet-proof, scared-but-not-admitting-it, pilot. I'm the whole Lafayette Escadrille, not the hooch-maid organizer.

Major Naumann went on and on and on and on and on and on about hooch-maid rules. What rules did I really need? Collect money from boys to pay girls for cleaning. How hard was that? I kept looking at my watch. This waste of time extra duty assignment was becoming far more complicated than it ever needed to be. Finally, I screwed up my courage and said,

"Major, I've got about twenty minutes to get to Pleiku to catch my dad flying over. Is it okay if we continue this when I get back?"

Major Naumann shook his head "yes" and then said, "Just one more thing, lieutenant."

"Please, major?"

"Okay, Frank. Go."

Zoom! Gone!

I took off from Holloway to the east, turned north and leveled off at a 1,000 ft above the ground. When I contacted *Pleiku*'s tower they asked me if I was the lieutenant whose father was scheduled to overfly shortly.

"That's me," I said.

"Okay Army, enter on a right downwind and you're cleared to land."

I made another left-hand turn to fly parallel to the runway in the opposite direction of landing. The runway was on my right shoulder, that was a right downwind. Then a descending right-hand turn about a half a mile from the end of the runway. That was called base leg. One more descending right-hand turn to line up with the runway, final approach, with landing flaps set and the engine at idle. I cleared the runway right after touchdown. (Bird Dogs don't ever go fast except when they're aimed straight down at the ground.) A gray Air Force pickup-truck with a big "Follow Me" sign on the back of it led me to the base of the tower.

The Air Force tower crew had made it easy for me. Before you assume that their courtesy was unusual let me assure you that there was nothing unusual about this at all. We were aware of what was going on at home, the anti-war protests, the public's disdain for what we sacrificed while we were in Vietnam, and the disrespect that greeted us when we returned. We had only one another to lean on, to care about, to look out for, and to protect from harm. I fought for John Meyers and Phil Phillips and Doug Krout and Ben Brown and Michael Buckland and Arlie Deaton and a whole lot of other guys whose names I don't remember. They were my friends, and even though fifty years have erased many more names, I loved them all.

"*Pleiku* Tower, this is TWA," and then my father's voice said his flight number. I brought the mic close to my mouth and said,

"TWA (flight number), this is Headhunter Four-Five."

That was my call-sign. I thought it sounded very combat-y. My father laughed.

"Who?"

"It's me, Dad. Frank,"

No way I was going to call myself "Frankie." Only my mother, Celestina, and my nana, Clara, were allowed to call me by my family nickname. The three tower operators were listening to every word, and I had no intention of giving them the chance to tease me about "Frankie." I may have looked like I was 15 (I was really 24), but I was still a lieutenant. And then Dad's questions started.

"What are you doing? Who are the people you're flying for? You are being careful, right? You aren't trying to be a hero, are you? Are you being careful? Your mother doesn't like the idea of you doing something dangerous. You're not doing anything dangerous, are you?"

Dad understood danger. Twenty-seven years ago, over Burma, he had contended with Japanese Zeros, their machine guns blazing, diving out of the sun at his B-24.

He wasn't done yet.

"Where are you going on R&R, and when are you going to go? Your mother and I want to come to wherever you'll be. When are you going? Do you know yet?"

The three tower guys started laughing, and the Tower Chief said, "Mommy wants to see her little boy."

I tried leveling my best Junior Lieutenant stare at him. The Tower Chief just laughed harder.

I felt like I was back in high school again. It was a Saturday night. I wanted to borrow the car, but the only way to get it meant I had to swear that I was going out with a nice girl and not taking her to the drive-in movies. I tried to be as sincerely non-committal as I could be, evasive but not exactly lying.

"I don't know yet about any of that, Dad. Probably not until spring, I think."

That part was true. The lying part had to do with what I was going to do once I got to wherever it was, I was going on R&R. I had a very clear idea of what I wanted to be doing, however. And I really didn't want my mother in the next room when I was doing that.

"I'm tape-recording this, Frankie."

Dad's "Frankie" announcement was met with loud snickers. I leveled the same Junior Lieutenant stare at the tower guys with the same results as before. So, I said, "I love you, Mom. I'll be home in nine months. I promise."

I needed my dad to tell Celestina that.

Static started to hide the words. His transmission began to break apart, with words now being lost to scratchy noise, as Dad flew out of range. Then too far away. Gone. I think he knew that I was lying about what I was doing. I was always a bad liar. I used to look at my shoes when I did. He couldn't see me in the tower, but I bet he pictured me looking at my shoes. Not brown penny loafers this time. Black leather boots. I replaced the mic. At least, I thought, he had my voice on tape. He had my voice. And an "I love you," unspoken by us both.

I talked to my mother the following spring on a ham-radio relay phone. I didn't talk to Dad again until I landed in Seattle, my first stop on the way home, in September 1970. The Christmas flight would have then been eight long months old.

In Vietnam a Christmas truce was in effect. No flying mortar watch over Camp Holloway this holiday night. I thought I lucked out not having to pull Officer of the Guard. I sat in our little bar pretending to nurse one scotch after another. A few other guys were there, but nobody was talking. I realized that I would have been better off pulling guard duty or flying mortar-watch. It would have given me something to do and would have saved me from a searing morning headache. I thought about my mother Celestina and my father Francis, my brothers Terry and Glenn, and my sister Kathleen. The Ravioli and Roast Pork DeGuiras, the Finnan-Haddie and Banana Cream Pie Dohertys. About how much I missed them. I thought about survival, about being afraid. I thought about my dad's voice fading away as he flew out of range. I thought about the big Christmas tree at home, covered with lights, just before the long hill on Fiddlers Green Drive. The caroling. Our friend Bob the Cop Anderson dressed up as Santa Claus. And snow. No snow in the Central Highlands. The worst night in Vietnam so far.

Eventually the Doghouse emptied. I was left alone with a can of stale potato sticks, a half-filled bottle of scotch, and enough self-pity to last at least a month. I had been away from home on other holidays, but never on Christmas. Memories didn't tease me so much as they tormented me. The girl who lived at the top of Richard Lane, who I still loved. What was she doing? Who was she with? A battalion of "what ifs" was holding a full-dress parade across my heart.

Then I asked myself a question that had nothing to do with feeling sorry for myself. A simple one, not jumbled up by the scotch I had consumed.

"How'd I get here?"

I asked out loud, looking at my face, which was looking back at me from the mirror behind the bar. The answer was as simple as the question. My father. That's how I got here. And the irony of that was not lost on me. Because my parents hated my being here, and they never disguised their feelings. I was here for reasons that were, for the most part, a lot of nonsense: adventure, honor, manhood. Baloney.

I wanted to be like him. My brother Terry redefined that for me years later, standing in front of an isolated Alaskan cabin, watching an eagle maneuver among angry seagulls to pluck pieces of a salmon carcass from the rocks.

"You always wanted to be Dad. Not be like him. Be him. That's why everything he did, you did."

He surprised me. Was I that obvious? I guess I was. Over another glass of scotch, or maybe more than another glass, because it was the worst Christmas night ever, I thought about how, as a little boy, I never stopped watching him. Because I wanted to see what he did, so that I could do everything he did. I wanted to be him.

# Chapter 4

# Be Like Dad

I followed my father around when he was home. We didn't talk much, but he let me follow him: mowing the lawn, starting a fire in the barbecue grill. Sometimes he let me steer the boat we'd rent when we went fishing with Pa, my Irish grandfather, who always fished in a suit and tie, and always wore his bowler hat.

Dad's work wasn't nine to five like other dads. Flying for Trans World Airlines took him away from home for a few days, but then he was home for a while. Unless he was training on a new airplane. Then he spent weeks away, in Kansas City, where the training center was. Dad didn't dress like the other dads who lived where we lived. Levittown, in 1950. When Dad would go off to work, he wore his pearl gray uniform with the stripes on the sleeves, a white shirt and a tie, and a hat shaped like a dinner plate with a peak in the front and a black bill. And a silver strap that went along the front, held in place by silver buttons with Indian headdresses on them. On the peak there was an Indian Head emblem and the letters TWA. He always had a suitcase and another fat rectangular bag. I didn't know what that fat bag was for. (I would later laugh about it. I called it my brain bag because it held my flight manuals and charts.) Dad would get in our car and drive off to the airfield. And after a night or two away from us he came home.

A man across the street, Mr. Howydell, wore a company shirt, yellow and brown, that said O'Donnell Movers. But that wasn't a uniform. It was just a shirt. Mr. Howydell didn't wear a tie, and he came home every night.

One day Mom drove Dad to work so that she could have the car. I was no older than 7, I think, and that was the first time I ever saw an airport. My father always called it an airfield. There was a green and then a white light that flashed on the top of Idlewild Airport's glass-windowed tower, its repetitive wink hypnotic. There were barn-like buildings with huge doors and gently curved roofs. Airplane hangars. More airplanes in front of a

36

building where people were going in and out. The airplanes had propellers, and one of them had TWA painted on its side, like the TWA on my father's hat. Some kids made truck noises when they played. I did that. But after that day I made airplane noises too. And I stuck my hand out of the car window to make my hand "fly." I can't help myself. I have never been able to stop doing that.

"Frankie, would you like to come to work with me? I'll pick you up on Thursday afternoon, at two. I'll give you a note for Sister. If I'm not there by two, then my schedule has changed. Otherwise, be ready," Dad said.

It's 1956, I'm 11 years old, and in the sixth grade. I can't sit still because I'm waiting for Thursday afternoon. Waiting for the afternoon which, for a little boy, changes his whole everything.

Thursday. Finally! I'm staring at the wall clock, and then checking the classroom door. I should be listening to Sister Athanasia. But I haven't listened to her most of the day.

It's two o'clock. Dad said he'd be here by two. If he isn't here by two, then it isn't going to happen. I feel myself getting small. Trying to hide from the disappointment that's starting to envelope me. And then I see him, framed by the door's window. He's in his uniform. We're going.

The drive to LaGuardia is quiet. I'm too excited to trust my tongue. We park the car in the crew lot. I can see a winking green and white light on the top of LaGuardia's tower too. Just like the one years ago at Idlewild. Dad has his hat and flight bag. I'm supposed to bring my schoolbooks so that I can do my homework on the plane, in the cockpit. Not much chance of that happening. Dad looks at me, then at the schoolbooks. A small smile softens his face.

"Leave them, Frankie." So much to see.

Dad sits in the left seat. The copilot is on the right. Duplicate flight instruments on the panel in front of them. The flight engineer is behind the copilot but sideways, facing another panel of lights, switches, gauges, and dials. And I am in the jump seat, right behind my father.

The airplane is beautiful. A "Connie," a Lockheed Constellation. The fuselage, almost dolphin-shaped, is white with red stripes. TWA blazed in red above the passenger windows. Four large eighteen-cylinder engines, two to a wing, each engine with a giant four-bladed propeller. My heart is just pounding because everything about this is magic.

The Connie's engines are started and throbbing, an unmistakable pulsing unlike the sound of anything I've ever heard. Seat belts and shoulder harnesses are on, checklists are read, and responses are made. We're on the runway. Dad's right hand is on the throttles and his left hand is on the steering yoke. We take off to the north toward the Whitestone Bridge. The flight engineer moves the throttles to adjust the power setting. The copilot talks to air traffic control. My dad is flying. His hands and feet are on the controls. He's making the Connie turn. He's making it climb. My dad. This is what he does. This is how it works.

We're going to Columbus, Ohio, and then returning to New York. The route takes us over Pittsburgh. The flight engineer tunes up the Brooklyn Dodger-Pittsburgh Pirate baseball game on a spare radio. Jackie Robinson and Peewee Reese. We fly right over Forbes Field, and I can see the ballpark. I can listen to the game, but I don't. Because I'm in the cockpit of this airplane, with my father, who is the captain. I know at this very moment that I am in love with flying, and that I am going to be a pilot. Then the "Hostess" brings dinner for the three crew members. And for me too.

On approach to Columbus, landing over farmland, the runway stretches out in front of us. It's lit up even though it's daylight. The landing gear is lowered. Wing flaps are extended. The flight engineer cups his hand mimicking the wing's shape. He explains that the flaps give the wing a curve so that it can still produce "lift" as we slow down. A herd of cows slowly moves off as we cross the airport boundary. They've seen this performance a zillion times.

On the way back from Columbus, I lookout the cockpit's window as little lights wink on and the afternoon slips into night. I may be only 11 years old, but I know magic when I see it. I don't want this day to ever end. And I know that this was where my life is going to be, in a space like this, filled with switches and gauges and dials and needles and radios and a weather radar and throttles, a yoke and rudder pedals. The same little space my father is in this very minute.

Flying became all I ever wanted to do. Nothing would compare to this experience. And nothing ever could. The sunrise poetry of flying, the engine song of flying, the cloud dance of flying. The sheer romance of flying. From the first moment I stepped into the cockpit I was bewitched by all that I saw. I was in love with flying. There would be airplane noises forever. Always.

About a week after going to Columbus in Dad's cockpit he and I were working outside, planting rhododendrons and mountain laurels alongside a path that led into the oaks and dogwoods behind the house in Lloyd Harbor. I was digging the holes while my father made sure they were the right size. I hadn't yet figured out that this was always going to be the way of it. Me digging and him critiquing. And anyway, I was showing my father how strong I had become.

After we eased the root ball of a laurel into its hole, we both straightened up and my father said,

"You know, Frankie, I'm really not much more than a bus driver."

Nothing further. No explanation. Just those words left hanging out there for me to think about. To wonder what he didn't say. Was this a challenge, to make more of myself than he made of himself? That couldn't be what my father meant. He had a twelfth-grade education and was pushing racks of clothes in New York's garment district before the Army Air Corps. Now he was getting ready to go to Kansas City for a month, to check out, to become qualified, on a brand-new Boeing 707. He would have to recalibrate his brain to think at jet engine speed instead of at propeller speed. Years later I realized what an accomplishment this really was. A young man who survived flying B-24s during the Second World War, who really needed malpractice insurance before he picked up any kind of tool, figured out how to fly a mechanically complicated, mentally challenging, very fast jet. I had marveled last week at what went on in the cockpit of the Connie on the way to Columbus. On that spring day in 1956, after listening to my father's bus driver remark, I discounted it out of hand.

He wants more for me than what he has, I decided. I filled in the dirt around the laurel's root ball and got ready to dig the next hole. Dad didn't say anything else. He doesn't really mean that, I thought. This house, these trees, the boat in Lloyd Harbor, the beach on the Sound. The permanence of these rhododendrons and laurels that we're planting along the path into the oaks and dogwoods. I didn't believe he meant a word of that.

In the years after grade school, I attended Chaminade, an all-boys Catholic high school. Then went off to the University of San Francisco, USF, the Jesuits. My mother and father told me that these schools weren't choices that were mine to make. They were part of my parents' plan for me. But later, after all the "you have to" decisions they made for me, I was going to put one hand on the throttles, the other on the yoke, my feet on the rudder pedals. Just like my father. I was going to wear aviator sunglasses, just like my father did. I wanted to be good at something too. Just like he was. I didn't know it yet, but I would have to go to war just like he did. I was going to go flying, just like he did. I was going to be just like him.

My parents handed me my marching orders and I was enrolled at USF in the fall of 1963, but I didn't really start being a student until my junior year. Prior to that I was just taking up space. That I managed to squeak by academically those first two years was nothing short of a miracle bolstered by all-nighters and coffee. That I became brilliant as a junior did little to erase the mess that I had made of my first two years. The inevitability of Vietnam, an inevitability of my own making, hadn't hit me yet, so I decided to save a few bucks during my sophomore year and the first half of my junior year by eschewing haircuts. By the time Christmas rolled around in my junior year, in 1965, it had been almost sixteen months since a barber had come near me.

I took the all-nighter from San Francisco to JFK, then waited for Dad to pick me up in front of the TWA terminal. I saw him coming. His car slowed down but didn't stop. He was peering out the window at me, my ponytail, and my round, rose-tinted, hippie glasses. OK. What do I do now? Call Mom? He came around again, and I hoped this wouldn't be another drive-by. This time he stopped, and as I lifted my suitcase, he frowned at me over the car's roof.

"What are you supposed to be?"

Back at school for the beginning of the winter quarter, the Draft, the Army, and Vietnam were all staring me in the face. Grad school was not an option. Two years of seldom opening a book took care of that. I got an Army approved haircut and enrolled in ROTC (Reserve Officer Training Corps). I didn't talk to my parents about this. I didn't ask permission. I just did it.

Dad picked me up at Kennedy again, at the end of my junior year. This time he stopped the car, got out, and asked,

"What are you, some kind of fruitcake?"

My hair was short. Not a little short. Crewcut short. And I had given the rose-colored glasses away to a stewardess on the flight back to San Francisco after Christmas. I could tell by the way Dad was eyeing my haircut that he had figured out what I had done. Hoping to buy a little time I told him that I'd explain when we got home. I wanted to wait so that I only had to go through this song and dance once for both my mother and my father. Because I knew my parents were going to be upset with my decision. Especially my mother. All the rationalizations I made, about two years of bad grades, about really doing so much better now, about it being too late to convince anyone to accept me into a Masters in Psych program, about the threat of the draft, about going in the Army as an officer, none of that made a bit of difference. When what I had done sank in, Celestina's face drained of color, her eyes filled with tears, and she slapped me. She had never ever slapped me before. Dad walked out of the kitchen, a string of God-damn-its trailing after him.

We settled into a distant but cordial truce. I went back to the same summer job I'd had all through college. Back to West Neck Beach as a lifeguard, with a new group of 14-year-old girls camped out daily around the white guard tower. Calm remained until I had to pack up for ROTC summer camp. Six weeks at Fort Lewis, Washington.

"I hate that you are doing this," my father shouted.

"I'm not going to Canada. I'm not running away. I can't."

I really meant that. My friend Bunky Egan drove me to the airport at Kennedy because Francis and Celestina refused.

Just before leaving for my senior year at USF my father and mother asked me again if I was sure that volunteering for the Army was my only option. I explained myself again.

"I made a mess of the first two years at school. I dug myself a hole and I'm only half-way out. I know I'll be drafted as soon as the Army finds out after graduation that I'm not enrolled in grad school. I'm going as a second lieutenant and I'm going to get the best deal I can get."

I didn't say a word about flight school or trying to switch to the Marine Corps. Just stop talking, I told myself. Graduate from San Francisco and go from there. So that's what I did.

I came home for the summer after graduation. My last summer in my parents' house. I returned to San Francisco in early September. Then polite letters, soft voices on the telephone, avoiding the subject of my gold second lieutenant's bars during a Christmas visit. Our cautious truce lasted until I came home at the end of February. My report date for active duty was approaching, and the tension between my parents and me increased daily until we barely spoke to one another. Did I want to leave? Not really. Did I need to leave? No, I had to leave.

On 17 March, in 1968, Finnegan's, an Irish bar in Huntington Village, was probably packed for St. Patrick's Day. It had been packed on every St.

Patrick's Day since it opened in 1912. It was packed most nights, and I was positive that tonight was standing room only. A lot of my friends were sure to be in the bar, standing, balancing, swaying when necessary, trying not to spill a drop of their pints. I'd been in Finnegan's on other St. Patrick's Day evenings. The room always throbbed like a beating heart. And those of us in that room on Erin Go Bragh night throbbed in time with it. On this St. Patrick's Day, I was nowhere near Finnegan's or the top of Richard Lane (I was still so in love with a girl who lived there) or Huntington or Lloyd Harbor or New York. I was in Kentucky, at Fort Knox, at Armor Officer Basic School. I was a second lieutenant. I was in the Army.

Mom and Dad drove me to LaGuardia. We were not celebrating St. Patrick's Day or anything else on that drive. I had to fly to Cincinnati, then take an Army bus to Fort Knox. The conversation in the car, some quick questions on their part and even shorter answers on mine, was so strained. The drive to the airport must have been torture for them. Nothing calmed them, and there was no turning the car around. The war in Asia was building up. The *Tet* Offensive was all over the news. There was no mistaking the skepticism in television news anchorman Walter Cronkite's voice. My father concentrated on the Long Island Expressway. My mother exchanged words for sobs.

I had a hard-sided suitcase crammed with underwear, socks, sweaters and shirts, a belt, and a hanging clothes bag with my officer's uniform, a blue blazer, slacks in charcoal and taupe, and several ties. Almost everything sported the same label, Brooks Brothers. I was wearing my tasseled Weejuns. All prepped up. The next morning, I would be dressed in olive green, with my head shaved, just like every other second lieutenant in my Basic class.

As I sat in the barber's chair that first morning at Fort Knox, I smiled at the barber.

"Tighten up the sides and take just a little off the top."

He snapped the caftan-like bib around my neck, fired up the clippers, and, going from front to back, cut a racing stripe from my forehead to the nape of my neck. Not exactly the fashion statement I wanted to make.

Standing in line in the officers' mess, the young lady behind the counter pointed to what looked like corn and asked,

"Hominy?"

I asked her for two, please. She looked at me like I was nuts.

"Hominy?"

"I like corn. Two helpings please." I replied. I thought she said, "how many." The lieutenant in line behind me punched me in the back "She said hominy, dumb-ass, not how many."

The furthest south I'd gone? Pasadena, in Southern California. What did I know?

Sitting in the grandstand being schooled on map-reading, the sergeant giving the class opened his presentation with, "awlraht yew mens." I bit my tongue, so I didn't laugh out loud. We sat through a lecture on night vision. Something about the rods and cones in our eyes and aiming tank cannons in the dark. Why I hung on to this all these years, I have no idea. But after all these years it's still funny.

There were things I learned at Basic that were really, significant. Those things had nothing to with map reading or night vision rods and cones, with "awlraht yew mens" or "hominy." They were only the most important rules an officer lived by.

"Never ask your men to do something that you either won't or don't want to do. You are the first man on the battlefield and the last man off. Your men eat first, shower first, get clean clothes first. Your men come first. They always come first."

My orders, after I completed Basic, had me assigned to the 3rd Armored Division. In Bavaria. Not in Vietnam, in *Kirch Gons*. I was safe, except that I wasn't. I never for a minute believed I'd get to stay in Germany. Tanks kept me from wading through rice paddies. I wanted to fly over rice paddies. Not walk, wade, or drive through them. The next step was to make a phone call. To Armor Branch headquarters at the Pentagon.

Armor had only two slots in every fixed wing (real airplanes) class, but all the slots it could ever want in helicopters. I wanted one of those two fixed wing slots. I was connected to a Colonel Patterson. He handled the flight school assignments.

"You want to go to fixed wing, don't you?"

"Yes sir. That's why I'm calling. I've passed the flight physical and the written aviation aptitude exam but haven't submitted my paperwork.

I wanted to talk to you first, sir, to be sure I got one of the fixed wing slots. My father was in the Army Air Corps in the Second World War, and I'd like to do what he did."

"What did your father do after the war, lieutenant?"

"He went to work for TWA, sir. He is an airline pilot."

"Young man, the future of Army Aviation is in helicopters. That's what you should be doing. And you're never going to be able to fly commercially with the training you'll get in the Army."

"Colonel, I really want to follow in my father's footsteps. I'll request a transition to helicopters after I finish Fixed Wing."

I was tap dancing my way through a big fat lie and I was sure Colonel Patterson knew that. A pause that took forever, and then, "Alright, lieutenant. You'll have a slot sometime this summer. And son, tell your father and mother that after flight school you will be going to Vietnam."

Vietnam. I wasn't surprised. That was what flight school promised without Colonel Patterson needing to say so. I knew what I had done. I had a beer or two after chow in the little Officers' Club Annex close to our barracks. Only junior officers hung out there. It wasn't Finnegan's, and it wasn't St. Patrick's Day, and I really missed the girl at the top of Richard Lane, and I hadn't composed the speech I was going to give to my parents yet, and I didn't want to think about any of that tonight. Well, that's not true. I always thought about the girl at the top of Richard Lane.

A week later the captain in charge of our group of officer trainees called my name. I stood and he handed me a change of orders. *Kirsch Gons* was crossed out and my next duty assignment was Fort Stewart Georgia. Just south of Savannah. Primary flight school. I also got an additional two years tacked on to my military commitment.

I dialed home during our morning break from class, my brand-new orders in my sweaty hand. Dad answered the phone. That was lucky. I wanted to tell him, and not Mom, first. Telling Dad first was like the dress rehearsal of my announcement. I knew he was not going to be happy, but I was frightened to death at how Celestina would respond when she heard the Vietnam part of my explanation. I could see her explosion followed by her charging out the door on her way to D.C. to tell the colonel to forget it. At least she couldn't reach through the phone to slap me again. When my father answered I figured that if I just started talking and kept on talking until I said everything I needed to say, he wouldn't be able to ask any questions until I finished. That way I could get the flight school part all out without tripping over my words. I managed it all without interruptions.

"I'm going to have to sign on for two extra years, Dad."

The Army got paid back for flight training in time.

"And I'm going to have to go to Vietnam. For a year."

My father said that he thought I would. He was quiet for one of the longest minutes in my short life.

"Do you want me to tell your mother?"

I was stunned by his offer to make this easy for me. That was not the way these things ever went before. If I had done something I had to own up to whatever that something was.

"No, Dad. I have to do that. Is Mom home?" (Hail Mary, full of grace...)

A split-second later Celestina was on the phone.

"Mom, I..."

"I know. I heard."

Her voice, almost ragged around its edges, was surprisingly controlled. It must have taken all the willpower she had.

"Mom, I've always wanted to fly. Always, Mom."

"You've made a bargain with the Army, Frankie. Now you must make a promise to your father, and to me. Especially to me, Frankie. You must come home from that place. Do you hear me? Don't leave any part of you over there. Not one little piece."

The first weeks of flight school give me goosebumps, because it is as if laughter has wings. Take-offs, landings, simple maneuvers, a great first instructor, everything coming easily. And then, just like that, initial training isn't so much fun anymore. I'm not running to the airplane. I am trudging. I don't know what causes my new instructor to disregard me, to dismiss me, to abandon me. But he does. I ask him why. He glares, answering with silence. He leaves me to figure everything out for myself. I do, almost. But almost isn't enough.

The early November sun is hot. I am sitting on the back steps of my class's briefing room. There's a little shade from the roof over the back door. But it doesn't help much because I'm sweating from embarrassment and disappointment. I've never failed at anything in my life. Never. Until today's check ride on the maneuvers portion of the second phase of initial flight training. I'm dreading facing my classmates. There's no way I'm going to be able to tell my father.

The first phase of initial training, which began in September at Fort Stewart, Georgia, is to learn how to take off and land. That makes sense. Taking off is the easy part. But sooner or later I had to get the Cessna trainer back on the ground. So, learning to land is important. It's also fun. When my instructor Sheldon Hanneman, a civilian pilot, decides that I'm ready, he asks me to pull off the runway and stop. We don't taxi to the parking ramp. Instead, he opens the door and climbs out. Before walking away, he tells me to make three takeoffs and landings and after the third landing to taxi to the ramp and shut the airplane down. Mr. Hanneman is sending me off to "solo." I am overjoyed! This is a big deal, a big vote of confidence, one big step for me. Three landings, then park the airplane on the ramp, where Mr. Hanneman is waiting for me. He doesn't just shake my hand. He hugs me.

My instructor for the second phase is a captain just returned from Vietnam. He is nervous, unfriendly, cantankerous, rude, and condescending. All the attributes one could want in a teacher. We fly together maybe twice a week over a three-week period, and he teaches me absolutely nothing. When we climb into the airplane for the first time, before we put on a seat belt or read a checklist or start the engine or taxi out for takeoff, he tells me (and I will never forget his words),

"They didn't kill me in Vietnam and I'm not going to let you kill me here either."

I don't respond. Even if I want to, I am so stunned that I just look out the window, over the nose of the airplane, and start to sweat.

We level off at about 3,000 ft and my instructor, Captain Somebody, takes the controls to demonstrate the first upper air work maneuver. A *Chandelle*. French for candle. A lovely name for not too hard an exercise. Raise the nose but don't climb. The airplane sort of hangs on its prop. Not enough engine power to gain altitude, but enough to keep the airplane from descending, barely moving forward. And just for the fun of it, make a turn to go in the other direction. The point of this instruction is to teach the student how to coordinate the controls. Doing this right means that climbing and turning had to work together equally. Coordinated. Smooth. Precise.

Next is a Lazy Eight. Lay the figure eight on its side and aim the nose right at the crisscross in the middle. Then trace the lines of the figure eight with the nose. My instructor doesn't have me follow him on the controls – my feet on the rudder pedals, my hand on the yoke, and my other hand over his on the throttle – to feel what he's doing. He doesn't talk as he moves the airplane through the maneuver. He doesn't explain anything. He just does it. I hear the engine rev up and then idle back. I feel the airplane climb and turn, then descend and turn. But I have no idea when or how or why. I have no idea at all. But my instructor is coordinated, smooth and precise.

One demonstration for a *Chandelle*, one demonstration for a Lazy Eight, and that's it. They're complicated, but not for him. Just for me. Because I have no idea what we just did. No verbal explanation about coordination or power, no staying on the controls with me so that I can feel my instructor's corrections. No critique. No nothing. I try to do what I think I am shown but my attempts are not remotely close. Do I receive any further instruction? Nope. We fly together two more times, and there is almost no instruction then either.

There are other maneuvers too. Maneuvers that are demonstrated but never explained. My instructor says,

"This is a Pylon Turn."

And then he does one, silently. I figured out how to do this and the other required maneuvers, like Wind Circles, on my own. I get these right away. What I need my instructor to show me again are *Chandelles* and Lazy Eights. No help whatsoever. But he and I are even, I guess. He doesn't teach me a damn thing, and I manage not to kill him.

The flight test to show proficiency in upper air work takes place the day after my last training period. The examiner is Major Arlie Deaton. I meet him for the first time this check ride day, and our paths will cross again and again over the next year. He will be my commanding officer in Vietnam, and Arlie and I will stay friends for almost half a century. The maneuvers I know how to do I do with almost no mistakes. Then we climb up to 3,000 ft and I do a *Chandelle*. In name only. The Lazy Eight is equally unrecognizable. I stop throwing the airplane all over the sky and feel myself shrinking. But it's a little airplane, and there's no place to hide. Deaton is draped over the yoke, looking at me with a bewildered smile. Then he says,

"Watch."

He does a *Chandelle*. Ah, so that's what it's supposed to look like! He tells me to do a *Chandelle*. I do what Arlie showed me. And it is what it's supposed to be. Next a Lazy Eight. Now I see. Arlie tells me to do one. I do, and it is what it is supposed to be. We return to Fort Stewart's airfield, and I make a nice, smooth, gentle landing. Taxi, park, shut down, check lists, then back to the briefing room. Except we don't go inside. We go around to the back door and sit on the steps. I am afraid I know what he is going to say.

He is going to tell me that check-pilots can't instruct. That's always the rule, he will say. I expect that Arlie will tell me that I have failed the ride. And that's exactly what he does. But having to hear him say this is crushing. He tells me that he knows I am going to be a good pilot. He says that my being able to do what he explained, the *Chandelle* and the Lazy Eight, proves that. He says that he will make sure that I am recycled into the pilot class just behind me so that I can repeat these last three weeks with a better instructor. He tells me not to let him down. He saves me from being washed out of flight school. I am badly wounded, but I am not dead.

And I am not going to call home with the news, because I have never had to tell my father that I have failed anything. So, I don't. I don't call. I guess telling my father that I have "busted" a check ride is really the one thing I can't do. I never tell my father, and I never fail another.

Arlie keeps his promise. I am recycled to repeat the second phase, to learn the maneuvers I was never taught. My instructor this time is another civilian. He has a pencil-thin mustache and iron-gray hair slicked down on his head like a helmet. His name is Mister Weaver. I never learn his given name and have no intention of asking. He is as thin as a fencing sword and the index and middle fingers of his flight gloves are stained nicotine yellow. Camels, one right after the other. I don't care. I just want him to teach me.

That is exactly what happens. It's amazing. Mister Weaver has little cardboard discs that he uses to cover up the altimeter and airspeed indicator.

"Look out the window and tell me how high we are. Listen to the air as it passes over the cockpit and tell me if you think we have enough airspeed. Feel the airplane. It will tell you what it wants. It will tell you what to do."

He teaches me to fly like a pilot, not like a robot.

The three weeks with Mister Weaver are funny too. His manner is easy and calm, but he has one strange quirk. His head constantly moves, and his eyes constantly search. Up above us, on either side of us, below us, behind us. I screw up my courage and ask,

"Mister Weaver, what are you looking for?"

No smile in his answer.

"Messerschmitts, kid, Messerschmitts."

Swastikas and Iron Crosses. Mister Weaver was a fighter pilot (P-38 Lightnings) over Italy in the Second World War. I'm in awe!

The repeat check ride is a non-event. The check pilot (not Deaton) is friendly, and I am at ease right away. The *Chandelles* and Lazy Eights and Wind Circles and Pylon Turns and Grass Strip Landings are fun. My second phase of flight school is finally over. We are sent from Fort Stewart, which is just below Savannah, to Fort Rucker, in Alabama, which is still embroiled in the Civil War, or, as Alabamians call it, "The War of Northern Aggression." I never see Mister Weaver again, and I am sorry for that, because his lessons never leave me. Graduation, and then Vietnam. Mister Weaver helps me survive the war.

Eighteen months later I am assigned to Fort Rucker as a Bird Dog instructor pilot. I walk into the airfield's little coffee shop, a converted double-wide trailer. It is raining so my students are just hanging out, waiting for the morning's flying to be scrubbed. A familiar voice calls my name. It's Morty, my flying partner from before I was "left back." My flying partner who received great help from the same instructor on everything that I didn't. And because the world can be map-dot small, my former instructor, the one who didn't die in Vietnam and whose students obviously didn't kill him, is having coffee with Morty. The disappointment and humiliation come thundering back. I am sitting in the hot sun on the rear steps of the briefing room again, knowing that I am about to fail that check ride.

Morty slaps me on the shoulder and tries to crush my hand when he shakes it. Morty is a big guy. He motions to my instructor and asks me if I remember Captain Somebody. I look down at my feet to gather my composure. That failure never left me, and I am an expert at carrying a grudge. Then I look at him and say,

"I'll never forget you."

It's been fifty years since that sweaty Georgia afternoon. I'm Irish. I don't forget; I don't forgive. Not that miserable prick who taught me nothing. No point in pretending that I ever will. At least I didn't kill him.

The truth is that I wasted very little time thinking about "Captain Somebody." I didn't take thinking about him to Vietnam with me, that's for sure. Flying this mission across the border into Cambodia and later Laos demanded total focus. Getting shot at was expected. It was Arlie Deaton's words that I took with me. "Don't let me down, Dawtry," became a promise I made to him, to my dad, and to me. "Don't let me down," reminded me to keep my brain engaged and think everything through.

Arlie's words reminded me to always do what I promised others I would do. I expected everyone else to do the same and it was just so unexpected when some people didn't. I realized that the values espoused by people who mattered to me, who were here in Vietnam, confronted by an awful war, like Sister Angela and Arlie, their values were anchored in altruism, in honor, in selflessness, in doing the right thing. And doing the right thing allowed me to live with myself.

A few days after my pre-Christmas conversation with Dad as his 747 flew over *Pleiku*, I crossed the border back into Vietnam, out of small arms range, on my way to the Special Forces compound at *Du Co*. I had been flying since early morning, working along the North Vietnamese infiltration route east of the *Ia Drang* Valley. It was lunchtime and I was hungry. I allowed my mind to wander a little, day-dreaming this time about home, about Sunday dinner in Nana's and Pop Pop's dining room. About ravioli and meatballs and fennel sausage and roast pork. I was hoping that I would at least find franks and beans or, better yet, pretend Italian meatballs and spaghetti in what remained of the C-Rations at *Du Co*. The helicopter crews always got to the C-Rats first and always snatched all the good stuff. Please, I prayed. Anything but those olive-green cans of god-awful pressed ham and lima beans.

I didn't expect to see another airplane out here. *Du Co* was right on top of the border, and really close to the Ho Chi Minh Trail. I wouldn't have been anywhere near this area if I didn't have to be. But the part of me who speaks before he thinks opened my big mouth and volunteered. That part of me wanted to be a big hero. Sometimes I wished that the big hero part of me would learn to just shut up. I stopped eating imaginary meatballs when I saw a Bird Dog several thousand feet above me. I could make out the red, white, and blue vertical stripes on its tail, its vertical stabilizer. 223rd Aviation Battalion markings, just like mine. This guy was almost certainly from my unit, the 219th Reconnaissance Airplane Company, a Headhunter. He was too far north to be out of *Ban Me Thout*, a 185th Pterodactyl, and too far south to be out of *Phu Bai*, a 220th Catkiller. He had to be a Headhunter, one of our guys.

The mystery Bird Dog was west of me and as I watched him, I was all the while getting closer to him. He was doing acrobatics. Loops, Wingovers, Split-S's, Spins, Steep Turns and Stalls, Lazy Eights and *Chandelles*, things I loved to do too. I had no idea if he had seen me or not, but as I got closer, he kept right on having fun. This was something I did after finishing whatever I was supposed to do. Not every time, but every now and then, and always after my mission was completed. Just to use up my leftover adrenaline. Except that seeing this airplane here, in this sector of our operations, just didn't feel right. As far as I knew there was nothing going on here now. So, doing acrobatics well above small arms range? Maybe this wasn't just getting the beans out. It seemed to me that this was more like hiding out.

I don't know why I was surprised by this airshow. But I was. Maybe I was just too altruistic. Maybe I was just too naive. Too many maybes for one day. I thought everyone did what they were supposed to do. Pilots and crew chiefs, clerks and cooks, everyone. It never occurred to me that someone wouldn't before now.

Several days later I saw a Bird Dog doing loops over the same place, at the same altitude, and at about the same time. This morning mimicked the morning when I first saw the single airplane air show going on over the *Ia Drang*, the same uneasy feeling. The only real difference between that morning and this one was that today's ground fire was lighter. There weren't as much shooting at me this morning. No ground fire would be better than some ground fire, but I'd settle for some ground fire rather than a lot. I didn't think whoever was in that Bird Dog saw me this time either. But my curiosity was nudging me.

"Who is that? Could it be the same guy?"

I walked into the Officers' Club after dinner and sat down next to Captain Don Shipp, our executive officer, ordered a beer for myself, a bourbon for Don, and started a question. I told him about the air show out beyond *Du Co*, told him exactly where I saw the air show, and the time of day that the performance took place. I explained that when I finished a mission, I often liked to play with the Bird Dog, pretending I was in a whirling fight with the Red Baron. But twice now, in the same place? And high enough to be zipping around the little cumulus clouds that floated over the mountains?

"Does this seem strange to you?" I asked.

"If you see the airplane again, try to get the tail number," Don answered.

No finger pointing without evidence. All our airplanes have numbers stenciled across the vertical stabilizers. The airplane I flew most often was 001534. I can never remember my blood type, but I remember that tail number.

"I'll try."

Was he just blowing off steam? I began to regret bringing this up. Maybe I needed to listen to the stunt pilot's explanation. I was never fond of whiners or tattletales, and I was beginning to feel like one.

Back again a few days later over Cambodia, east of the *Ia Drang*, working the Trail, I was looking for trucks and troops in the early morning, and getting shot at. A lot. I could see holes in my airplane's sheet metal, out near the left-wing tip. On the way back to *Du Co*, sure enough, there was the Bird Dog, spinning three revolutions in a dive, stopping the spin, and then leveling off. He was just slightly above me, off to the north of me, and close. Close enough for him to be able to see me, and close enough for me to be able to read the airplane's tail number. I would be able to cross-reference its maintenance log with the dates of the airshow performances and figure out who was flying. That's what I did, and the stunt-pilot was identified. He was a boy, my age, who was no doubt carrying around the same fear that I carried, probably that we all carried. I struggled with what to do next.

I didn't go back to Don to tell him what I had figured out. I needed some time to think through how what I saw made me feel. Instead, I did a little snooping, asking members of this young man's platoon where they had been working, what they had seen, if enemy activity had increased, if they had received any AK-47 or .51 caliber machine gun fire. I used my mission, looking for traffic along the Trail, to cover my tracks. I related my questions about their mission to what I was doing. And it became obvious to me that the acrobat was nowhere near where he was supposed to be and not remotely doing what he was supposed to be doing. I thought that maybe he was hiding.

I was still not ready to talk to Don Shipp about this, so I avoided him because I was afraid that he would ask me about the stunt pilot, and if I had figured out yet who it was. I concluded that for the time being I was going to keep the identity to myself. All of this had made me uncomfortable. So far, I had unintentionally discovered a pilot not doing what he was supposed to be doing and had brought this discovery up to Captain Shipp, my second in command. Then I uncovered the pilot's identity. I didn't know yet why this pilot was hiding. And that's what made me uneasy. Why?

I felt as if I had walked around for days with my chin on my chest and my hands in my pockets. It didn't matter what I was doing. Flying, eating, drinking beer. All of this with my chin on my chest and my hands in my pockets. And my smile was absent without leave. On the one hand I reasoned that maybe the stunt man had small children or had decided that sticking his neck out wasn't worth it. Maybe he was doing loops and spins because he didn't believe in what we were doing here anymore. On the other hand, maybe he was just scared. A crisis of conscience I could accept. A lack of courage was something much harder for me to swallow.

So okay, I didn't have children yet. But what if my chances of dying increased and my children didn't get to be born because the stunt pilot was ducking his responsibility? How was that fair? What exempted him from the risks I had to take? Flying in combat was flirting with death, period. And we all volunteered to do this. Nobody got drafted as a pilot. This was a conscious decision that every one of us had made. It didn't matter that my missions across the border were inherently more dangerous. Flying in combat was inherently dangerous no matter where one flew. If the stunt pilot had decided that he had lost faith in this war, he could ask for an administrative job. He could be the supply officer or the motor pool officer, jobs currently occupied by pilots who didn't like combat flying either. Those jobs had to come open sooner or later. And if he was afraid? Well, so what! Me too, every day. But I couldn't see myself allowing someone else to carry my share of the danger just because I didn't want to. What was the big rule that we were told in Officer Basic Training? You should never ask someone else to do something you yourself wouldn't do.

My feelings about this war were a tangled mess of questions too. Were we right? Were we wrong? Were we risking our lives for something that mattered? Or did one guy doing barrel rolls make any difference? His justifications belonged to him. I decided that whatever issues this young man had, he would have to resolve them for himself. I knew that I didn't want to be any more involved than I already was. It wasn't going to be me who was going to expose him.

"Do you mind if I sit down, lieutenant?"

I looked up from my metal dinner tray at a boy my age.

"Please. That would be great."

I got to my feet in our almost empty mess hall. He was a captain. This public display of courtesy was correct. Respect for rank, for discipline, for order.

"I know you saw me. Thank you for not saying anything,"

It was simple for the acrobat to figure out that I was the pilot who watched his airshow. There were only two of us from the 219th who were flying this weird mission, only two of us crossing the border into Cambodia. Check the mission logs, just as I had.

The humiliation at being caught, which I read from the expression he wore all over his face, and the fear of being exposed that I saw in his eyes, erased whatever doubts I had about whether to report him. I knew I couldn't, and I knew I wouldn't. I looked at him, a boy just like me, then down at my metal tray, and then back at him.

"You know what I thought about while I tried to sort out what to do?"

He just shook his head from side to side.

"I thought about the last guy who will die here. What a family would do knowing that their son was the last one dead. What could anyone tell them?"

And then I gave him absolution, sort of.

"It's not up to me to decide for you what's right or wrong, captain. Your right and wrong belong to you. You get to pick. You own your reasons. And you own their consequences."

Relief. I saw relief relax the muscles around his jaw, around his eyes. He didn't say anything else, just extended his hand, which I shook. I wouldn't think of not shaking his hand. Respect for rank, for discipline, for order. Nothing further was going to come from me.

I finally left Holloway for *Kontum* just after Christmas, with eight months of my year remaining, and reported to Captain Charles Slimowicz, who ran the 219th's second platoon. I had put the stunt pilot episode aside, but not the notion of the last body shipped home, the last family standing at the graveside of the last soldier to die here. As my year progressed, and as the secret war became bloodier, as the casualties mounted, and as my sense of the futility of this war grew, the horribleness of being the last man dying was like an unrelenting stomachache. I was sure the war would go on after I left, so I might die, but I wouldn't be the last dead guy. Hardly consoling. There were peace talks now in Paris, but the negotiators couldn't even decide on the shape of the table at which they would argue. Not much chance of a ceasefire before my Vietnam ended.

I decided, no acrobatics instead of missions for me. No hiding. I volunteered for flight school. For Vietnam. I took an oath, I gave my word, and I could never renege on my promise. I would see all of this through. That meant never letting my guard down. I could let my mind wander a little when I was flying out of range of small arms fire. But my eyes could never stop looking at everything that was going on around me. My ears could never stop listening for the crack of rounds going by me. I could never tell anyone about the secret sorties I was flying. And the part of my heart that understood honor would never let me break my pledge.

I had another promise that I had to keep as well. A promise that was more important than any other. The one I made to Celestina, over the phone, when I called home from Fort Knox. When I told my mother and father that I was going to flight school, and then Vietnam. This promise was why I had to stay alert, to pay attention, to figure out how to survive. Because I remembered exactly what Celestina demanded of me. My mother's voice was almost ragged around its edges, her words wet with tears.

I made a lot of promises. Promises to the Army, to Arlie Deaton after my failed check ride, to myself, and to my parents.

"Come home to us, Frankie."

I swore an oath to defend my country as gold lieutenant's bars were pinned on my uniform. I promised Arlie that I would live up to the faith he had shown in me. I promised myself that I would honor the commitments I had made. I promised my parents that I would come home in one piece. I cared about them all. I wanted to keep them all. If I broke a promise, a promise I had made, I would never be able to shrug that off, to pretend that the broken promise didn't matter. Turning away from the bargain I made with the Army to do what I said I'd do, or with Deaton.

"Don't let me down, Dawtry."

Or with myself to honor my word, would really diminish me in my own eyes. To go back on my word to my mother and father? That would destroy me because it was the one promise that I knew wasn't a sure thing.

# Chapter 5

# MACVSOG

**Overview:** *Kontum*

It's after 0100. My alarm will go off soon. It's set for 0315. Time enough to get to the showers. Let's hope the showers are turned on. If not, maybe I can find a faucet at a sink that is working. Cold water is better than no water at all; hot water would be amazing. Just to get soaped up and scrubbed off with a washcloth would be a luxury. And for a few moments I wouldn't smell. At least not until I put on my flight suit. It's so gross that it is standing at attention in the corner of our hooch, rigid with salt and sweat.

There's time yet before the alarm goes off; before we careen through the pitch-black night from our hooch to the airfield. Zooming past the cemetery we will turn off the jeep's headlights. Besides the dead there are living people in there too. They have AK-47s. They know we are coming. Maybe they are waiting for us. I hope they have fallen asleep. I hope we don't run into something on the road.

There's time yet before the alarm goes off. I think back to November, when I first got to the Central Highlands. My heart was pounding out of my chest. I was certain everybody could hear it. So scared I couldn't focus, I couldn't talk. That first time flying over the Ho Chi Minh Trail, the mission Don Shipp asked me to volunteer for, when we inserted a recon team that was in trouble immediately, they were screaming over the radio, almost drowned out by the staccato of small arms fire. The FAC marked positions with his rockets for the F-4s. They stopped Charlie. Med-Evac helicopters hovered in the landing zone; gunships strafed the tree line. The team, or what was left of them, were on the choppers. We got them out. I thought then that it would be a miracle if I lived through eight more months of this.

There's time yet before the alarm goes off. I think about how quickly I have become fatalistic. It has taken a month at the most. I can picture the ways I am going to die. I want whatever is going to happen to me to be quick. If I am shot down and captured, the North Vietnamese are going to kill me. But they will take their time, and it will hurt too much. So I save a bullet in my .38. My heart still pounds, but now I'm the only one who can hear it.

There is time yet before the alarm goes off. Somehow, I am still alive. The parade of dead people continues unabated. Body bags in twos and threes lay by the side of the runway but so far, I'm not one of them. I lay staring at part of the wall alongside my upper bunk, populated by pictures of naked girls. Illuminated by my cigarette, reminding me that I have something to look forward to.

There's time yet before the alarm goes off. Soon it is summer. I won't have too much longer to go before I don't have to do this anymore. My heart pounds louder than ever. My fear of dying grows again because I think that maybe my death is not a sure thing. That maybe I'm not going to die. I think that maybe I might, I just might, go home, and keep the promise I made to Celestina. In the glow from another cigarette, I give this feeling a name. I know what it is. I know it now. I know what this feeling is. Hope.

**January 1970, Fifth Month**

A jeep dropped me off in front of the FOB 2 compound, the first day of January and my first day in *Kontum*, about two miles from the airfield. FOB 2? I had no idea what that meant, but this place had more razor wire than San Quentin and was guarded by guys who didn't look very Vietnamese to me. That's because they were *Montagnards* from the *Rahde* tribe, mountain people with a primitive culture who hated the Vietnamese as much as the Vietnamese hated them. *Montagnards* were fierce fighters, and the CIA (yes, those guys, I later learned) paid them very well.

I reported to the camp commander, Colonel Abt, who was wearing cut-off fatigue pants, an olive-drab T-shirt, and shower shoes. He was dressed for the beach even though there wasn't one remotely close to here. We exchanged a salute and a handshake, and Colonel Abt welcomed me to Command and Control Central, Forward Observation Base 2. (Aha! So that's what FOB meant.) He made a little small talk and then walked me over to the S2, the intelligence officer, a Green Beret major who was a dead ringer for Colonel Potter from TV's Mash. Major Gole, I think his name was.

The major and I stood in a darkened room with a big, dimly lit wall map. He told me that this was a top-secret briefing. I was not to talk to anybody about what I heard. How could I talk to anybody? I didn't know anybody yet. And I haven't seen his wall map yet either. I mean, come on.

Lights now illuminated the major's big map. He pointed to different places that meant nothing to me so far. They would though.

"This is Leghorn, our mountain-top radio relay site. This section of the Trail is the Bra."

The S2 explained while tapping at the map with a skinny bamboo pointer. Naming anything after lingerie always got my attention. It was called the Bra because the trail made a double U turn around a river. But wait a minute! Trail? The Trail? That Trail? Hold it!

"This is Salem House, and this is Daniel Boone."

Now I was really focusing. Salem House my ass! That was a little slice of the northeast corner of Cambodia. And Daniel Boone? That was a big slice of the southeast corner of Laos. Where was the Vietnam part of the map? Didn't I need that?

Our presence in Laos and Cambodia was a deliberately unadvertised adventure, a secret war within a war. If I was to die across the border, an officer in an Army-green sedan would stop in front of our house. The officer would have to tell Celestina that I was killed, but not in Laos or Cambodia. Near the border but not over it. Never over the Vietnamese border.

Jesus, Mary, and Holy Saint Joseph, what had I done? I'd allowed myself to be suckered by Shipp was what I'd done. I realized that my boredom flying transports for the 18th had overcome common sense. The S2 explained that the mission that I had been flying from *Du Co*, called Command and Control South, came under the same umbrella as this operation. And there was a third contingent, Command and Control North, which operated into Laos from *Da Nang*. The umbrella had a name too. It was the Military Advisory Command Vietnam Studies and Observations Group. MACVSOG. Or just SOG. The object of the operation was to tie up traffic all along the Ho Chi Minh Trail, the NVA's main supply route from North Vietnam to South Vietnam. And I was going to be part of this. Oh my God!

I talked my way out of the 18th (Otters) because I wanted some excitement. It appeared that I was going to get a full dose of that. I was only half-listening as the different missions I had volunteered to fly were outlined. My brain felt like it was paralyzed. Probably in shock from fright. Fright wasn't the half of it. Now I was sweating. A lot. And my stomach was doing steep turns. The Green Beret S2 finished his briefing and then rummaged around in a box. He came up with a unit patch which he handed me.

"This is yours, lieutenant. But don't sew it on your flight suit."

Thank you so much for this! A white skull on a black background, with fangs dripping blood, wearing a green beret, bordered in red, yellow, and green shaped like lightning bolts. Across the bottom was a banner legend that said "CCC," and "SOG." The unit patch for this Special Ops Group, and I had no intention of sewing it on anything. If I was captured, I could just as easily have held up a sign that said, "Shoot me." Only later did I find out from Phil Phillips, one of the other pilots, that the NVA had placed a bounty on the guys who were flying these missions as well as the Special Forces troops on the ground who were conducting them. Wear the patch, not wear the patch? What difference did it make? Probably not much. But I was still not wearing it on my flight suit.

What did SOG study? Well, it studied the Ho Chi Minh Trail. It studied who traveled on it, how they traveled on it, and when they traveled on it. How did SOG study it? By inserting a recon team into either Laos or Cambodia, and I flew the initial reconnaissance over the area the team would go. The team sneaked up on the Trail and watched. Sometimes they "snatched" a prisoner. Then they sneaked away to an LZ (landing zone) where helicopters picked them up. Tying up traffic on the Trail slowed the flow of men and ammunition to NVA units in the South. Traffic jams bought time to get the South Vietnamese ready to take over from the US Military, which Nixon had begun to withdraw from the war.

Sometimes the NVA discovered a team because they watched landing zones. They deployed trackers, and occasionally the trackers used dogs. And then a firefight erupted, usually at very close range. People were shooting everywhere but mostly at each other, at the helicopters, at the helicopter gunships, and shooting a lot at the unarmed airplane who directed the show. When it was a Vietnamese recon team, that was me. But the intense ground fire was the proverbial chicken that came home to roost on the very first mission I flew.

Essentially my missions were all the same. Each one was across the border where we weren't supposed to be, all flown on the treetops, all with a lot of bad guys shooting, mostly AK-47s, aimed at my airplane. I was also told that I was detached from the 219th. My callsign wouldn't be Headhunter Four-Five anymore. I was officially flying in support of CCC and my callsign was now SPAF Two. The number two pilot in CCC's Sneaky Pete Air Force.

Thank God Major Gole had finished his briefing because I had to go to the bathroom. I saluted the major and found the latrine, a plywood out-house with a door that closed. Thank you for the privacy. I started to read the graffiti on the walls. Someone had written

"Hooray for the Green Bidets."

Really. Here in the middle of nowhere someone knew what a bidet was, painted it green, and pinned jump-wings (a parachutist insignia) on it. This made me laugh. Scared to death, but I was laughing.

After my "Oh my God, that's Laos" briefing with the SOG intel officer I was shown to our hooch. I dropped my duffle bag and steel pot on the floor, leaned my AR-15 against the wall, and looked at the only empty bunk in the room. An upper bunk, with a giant poster just above it. A naked woman, lying on her stomach, leaning on her elbows, smiling out at anyone and everyone. It occurred to me that my pillow would place my face alongside her perfectly rounded fanny. Every morning and every night, my face and her perfectly rounded fanny.

I found the mess hall. This might have been the only time I ate there. I didn't know it yet, but I was going to be airborne from dawn to dusk, and the mess hall would be closed when I left the compound and closed when I got back. Later that evening I met the other two SPAF pilots for the first time, Claude "Phil" Phillips and Doug Krout. They returned from a mission and the mess hall was shuttered, my first indication that dining options were limited. C-Rations and beer for dinner.

This wasn't the first time I ran across Phil Phillips. Phil was a couple of classes ahead of me at Fort Knox, at Armor Officer Basic. I saw him once, at a little officer's club not far from our Bachelor Officers Quarters (BOQ). I remembered him because he rolled up to the outside patio on a big, loud motorcycle. The bike, a black and silver Harley, was a perfect mode of transportation for the young lady perched on the back of it, snuggled behind Phil.

Phil looked like a drug smuggler or maybe a foreign legionnaire, like somebody who could be a character in Rick's Cafe, Bogart's Casablanca bar. The girl on the back of his bike could have been inflated with a bicycle pump. All peaches and cream and boobs. When I looked at her, I saw only

60

arcs and curves. Not one straight line. Anywhere. They only stayed for a minute or two, then rumbled off into a Kentucky late spring evening. And that was that I thought.

Until now, in this hooch, at FOB 2.

"Were you at Knox last summer? Did you have a big bike?" I asked.

"Yeah, I was there, and I still have the bike."

"The Harley! I thought I recognized you. Is that the girl who was with you at Knox?"

I pointed to the poster.

"Yep. That's my wife Sandy."

I lived with that poster for almost eight months, and she became "Naked Sandy" from that moment on. The odd thing was that eventually I stopped seeing Sandy naked. I just saw her. The only "naked" part of Sandy was the name I gave her.

If you asked me where Phil went to college or if he even went to college, I couldn't tell you. Did he have brothers and sisters? I don't know. Was he from Knoxville or Nashville? Not sure. Maybe Memphis. Was he Reserve Officer Training Corps or Officer Candidate School? No clue. And it wasn't just Phil. I didn't know anything personal about Doug Krout or John Meyers or John Plaster or Greg Glashauser or Michael Buckland. I didn't know anything personal about anybody. If you asked those men the same questions about me, I doubt they'd be able to answer them either. Don't get too close. Because dying was every day. So don't let anyone get too close.

I seldom flew a two-ship mission with Doug. I don't know why. It was just the way the mission assignments went, I guess. If we flew a SOG team leader, a one-zero, on a recon of the area he was going to be looking at, we flew as a single airplane. Phil and I flew some of those, but mostly Doug handled them. I always seemed to be assigned photo reconnaissance or a bomb damage assessment, a two-airplane mission, and Phil usually flew the second airplane. If I had a few beers at night, it was usually just with Phil. Doug would disappear. He never said where he went or what he did. If he wanted me to know, I thought he would tell me. But I never asked, and he never said. If the three of us talked, we talked about flying, the Trail, the mission. Sometimes we didn't talk, and we always kept our hearts hidden. I believed then that the less I knew about someone the less painful it would be if something happened to him. Like being killed. The more impersonal a relationship the less devastating death would be.

I tried not to think about death. Mine, or someone else's. But there was no escaping the image of body bags stretched out beside a runway, waiting to be picked up by a Medevac Huey. I might have known who was in the body bag, but I had no intention of unzipping it to say goodbye. The image was powerful because the body inside the bag was obscured, and all I had then was the mental picture I carried of the dead person. I could close my eyes to the boy in the body bag, but I couldn't erase the picture of him that was immortalized inside the photo album of my brain.

At arm's length, that's where we kept one another. At least it seemed to me that we did. Like we all lined up on a parade ground. Dress-Right-Dress. Our feelings spaced apart as if we were new second lieutenants in formation. This way we could keep doing what we promised to do despite the body bags alongside the runway.

By volunteering to fly for SOG I allowed testosterone to overrule caution. Even though I found out from Doug and Phil that there were other guys who stepped up to do this but left quickly. Sometimes after only one day. I was not able to leave. I gave my word, so I had to see this through. I knew myself. I couldn't conceive of the self-recrimination I'd heap upon myself if I left. And God help me for admitting this but for as frightened as I felt, I was thrilled by the notion of riding in on a white horse to save the day. King Arthur, Sir Frankie was here.

I was over Laos flying one of my first SOG missions, only a day removed from that initial briefing in *Kontum*. The big side windows in my Bird Dog's cockpit were wide open, allowing the muggy mid-morning air to rush through the cockpit. It didn't cool me off. I could hear the rounds snap as they went by. I could see the muzzle flashes from the AK-47s that were trying to kill me. Or shoot me down so that the NVA would be able to kill me when I crashed, provided I didn't die in the crash.

I wasn't expecting this. I didn't know what I was expecting but this wasn't it. The intelligence officer, Major Gole, told me in his briefing that taking some ground fire was an everyday occurrence, but there was nothing "some" about this amount of ground fire. This was every damned gun that the North Vietnamese had, all jammed into one clearing in the jungle, and every one of those guns was trying to blow me out of the sky, and I was terrified.

I was also sweaty. Dripping into my eyes, running into my belly button, sweaty. My airplane was standing on its wing tip, just about ninety degrees to the ground, and I was looking over my shoulder. My left hand reached up to the red-capped toggle switches that are over my head, moved them forward, and armed my rockets. I didn't need to look; I knew exactly where the switches were.

My hand dropped down and found the throttle. I eased the power off as the Bird Dog continued over onto its back and then rolled upright, diving at the target. I brought the grease pencil dot on my windscreen, my home-made gunsight, onto the place where I saw the wink of fire from the barrels of the AKs. We slowed down a little, on purpose, in the dive. Slowing made the Bird Dog more stable and improved my aim. Two rockets, with seventeen-pound high explosive warheads, whooshed from the outboard tubes under my wings. Now the Bird Dog had leveled off, staying low, its wheels skimming the jungle canopy, making quick, zigzagging turns right and left. I wasn't going to give the AKs the big bullseye of my underbelly to hit, so I stayed on the treetops. To climb now would mean slowing down, and I couldn't let the airplane slow down. Slowing down could kill me and my Bird Dog. I didn't think about doing any of this. Even though I was scared beyond belief. And racing to get away, I flew the Bird Dog like monsters were chasing me. I just did things without really thinking. I just did things.

The way the game was played changed when I moved from flying the U-1 Otter with the 18th to the 219th. The Otter hauled passengers to and from relatively secure airfields. There was a risk of being mortared at night but flying for SOG meant that bullets shot at my airplane and nighttime mortars tried to kill me. Survival didn't depend on just crawling to a bunker. Survival was now also contingent on knowing exactly what my small airplane and I could do. Because now the airplane and I were partners in the struggle to live.

The only way to understand what the Bird Dog could do was to apply what I was shown in flight school. So, I reviewed what my instructors, Sheldon Hanneman, Mister Weaver, Ray Caryl (a 220th Catkiller FAC), and Arlie Deaton, taught me. And when I went flying, I experimented. I asked, "what if?"

Every day, for the first two weeks of November, relearning the Bird Dog, learning the Central Highlands, I asked myself "what if?"

What if my elevator cables were shot away? The elevator, when the control stick was pulled back to me, made the nose go up and the airplane would climb. If I pushed down, the elevator made the airplane descend. This was how pitch was controlled. If I pulled the throttle back to reduce engine power, the nose would fall. Increasing power pushed the nose up. I practiced moving the throttle on and off. The nose went up and down. Another way to control pitch. In a pinch I could use power to make the airplane climb or descend. I very carefully practiced flying an approach to the runway at Camp Holloway using the throttle to control up and down. This was a lot of fun!

Did you ever stick your hand out the window of your parents' car, cup your hand, and make it go up and down? Or hold your hand flat, point your fingers a little left or right, and feel your hand zoom off in the direction you were pointing? Since that first visit to Idlewild, when my mother drove my father to work, and I was a little boy, I had always done that. Sometimes I still do. I tried that in the Bird Dog too, because what if my aileron and rudder cables were shot away? First, I linked my thumbs together and held my palms flat, out the window, facing forward. The airplane turned very slowly, but it turned. Next, I grabbed the maintenance logbook and held it out the window, flat, and facing forward. We turned a little faster, the wings stayed almost level, and the airplane didn't climb or descend much either. We just skidded through a turn. Finally, I pushed my cockpit door about a third of the way open and held it there. We made a big skidding turn to the right because the door was on the right. When I returned to Holloway I lined up on approach to land, aimed the nose at the runway's centerline of faded paint, and used both the throttle and the door to control up and down, right turns and bigger right turns.

Landing safely like this was not going to happen though. I decided that if I found myself down to a throttle and a door for control of my Bird Dog, I might not be able to keep the airplane on the runway. The Bird Dog and I would probably be in the weeds after touchdown, maybe rolled up in a ball. If something like this were to happen, I decided I would opt to accept a crash after landing as a fact. I would make sure I set the airplane on the ground as slowly as I could so that I didn't really hurt myself.

On the last day in December, after arriving at FOB 2, I occasionally had a Vietnamese Special Forces observer ride in my backseat. He looked like he was barely out of high school. "How old are you, *Trung-uy* Kung (lieutenant in Vietnamese)?"

"I am twenty-four years old, *Trung-uy* Doh-tee." We were the same age. "You look like you are almost a baby, Kung." He laughed.

"Maybe you are a baby, Doh-tee. Baby *Trung-uy* Doh-tee."

Two boys, now soldiers, playing at the "for real" of life and death. I liked Kung very much.

After an early morning mission over Laos in support of a Vietnamese SOG recon team, it occurred to me that I should try to show Kung how to fly the airplane in case I got shot. Another "what if." The airplane had a control stick, rudder pedals, and throttle, for the back-seater. I slumped sideways against the left window and announced over the intercom,

"Hey Kung. I'm shot and I need you to fly!"

I watched him as I said this, and I thought his face was going to fall off from surprise.

"No, no, no, Doh-tee."

I wouldn't let him off the hook.

"Come on Kung. You're flying."

He had to loosen his lap belt and sit on the edge of his seat so that his feet would reach the rudder pedals and his left hand could adjust the throttle. His right hand was choking the control stick to death. We were all over the sky for a minute or two. But I kept talking to him and as he relaxed so did our gyrations. We did this almost every time we flew together. I'd take over at about 100 ft above touchdown and land the airplane. I was convinced Kung could get us on the ground and chop the power. Staying on the runway was not very likely, but it would have been a bonus.

Kung was so small that he could barely see over the back of my seat to look at the flight and engine instruments. He just disappeared behind me. I couldn't see him unless I turned all the way around. He only spoke when we were conducting an insertion or extraction of a Vietnamese team. We decided on a plan, and he translated it to the men on the ground. When we finished, the flight back to *Kontum* was Kung's nap time. Sometimes I would forget that he was in the airplane. I was lost in thought, considering what we had done that morning, how the mission went, and what I could do to protect the recon team, Kung, my Bird Dog, and finally, me. Then, forgetting all about Kung asleep behind me, I decided it was play-time. I loved to race the clouds. Or it was "make the airplane go upside-down" time, or "stand the airplane on its wing-tip" time, and maybe "do a split S or a loop" time. My mission was completed. It was "screw around" time. I have no idea why I thought Kung would sleep through all these gyrations.

There was no way he could sleep back there, and when he did open his eyes, terrified, he would heave up every kernel of rice in his stomach.

Kung got sick just as I flipped the airplane upside-down and let it spin a little. The second time his stomach came apart was in the middle of a barrel-roll. My Bird Dog didn't roll gracefully but it would roll. I was having a great time. I was the only one in the Bird Dog having a great time. There was Kung's ashy-gray face in my little rearview mirror, his eyes narrowed and angry. After landing I helped Kung clean up and then invited him to lunch in our mess hall.

"I am not hungry, Doh-tee."

Kung wasn't smiling. And my apologies were not helping. No more barrel-rolls when Kung was with me. I promised him.

We flew together a few days later, and after work he insisted on taking me to a local roadside stand not far from the airfield. He ordered a stew which smelled delicious, and two bottles of Vietnamese beer, which had a faint formaldehyde taste. I ate all my stew, and as I put my spoon and chopsticks down, he smiled broadly.

"*Con khi*, Doh tee."

Kung began to laugh. The man who made the stew and the woman who served the stew were laughing too. I smiled weakly back at the three of them. "*Con khi*." I knew what that meant. Monkey. Kung evened the score, and I thanked God his version of revenge wasn't served cold. This was the last time that I saw my friend. I don't know where Kung went or what happened to him. I asked, but the Vietnamese officers I asked just looked away.

As time made its way through the last few days of December I thought less and less about "what ifs," and more and more about lessons I was taught in flight school. Arlie Deaton told me to trust in my ability, to believe in myself. Sheldon Hanneman had the confidence in me to get out of the cockpit and send me on my own to take off and land, to "solo." Ray Caryl, fresh from combat, insisted that I concentrate on everything around me, because in Vietnam, he said, a FAC in a Bird Dog was a bullseye with a propeller. And Mister Weaver? He taught me to fly by feel, by sound, and by sight.

"Listen to the airplane. It will tell you what to do."

The little discs he placed over the flight and engine instruments required me to sense where I was and where I was going.

"Feel the airplane. Whirl around the dancefloor with it."

66

I thought, good God, how I loved to fly!

"Make your airplane an extension of you, lieutenant, because when everything goes to hell in a handbasket, all you have time to do is think about surviving."

I wished I could tell Mr. Weaver that going to hell in a handbasket happened every day.

# Chapter 6

# Celestina

"You've made a bargain with the Army, Frankie. Now you must make a promise to your father, and to me. Come home from that place. Do you hear me? Don't leave any part of you over there. Not one little piece."

Celestina DeGuira, 30 March 1968

**January 1970, Fifth Month**

That was the promise my mother had demanded of me when I called from Fort Knox to tell her that I was going to flight school, and that I was sure I would have to come here. Celestina's words nudged me from time to time, echoed across my brain every now and then, and, when I held them up as a reminder of my promise to her, they filled my heart because her words showed me how much she loved me. Shortly after the New Year I held a telephone to my ear and spoke into the mouthpiece and told her that I loved her too.

I was able to make a MARS Station call to anyone "back in the world." MARS stood for Military Auxiliary Radio Station, and we had one on the Special Forces compound where I now lived. Where I now lived? That sounded funny. More like where I burrowed underground to avoid mortar rounds and rockets and occasional small arms fire directed our way. Saying this compound, so close to the Laotian border that I could throw a rock across it, was where I lived? That made my whole existence seem way too normal.

An antenna reached 50 ft into the air, and a small open tent next to it sheltered an olive-drab colored box with dials and gauges, which was wired to the antenna, and which cradled a regular looking phone. The phone reached across the world. It reached all the way to where my mother was.

It reached to the tears that I knew would come when Celestina heard my voice, and when I heard hers.

It was my turn to call home and taking into consideration the eleven-hour time difference between *Kontum* and New York, I signed up for nine o'clock at night so that it would be eight in the morning in Lloyd Harbor. Mom would be getting my little brothers off to school. She was probably making their lunches. A good time to catch her.

My mother was home. She answered the phone. And even though it was almost half a century ago I remember our words so well.

"Mom, can you hear me? Over."

"Is that you, Frankie? Where are you?"

"Yes Mom. It's me. Can you hear me okay Mom? Over."

"I can hear you just fine. Where are you?"

"Mom, we're talking on a ham radio relay and then a thing called a phone patch. So, you have to say 'Over' when you're through with a sentence, or when you're through talking. Okay? Over."

"Over? Why do I have to say 'Over?' Where are you? Are you in San Francisco?"

I took the receiver from my ear and looked at it, as if it was going to explain "San Francisco." It must have made sense to her though. USF.

"Jesus, Mary and Holy St. Joseph, Mom. I wish I was in San Francisco. I'm in *Kontum*, Mom. Over."

"Why do you keep saying 'Over?' Where are you really, Frank?"

"I really am in *Kontum*, Mom. But it won't be long before it's early September and I'll be home. Over."

I lied. It would be nine months before September showed up.

"You said 'Over' again, Frankie. I'm not going to say that. I just want you back. I want you back safe, Frankie."

I almost sobbed.

"I'm doing my best to be careful, Mom. Tell everyone that I love them, and I'll be home for Kath's wedding. I love you, Mom. Over."

Our time was almost up.

"Come home, Frankie. Promise me. I need you to come home."

The same promise that Celestina had demanded of me before I left for Vietnam. The words were a little different that day, but it was the same "before flight school" promise. I put the receiver back in its cradle, walked out of the tent through the dark, out to the line of bunkers and rows of barbed wire that surrounded our compound. I could sit on one of the bunkers so long as I showed myself to the *Nungs,* the ethnic Chinese mercenaries who manned our bunkers, who guarded our base. I sang a little Creedence Clearwater, *Susie Q*, in English, so they wouldn't shoot. The night was clear, and because there was almost no ambient light every star in the universe seemed visible. The night sky had magical depth, and I wished I could have reached high enough to feel my hand go through that depth, up and up and up, to where God was.

Looking out from the wire, the tree line in the distance was just discernible as a different, darker degree of black. Maybe the density of the jungle gave the darkness more intensity than the black that rolled from the barbed wire across open fields of fire to the tree line beyond us. I sat on the sandbagged roof, careful not to wake anything that lived in the sandbags and listened to the night. It was noisy. Good. Nobody was out there, and if they were, they weren't moving. I thought about Mom and Dad, about the last time I saw them. My mother's tears, her angry voice, the sound of her fist banging on the walls of the jetway to the airplane that would take me away from my parents, and on the journey which brought me to this bunker. To this almost midnight in *Kontum*, in the dark.

I let my mind wander back to a beautiful Alabama June morning at Fort Rucker. We were graduating on this clear, blue-sky, 1969 day. Chairs and the dais for the speakers were in place on the parking ramp adjacent to one of the runways, just in front of the airfield's control tower. Behind this, O-1 Bird Dogs were aligned at "Parade Rest."

Prior to the ceremony I walked Mom and Dad out beyond the bandstand and bunting to an airplane, now my airplane. I opened the door to the cockpit and stepped back a little so they could see inside. A centered control stick and three or four engine gauges on the instrument panel. A compass, a turn and slip indicator, an artificial horizon, and an ancient radio transmitter-receiver. That was it. My mother leaned into the cockpit as Dad peered over her shoulder. And I, glowing in my dress-blues with my gold shoulder boards, silver first lieutenant's bars embroidered on them, said, "Now don't touch anything."

My father was a senior TWA B-747 captain, flying the most technically advanced commercial airliner in the world. He was looking into the cockpit of an airplane which was little more than a Tinker Toy. Mom disengaged herself from Dad's arm, laughed and said,

"You idiot."

Then she held me close and kissed me on the cheek. She was crying.

The commanding officer of Fixed Wing Training (airplanes, not helicopters) handed me my wings. I walked to where my parents were sitting and handed them to my father. I was now a pilot, just like my father was. Dad surprised me by handing them to my mother. She pinned them on.

I spent the rest of the summer at Fort Ord, on the coast just south of San Francisco, transitioning into a bigger airplane, the *De Havilland* Otter. It still had just one engine and an old-fashioned tailwheel instead of a nose gear, just like the little Bird Dog, but it held thirteen people and was used as a passenger transport, a liaison airplane, or a cargo hauler, a much safer, and what turned out to be a painfully boring mission.

Then summer of 1969 was over and Fort Ord flying was over. It was time to go. My parents had come from New York on the second of September to spend a few hours with me before I left for Vietnam. Dad worked hard at small talk over a lunch that no one was eating. Mom said very little. And now it was late afternoon at San Francisco's airport, with me in my uniform, and my parents in tears. Dad had few words now. He knew what was waiting for me. My mother was crying harder. Down the jetway we walked to the door of the airplane, and the flight attendant reached for my ticket. Dad's hands were on my shoulders.

"Come home to us, Frankie."

My mother's composure is gone now. Her rage in full throat, her fist pounding the metal wall of the jetway.

"I did not raise him for this!"

Again, and again.

"I did not raise him for this!"

I held her tightly in my arms, but she would not be consoled. Dad drew her to him. My mother's face was buried in his coat. I couldn't see either of them now. She had disappeared into my father's shoulder, and he into my mother's auburn hair. I stepped from sheltering, frightened, sorrowful parents, crossing from the jetway onto an airplane that would deliver me to a war that nearly broke my heart over and over again.

# Chapter 7

# The Central Highlands

The Vietnamese heat was wet and draining. The smells were intoxicating and nauseating at the same time. Jasmine and ginger, body odor and rotting vegetables. Pho, a noodle soup so good it could melt one's heart, someone's breath so sour it could melt glass. All at the same time. And then there was fear. People died here. Shot, blown up, napalmed, dead. I knew right off the bat, when I arrived in *Nha Trang*, that I was afraid. And over the next few months I learned that my fear came in different degrees of intensity, levels of being afraid, that were recognizable.

There was the everyday rolling stomach queasiness. Like the buzzing from an overhead fluorescent light. I heard it at first but got used to it. I didn't stop hearing the buzz, but I accepted it as my new everyday. This new everyday was sensing incoming rockets or mortars before the warning sirens howled. Being on the floor headed for the bunker as the warning wails split the night. Being almost to the bunker before the first whump of an explosion. Or, and this was considerably more mundane, getting a haircut but never allowing the Vietnamese barber to use a straight razor to trim hair on the back of my neck.

Combat fear, being shot at by AK-47s or .50 caliber anti-aircraft guns, was as intense as fear could get. The adrenalin-spike was like a flashflood, like going from zero to the speed of sound in an instant. Sometimes bullets took me by surprise, sudden green streaks from tracers arcing up at me. An instantaneous "what the hell was that" rush of chaos. Other times, when I saw a situation gradually unfold, fear built more slowly. If I couldn't do anything about what was taking place, fear made me feel like my cramping stomach was going to whoosh right out of my mouth.

When the fight was over, when the dead were counted, I experienced a depressing, almost crushing sense of fright. Because I knew that I got lucky that day. I was still alive. But there was tomorrow again and again for how many more tomorrows? That was different from anything immediate. That was anticipation fear. That was having to do this all over again fear. Like driving to the airfield in the dark of pre-dawn, having to pass a cemetery where a few weeks earlier somebody had shot at us as we careened by. We had slowed down before the cemetery and turned off the jeep's lights, letting our eyes refocus in the blackness, then had floored the jeep, praying all the while that a person or an animal or a booby trap wasn't in the road.

After Christmas I discovered my final type of fear. The fear that made me ask myself what took me so long to figure that out. I looked into my little shaving kit mirror and the boy looking back at me asked me a very direct question: "How could you be so stupid, lieutenant?"

*Kontum* airfield was just northeast of the main part of town, very close to the *Dak Bla* River. Phil and I loved the river. We bathed in it on scorching hot days even though the water was muddy. We washed the jeep that Phil stole in it even though the jeep might not have needed washing. We didn't drink the water however, because we knew young boys took their family water buffaloes for scrubbing there too. We went to the *Dak Bla* River whenever we could because the *Montagnard* girls washed clothes in the river. They were always smiling, sometimes at us, and they were always topless.

The runway at *Kontum* ran just about east and west, trying its best to cooperate with the prevailing easterly wind. It wasn't a dirt strip; it was covered with heavy sheets of perforated steel plate, which looked like metal Swiss cheese. When it was dry the steel plate was easy to land on. But when it was wet, landing was a slippery adventure. When it was wet and the wind was blowing sideways, like it usually did during the rainy season, landing was an inducer of soaring blood pressure. Running off a slippery-slick runway was the reward for a pilot who was careless in crosswinds. I was not careless.

I watched a C-130 land one afternoon and taxi onto the parking ramp. This was an unusual experience for me. Not because a big cargo plane had landed, but because it was afternoon, and I was not wandering around over Laos. My buddy Ben Brown, who was also one of our crew chiefs, and I were standing on little steps attached to my Bird Dog's wing struts, refueling my airplane. Ben had the avgas (aviation fuel) hose, filling the left wing-tank, and I was waiting to fill the right one. I took a moment to check out the four-engine freight hauler while cargo was off-loaded. As I scanned the fuselage, I noticed that the Air Force insignia was missing.

There was what had to be a removable panel where the emblem should have been. A blank one. The only crewmember I could see was the loadmaster who was supervising the removal of the cargo. He was obviously US. This wasn't too surprising, though. Everything that went on around here that had anything to do with the Special Ops Group was sneaky. I wondered where this airplane was going once it left here. I wondered who was flying it.

The big airplane was an attractive target. Too attractive for Charlie to pass up a chance to shoot something at it. Like a rocket made in Russia. A 122-millimeter rocket that sounded like a locomotive. Loud did not do justice to the chugging noise it made, especially when it was coming straight at us. Which it was. An NVA or Viet Cong (Charlie) soldier was hiding on a jungle-covered ridge just to the south of us, and he aimed his rocket launcher at the C-130. He missed. The rocket sailed over our heads and slammed into a dike on the other side of the runway. When Ben heard the racket made by the rocket zooming at us, he tossed the fuel hose to me, and said,

"It's all yours, *Trung uy*."

Ben jumped off the wing strut and ran for the sand-bagged revetments where our airplanes spent the night. I tossed the fuel hose on the ground, fired up the Bird Dog's engine and took off slightly lopsided because one wing-tank had fuel and one side didn't. The tower operators almost dove out of the tower so I couldn't ask for permission to take off. It really didn't matter because I didn't have my flight helmet, which I needed to be able to talk on the radios. I tried to find the gun emplacement and couldn't – but that didn't matter either because I hadn't loaded any marking rockets. And I couldn't talk to anybody to call in an air-strike because I still didn't have a helmet. No helmet, no talking, no radios, no rockets, no air-strike. But I tried. As I flew back to the airfield, I wondered how this place was defended and who defended it. It occurred to me then that the answer was obvious. Nobody. At least not during the day. And I realized as I returned to land after looking for the rocket launcher that there were very few perimeter defenses around *Kontum*'s airfield. No concertina wire, no bunkers, no gun emplacements, no guards. Nobody.

There were raised platforms that were manned at night by local militia, who used gongs to communicate with each other. The first time I heard the gongs I thought there had to be a Buddhist temple nearby. When I learned that the gongs signified "all is well" I laughed, and then I felt a little sick. Anybody could get in here, undetected, and sabotage my airplane. Isn't there one safe place for me? For my Bird Dog? One uncontested breath, one relaxed sigh for me? I realized that I could be killed anywhere. How stupid I had been to assume any place was safe.

Could the NVA have tiptoed between the guard towers? Tiptoed? At night? They could have marched a regiment between the guard towers. The towers had no searchlights, and *Kontum* had no ambient light. It had candlelight. Dim, non-illuminating, shadowy, little, candlelight. The airplanes, parked in three-sided, sandbagged spaces, were an easy target. Anybody could have booby-trapped them. Grenades, trip-wired to the ignition switches, trip-wired to the rudder pedals. Why did it take me so long to realize this? Mornings now became earlier for me. I had to be sure that no one tried to make a bomb out of my Bird Dog.

My flashlight had a red lens that was harder to see over a distance. I started going through D-cell batteries like no tomorrow. Because if I wasn't thorough, I wouldn't have a tomorrow. I checked every nook and cranny of my airplane. I bet I looked in places that nobody had looked in since the airplane came off the Cessna assembly line in 1950, when I was in kindergarten. Was this like morning sickness? I felt sick every morning, so I guessed what I felt counted as morning sickness. I was sweaty and my stomach churned. I had to put my feet on the rudder pedals and push them, one after the other, to the stops, to be sure that they were free and not binding, and that the rudder moved completely from side to side. My hands caressed the spaces inside the cockpit, around the rudder pedals, around the control stick, feeling gingerly for a wire, for a grenade. My eyes searched in the red glow, looking. I undid the engine cowling and slid my index finger gently along the one-inch opening, feeling for something that could kill me. Every switch, every control surface, front seat and back, before every flight, in the morning's dark. Then I strapped my AR-15 to the cockpit door, strapped myself into my seat, checked the fuel, scrunched my eyes shut, and turned the ignition switch to on. The Bird Dog didn't explode, and neither did I.

The daily pre-morning booby-trap inspection really didn't take too long. Then on taxi-out to the runway there were engine performance checks to be sure that engine failure didn't have me making an emergency landing in some patch of jungle. Before every flight an engine run-up had to be done. The brakes were mashed all the way down and the engine rpm was advanced to be sure the engine was running smoothly. No coughing or hiccupping allowed. An electrical check of these gadgets called magnetos was also made. The two magnetos provided a charge across the engine's spark plugs. The spark plugs ignited the fuel which made the pistons go up and down, providing power to spin the shaft which turned the propeller. The electrical charge put out by the magnetos had a minimum value that had to be met. Normal magnetos had a value higher than the minimum, and if the value was above the minimum the Bird Dog was ready to fly. As I taxied to the runway, I noticed that the value registered a little lower than it normally did. I almost always flew the same airplane and got to know my Bird Dog's quirks. A "mag-drop" would register with me. Over the course of a week the magnetos went from normal to "almost can't go."

I wasn't the only one who caught this. Phil Phillips and Doug Krout saw the same thing. We all suspected contaminated fuel, which was slowly fouling the spark plugs, so we flew to *Plei Djerang*, drained the gas tanks in our airplanes' wings, and used the avgas there. That cured our magneto problem.

That wasn't the end of the fouled spark plug problem though. We had been fueling our airplanes from big rubber bladders, light gray with USAF stenciled in blue across their middles, that sat on the ramp adjacent to *Kontum*'s runway. I had no idea how gas went bad. But ours clearly had. The magnetos proved that. What we also found out was that we weren't the only ones filling our gas tanks with fuel from these bladders.

The airfield had to shut down when the sky darkened because the runway had no lighting. We still took off and sometimes landed in the dark, but when the tower operators went back to the MACV compound the airfield commander yelled "Quitting time at Tara," just like in *Gone with the Wind*, and pronounced the airfield as officially closed. He did this every day. As soon as all the Americans left, an ARVN (Army of the Republic of Vietnam) officer and a few of his troops strolled onto the watch-tower-guarded airport. The officer pronounced the *Kontum* Airfield gas station officially open. A daily occurrence. The gas we used in our Bird Dogs worked great in the motor scooters, motor scooter trucks and the very rare car or two. *Kontum*'s residents couldn't resist. We had no idea the enterprising ARVN was operating this gas station for anyone and everyone. It only took a few days for us to find out.

After about four days all but a few vehicles in *Kontum City* had stopped running. To see the streets free of the tangle of scooters and the air absent of their exhaust was astounding. But best of all, the whiny snarl of their engines was silenced. I could hear birds chirping and dogs barking and people talking.

The fouled Vietnamese spark plugs were our fault though. I knew we'd get blamed. We weren't saviors. No. The Vietnamese saw us as an occupying army, and we represented everything that was wrong in their country. Like broken scooters. I wasn't surprised that the hand-gesture of universal disdain was flashed my way the one time I drove to the airfield in daylight. It was very funny. Our route from the SOG compound to the airfield took us by a house that was, I swear, really called *The Rising Sun*, and several of the girls, looking forlorn and bored, were sitting on the front porch. As we drove by, they waved single-digit hellos. I laughed my head off.

Now that I finally stopped shuttling back and forth between Camp Holloway and settled in at FOB 2 in *Kontum* I worked solely for Command and Control Central, whose missions were flown for the most part in Laos. There were almost always recon teams on the ground there. Usually more than one. They were supported by an Air Force FAC, his callsign "Covey," and an experienced SOG recon man, who was called a "Covey Rider." They were in contact with the "Spike" (recon) teams, ready to give them whatever help they could if something happened. The SPAF pilots, Doug, Phil, and I, always took the SOG recon team leader, the one-zero, on at least one early morning reconnaissance of the area in which his team would be inserted. We looked at the whole area the team would scout, possible routes of movement, potential ambush sites, and landing zones for insertion and potential extraction points. The recon team leaders knew what kind of LZs their missions would require so these were the areas we looked for. All marked on our maps with grease pencil. As spring snuck up on winter, any place that looked like a hole in the treetops was noted as well on our maps as a potential extraction point. Because as spring snuck up on winter, the Ho Chi Minh Trail got bloodier and bloodier. Our days, from before dawn until after dark, were spent over Laos, in our Bird Dogs, almost always within the kill zone of a rifle. Sometimes with a SOG team leader (one-zero), or a photographer, and every now and then with nobody in the back seat. If our back seater was a recon team leader, he was usually someone we hardly knew. We flew all day every day, got back to the FOB 2 compound after dark, drank some beer and ate who knows what out of a can or boiled rice and dehydrated vegetables out of a bag, showered if the water was on, drank more beer, and collapsed into bed. Until the alarm went off in the deep dark before morning. Then we got up and did the same thing all over again.

### February1970, Sixth Month

Days rolled one into the other with a sameness that was expected. But the days were never boring because getting shot at daily couldn't ever be boring. What was unusual was having very little contact with the outside world. What was even stranger was that I didn't care. Anti-war protests at home were more and more frequent. Kent State, Jackson State, the March on Washington. *My Lai* was being investigated and eventually fourteen people connected to the massacre were charged. If I was listening, I might have heard some of this on Armed Forces radio. If I was listening. Most of the time all I could hear was the sound of my Bird Dog's engine, bullets whizzing by the cockpit, or the Jaynettes singing *Sally Go Round the Roses* if the tape deck in our hooch was turned up loud enough.

Captain Glashauser, a SOG one-zero, rode in the back of my airplane once. He flew with me in the deep dark before morning in January. But first, a few hours before takeoff, he crashed into our hooch. He was our next-door neighbor. I thought Greg was nuts.

The "what do you call this?" where we lived was a long wooden shed divided into four spaces. You would have said they were huts or hovels. We called them a hooch. We called them home. Our hooch was protected by sandbags stacked to the eaves of the roof. The sandbags were supposed to stop shrapnel, flying pieces of red-hot metal, from mortars and rockets fired at night into our compound by the North Vietnamese. The wall that separated our hooch from the one next to us was a single, 8 ft sheet of half-inch plywood nailed to 2 x 4-inch studs spaced 4 ft apart.

It was about one in the morning. Our wall was being beaten to death by my friend Greg, who lived in the adjacent hooch. He was using the stock of an AK-47, which was made of solid wood protected by a metal plate on the part of the stock which went against his shoulder. Fortunately, he was not holding the AK in the firing position. He was using it like a battering ram. I was lying in my rack (bed) watching the hole get bigger. Pretty soon he was going to be able to climb through the hole he was making and stand in our opulent suite.

Gregory Glaushauser was a Green Beret captain. Very brave, and one of the best at what he did, which was operating in a jungle where a lot of people wanted him dead. Right now, he was armed, profoundly drunk, and standing over me with a box of saltines in the hand that was not holding the AK-47 which was aimed at my nose. I could see the clip of ammo inserted into his rifle, so I knew it was loaded. I was wide awake, getting anxious, with absolutely no idea of what was going to happen next. I held still and hoped that whatever Greg did wasn't going to hurt. I wished that Greg would put the rifle down.

It was hot in here, even with the big fan blowing a gale. I was very sweaty. I was always sweaty because Vietnam was always sweaty. And it was just Greg and me in this sweaty room. My one flying partner, Doug Krout, was spending the night at Holloway. He was finishing up his tour and getting ready to rotate home in a month or so. His replacement hadn't shown up yet. My other flying partner, Phil Phillips, was currently in Hawaii on R&R. And John Meyers, who was, until recently, Greg's sidekick and the pilot I replaced, was reassigned to Camp Holloway. I really wanted Greg to put the AK on the floor. With the safety on.

Greg's attention was diverted to the big poster on the wall above my bunk, momentarily mesmerized by Naked Sandy. Only for a moment. Greg snapped out of his reverie and turned off the fan.

Finally, he propped the AK against the only chair we had. At least now I knew that he wasn't going to shoot me. Greg opened the box of saltines and crushed a bunch of them into crumbs, then crushed some more, until he had enough crumbs to coat at least half a dozen plucked chickens. Or me. Before I knew it, I was ready for the deep fryer. I was coated with sweat-sticky saltine crumbs. All the while he was telling me, "It's time to pay the piper."

I had absolutely no idea what he was talking about. Then he stumbled back through the hole in the wall dragging the rifle behind him and fell into his own bed.

I had to be awake in two hours. I had to go flying, looking for landing zones in southern Laos and I had to take Greg with me. He would be running a mission next week in this area. Drunk or not, he was going. I shut off the alarm, got up, and headed over to the latrine, hoping to find a faucet with water when I turned it on. No working showers, as usual, in this damn place. A soaking wet washcloth was used to remove my crumb coating. Dressed now in my "unwashed for weeks because the water is turned off all the time" salt-crusted flight suit that just stunk, I climbed through the new hole in the wall to wake Greg up. Greg was still drunk. His new roommate, Lieutenant Fritz Krupa, helped me get my passenger dressed, and together we dumped him into my jeep. Greg was oozing scotch. He smelled just awful.

Captain Glashauser snored through the ride to the MACV compound to pick up Bob Hall and Ben Brown, our crew chiefs, snored through the ride to the airfield, snored as Bob and Ben plopped him into the back seat of the Bird Dog, and snored all the way to Laos.

The morning air was silky calm. We were flying west so the sun came up behind us. Such a beautiful place, this mountainous part of Laos, until parts of it got bombed into a crater-scarred moonscape. I recognized the area we need to look at from known landmarks and corresponding map coordinates. The Bird Dog's engine idled almost noiselessly as we glided down to get closer to the ground. My airplane's big side windows were open to the cool air, and I was as gentle as I could be as I eased the power up to level off about 500 ft above the mountainy jungle. I made notes in grease pencil on my map, marking all the possible landing and extraction zones. And Greg snored through all that too. I knew where he needed to go. I had his proposed route all marked on my map. I decided that I'd tell him all about it when he was awake. And sober.

The reconnaissance of the LZs was finished. There could never be just one landing zone. We always looked at multiple spots. The North Vietnamese used LZ watchers, camouflaged, and hiding nearby, who looked and listened for our Hueys, who waited for the insertion of our recon teams. Who alerted the rest of their unit so that our team could be engaged, so that a Huey could be shot down, so that the team could be overrun. And killed. We looked at several landing zones, trying to camouflage our intentions as well as the NVA camouflaged their watchers.

The Bird Dog climbed smoothly through the morning's still air, and I leveled off at about 5,000 ft, which kept me clear of the mountain tops. We were heading back to the border, flying into the early sunlight, going back to Vietnam. I put on my sunglasses (like the ones my father wore) and checked in with SOG operations through our radio relay site at Leghorn, advising them that I was enroute to *Dak To* for fuel. Greg was stirring in the back seat.

We crossed over the Laotian border into Vietnam. I could still feel the cracker crumbs sweat-glued to my skin. My left hand eased the throttle back to idle as my right hand nudged the control stick forward, putting the Bird Dog into a shallow dive. The airspeed was increasing. Good. Backpressure on the control stick brought the nose of the airplane up into a steep climb. Adding power slowly kept the Bird Dog climbing. It climbed until we were going almost straight up. I had the stick full back now. And Greg was moving around back there. The airplane was on its back and, as the nose led it through a loop, I heard Greg gag. The scotch still in his stomach must have been resurfacing.

We were just about out of the loop, and I pushed the rudder pedal all the way to the right. Go right, airplane. At the same time, I pushed the control stick all the way to the left, moving the ailerons. They told the Bird Dog to turn left. In its confusion, the Bird Dog flipped over on its back. I, however, was not the slightest bit confused. The Bird Dog was doing exactly what I wanted it to do. The airplane's nose pointed at the treetops, and it started to spin. Greg was no longer gagging. He was hanging out the back window. The remaining scotch in his stomach was gone. I stopped the spin and leveled off, then gently climbed again into the morning sky. I regretted making my friend Kung sick, and he paid me back with a monkey stew lunch. But not Greg. I mean, coated with saltines? You bet I needed to even the score, and loops and spins were the only ways I could. Greg asked for my canteen of water. I gave it to him, told him to keep it as a reminder of his first airshow, and to never ever do that saltine trick again, at least not to me.

It was hard to be upset with Greg. It was hard not to like a guy who had an all the time smile for everyone. Greg's saltine fiasco made me laugh, yes. But I wasn't happy. Because we could have been shot down. If that happened, I had no clue what to do in the jungle. If that happened, Greg knew exactly what to do. He knew how to operate in the jungle. I really needed Greg to be sober.

Greg's team was inserted the following week, and it was extracted a day later. They ran into trouble almost immediately. They were trailed by trackers using dogs, fought their way through an ambush, and made their way back to the landing zone. Helicopter gunships kept constant machine-gun and rocket fire on the NVA as the team was extracted. Captain Glashauser was lifted into one of the Hueys, wounded just under his left armpit. The AK-47 round took a chunk of Greg with it when it tumbled through his left side and exited below his shoulder blade. It didn't damage his lung, but it did break a rib.

I talked to Greg several times before I was pulled off the SOG mission, but I never took him flying again. He was back at FOB 2, and eager to rejoin his recon team as soon as he was able. The wound, however, would take a few months of healing and therapy. And I was ordered to return to Camp Holloway, to my unit's headquarters, for my last few weeks in the Central Highlands. Greg survived the war, but after I left CCC I never saw him again.

I have thought about Greg from time to time though. He has been one of the question marks in the bigger question I have wondered about for years after the war. Why did Greg do what he did? What was it that made him want to get off a helicopter close to the main infiltration route that ran from North Vietnam through Laos, and Cambodia into Vietnam? To get off a helicopter in the middle of the jungle, with enemy soldiers all over the place, to see what that enemy was doing, to see what supplies and troops the NVA was sending down the Ho Chi Minh Trail? To sneak up on and then slip away from those who would want to kill Greg and his team if they were caught?

A recon team could be on the ground in Laos or Cambodia for almost a week unless they were discovered and extracted early. The team rested and recovered after they were helicoptered back to FOB 2, and then started training for the next insertion, which might be a week or two away. Training was unlike anything I had ever seen. The level of intensity, the precision of execution, the integration of weapons, the outwitting of the enemy, and the economy of movement astounded me. I was witnessing, through constant repetition, a role-specific choreography of men acting and interacting in the ballet of survival. Slowly moving through the murky light of triple-canopy jungle as if in time with a muted Gregorian Chant. Almost a ritualized *Tai Chi* exercise. Then dancing a Jitterbug of fire and maneuver while they escaped an ambush of automatic weapons. Each man acted exactly as planned. Each man was sure that every other man on his recon team was doing exactly what was expected of him.

The stress of these missions was enormous. The team jumped from the Huey, and then the Huey flew away. The gunships flew away. And eventually the FAC and the Covey Rider flew away. And the team on the ground was alone with the quiet. Alone, amid people who would kill them if they caught them.

I came to the realization that running around in the jungle with painted faces was like playing a very scary post-adolescent game of Cowboys and

Indians. And the possibility of dying? That was all part of the adrenaline rush that Greg and his team craved. I really believed Greg loved it.

My own "why?" was, I thought, the bigger question. Why did I volunteer to fly the SOG mission? And the other guys who flew it when I did, Meyers, Krout, Ford, and Phillips? What could we all have been thinking? The pilots who flew in support of the SOG operation flew over Laos and Cambodia every day, low-level, in the small arms kill zone. Not once a week or every now and then. All day, every day. The stress of these missions was enormous.

My initial justification sounded good, patriotic, altruistic, selfless. At first, I flew this mission because I said I would. I volunteered, and my pride wouldn't allow me to go back on my word. I thought that I was doing something, if not to win the war, then at least for the guys with whom I served. I liked the way it made me sound sane and reasonable. It was so much garbage. I was hiding from what I knew was my truth.

It took me years to admit that truth, to say that truth out loud. I confessed to my wife Katie what I suspect she knew all along. That I wanted to be the *Lafayette Escadrille* and the *Flying Tigers* all rolled into one. And that combat, the proximity to and the possibility of death, was the highest of highs, an orgasmic rush unlike any other. It was a think-fast game that I had to win because the alternative was unthinkable. I was addicted to the cat and mouse we played in little airplanes. Because I was smarter, faster, better, tougher. I loved it. I did. I loved it.

Saying this out loud, to Katie? To my father? To anyone? Some of the most difficult words I have ever tried to say.

John Meyers was easily as funny as Greg Glashauser. They both said ridiculous things that they absolutely believed with all their hearts. Meyers swore that he was going to fly his Bird Dog beneath the lone bridge in *Kontum City* that spanned the *Dak Bla* River. Except that a Volkswagen bus couldn't be stuffed sideways under that bridge and the Bird Dog's wingspan was considerably bigger than a sideways Volkswagen bus. Greg Glashauser ranted that his first son was going to be named Wolfgang and that his son's first words were going to be "Fuckin' a Tweedie." Only Greg knew what that meant.

"Don't look back over your shoulder, lieutenant. If you do, you'll turn the airplane, and they'll shoot your ass down for sure."

Those were the first words John Meyers ever said to me. Because that is exactly what happened to a pilot who came up to *Kontum* to fly the SOG mission. The first time the new guy flew over the Trail he turned to look at a possible target and a machine gun found him. He was rescued, and after getting back to *Kontum* he packed his duffle bag and returned to Holloway. He volunteered to run the supply shop, a hateful job, and announced that he was never flying another combat mission for the rest of his tour. He didn't, and no one blamed him. That's why Meyers told me never to look over my shoulder. Grinning a maniac grin which scrooched up his whole face.

A week or so after Greg tried to turn me into fried chicken, I walked into the dim coolness of Camp Holloway's Officers' Club. It was empty except for a big lump of a guy sitting at the bar. Not quite eleven in the morning. A little early for a drink, at least for me anyway. The lumpy guy was Meyers. Our company commander, Major David Naumann, removed John from the Special Forces camp about three weeks ago, convinced that John was pushing his personal bullet-proof boundary to its farthest edge. He wanted to be John Wayne or Wyatt Earp or Butch Cassidy, or maybe all of them rolled into one. So, John took crazy-man chances because he was convinced that nothing could harm him. He flew his unarmed Bird Dog into battle, oblivious to the bullets and rockets zinging by him. Some of them hit the airplane, none of them hit him. John constantly thumbed his nose at fate. He was so convinced that he was unkillable, unhittable, indestructible, that every chance he took was a chance he thought worth taking. No matter how risky or how unlikely or how just plain nuts, he knew the bullets shot at him would miss. Somehow, again and again, they did. And somehow, again and again, God let my friend off the hook.

About a month earlier John, not yet dragged back kicking and screaming to Holloway, had taken Glashauser on a recon flight over a nasty area of Laos into which Greg's team was eventually going to be inserted. And then, after being coated with saltines, I took Greg back for a second look, which he saw through closed eyelids.

Most screwball ideas started with Greg or were instigated by Greg. And most of the time Meyers, easily egged on by Greg, was more than happy to go along with him. Glashauser decided it would be cool to bring a .30 caliber machine gun along on their recon. Just to shoot stuff. What stuff? Any stuff. So off they went, John and Greg, over the Laotian border, looking at Greg's next area of operation, and looking for stuff to shoot. A .30 caliber machine gun can be hand-held and fired. But not easily. Greg rested the gun on the sill of the rear window and then pulled the trigger. He shot the airplane. In the right wingtip. On full-automatic the gun bounced around the window opening like a whirling dervish. The wingtip was no big deal. Battle damage from ground fire, John would later lie. They were so lucky that they didn't shoot the wing strut in half. But luck is fickle, and God has been known to change Her mind, which is why Major Naumann pulled John back from FOB 2.

I was looking for an early lunch when I stepped into Holloway's Officers' Club. I'd been up since four in the morning and had taken off from *Kontum* in the dark. I spent almost four-and-a-half hours over southern Laos, then refueled the airplane at *Dak To* and flew to Holloway. I don't remember why. Right now, I was starving, and the Officers' Club had hot food. And my pal Meyers. I sat on the bar stool next to him and smiled.

Meyer's right hand was encased in an elaborate bandage. I sensed that he couldn't wait to tell me about why his hand was all but immobilized. I asked *Thuy*, the bar girl, about my dining options. I could have a hot dog, or would I like some *Pho Ga*, some Vietnamese chicken noodle soup? I opted for the soup and Meyers looked at me as if I'd ordered a hemlock salad with rat-poison dressing. He'd obviously never eaten anything that wasn't on the menu. The *Pho Ga* was terrific.

There was a rocks glass of cloudy brown liquid on the bar in front of John. I ordered him another of whatever that was and ordered a big glass of club soda for myself. I pointed at his glass.

"Okay. I surrender. What is that? What you're drinking? What?"

"Crown Royal and milk. I think I have an ulcer."

I laughed until my sides hurt. Milk with whiskey. An ulcer. Made perfect sense to me. His drink and my club soda arrived, followed shortly by my soup. I hadn't asked him about his wounded hand yet. I loved driving him a little more nuts, and John was becoming very anxious to tell me his story. I ate my soup.

I took the napkin from my lap – Army clubs had paper napkins while the Navy sissies had linens – and dabbed my lips. By now Meyers was visibly twitching, so I asked him how he hurt himself.

"Grenade launcher. I scrounged one with a sawn-off barrel and I shot it out the window of the airplane."

I don't know whose eyes were bigger, his because he was reliving this moment, or mine because I realized right off the bat how completely lunatic this was. John started his story from the beginning.

After the Glashauser-induced machine-gun debacle John became a man obsessed. He needed something with more oomph than our AR-15 rifles. He wanted something that exploded. Well, we did carry rockets in the rocket tubes under our wings. Two on each side. He could load up four high explosive rockets. Only four? Not enough. Not nearly enough.

An M-79 grenade launcher, now there's a cool gun. It looked like a chubby stump of a shotgun. It fired a grenade that looked like a chunky little Thermos. And John, no stranger to chubbiness himself, could carry maybe two or three dozen grenade-bullets in his helmet bag. He managed to borrow an M-79 from one of the recon team leaders. The gun had about two-thirds of its barrel sawn off so that John could hold it in one hand to shoot it out the window and fly with his other hand. A smart guy would have test-fired his new weapon using just one hand. And John was a very smart guy. Just not about this. He didn't test fire it at all. He wanted his new toy. He wanted to shoot it out the window. And win the war all by himself.

I looked at Meyers and I was frightened. Not for him. John was going to do what he was going to do. I was frightened for me. I could have easily grabbed an M-79 to shoot out the window of my airplane. Pretend I was a flying cannon. Stretched the definition of "Enough" to allow it to include this craziness. But I didn't. I believed in sacrifice if that meant saving the lives of my friends. That was a conscious decision I made when I looked down and saw Laos. When our guys were down there. Each day required an evaluation of limits, of knowing how far to go, and more importantly, of knowing how far was too far. I almost always knew. Almost. The farthest edge of enough? That was where John always seemed to be.

John's airplane had a sheet-metal patch where the .30 caliber's bullet holes used to be. He took his repaired Bird Dog and his sawn-off gun flying. Back into Laos again. John said he was about 400 ft above the ground, saw an abandoned bunker, and decided to fire the gun. And that's what he did.

To me the M-79 looked like a toy. It went pop, not bang, when the trigger was pulled. Every time I ever fired it I expected it to apologize to me for not putting on a bigger show, for not going *kapow* instead of *ploop*.

And the recoil was no big deal. Every gun had a recoil. Newton's law. Some recoils were not much. Unless the gun was being held in one hand. And the hand was not expecting it. The recoil drove John's hand upward and slammed it into the long strip of hinge that allowed the Bird Dog's big side window to be opened and latched onto the underside of the wing. When that hand, clamped around the butt of the M-79, crashed into that hinge a sharp piece of the hinge almost cut his thumb off. John and his bloody thumb had to fly back to *Kontum*, to the little dispensary. About an hour's ride, with his right hand getting more pumpkin-like by the second. John got a bandage and a shot of pain killer from the *Bac Si* in *Kontum,* and took another airplane ride as a passenger, to the hospital at *Pleiku* Air Force Base. The nurses and doctors asked him how it happened. I'm betting whatever he told them barely cruised by the truth.

I haven't made any of this up. Not a whisper of hyperbole or exaggeration. Meyers really did this. He was lucky he didn't hit the airplane with that grenade and blow himself out of the sky. For me, Meyers epitomized the mystery of survival. It struck me then that there was no rhyme or reason as to who died. Or when they died. Or how they died. Sometimes a guy would show up and be dead in a week, or a month. That guy could have been the greatest pilot since Chuck Yeager, yet a bullet still found him. Another guy who couldn't tie his own shoelaces would be unscathed, would last out his twelve-month tour, and go home. Meyers could tie his own shoelaces and everybody else's. With one hand all cut-up and bloody. John needed to be the gambler who always drew to a full house. He needed to win. Which made everything a challenge, and he loved to push every challenge to its farthest edge. When I admitted to myself that I loved the adrenaline rush of combat I thought of Meyers. John was hooked on the adrenaline rush, the winning. He loved the edges, but never considered the limits. Bullets set our limits. John just ignored them. The bullets and the limits.

I survived. I don't know how. From the late winter through the mid-summer of 1970, I was certain that I would die. I didn't. Somehow John survived as well. Maybe despite himself. No, not maybe. He definitely survived despite himself. John Meyers, with his Crown Royal and milk ulcer, his .30 caliber machine gun, his M-79 grenade launcher, his little unarmed Bird Dog, somehow lived. I don't know how. I think I know why though. I think God just liked him. I still do.

Glashauser and I may have had very little contact with one another for the rest of the time I was in *Kontum*, but somebody who coated my sweaty self with crumbled Saltines was not easily forgotten. Unlike Glashauser, John Meyers is someone I have seen on several occasions after the war. At reunions of Bird Dog pilots mostly, especially when Arlie Deaton was alive. My relationship with John was short on time but long on intensity while we were flying together in Vietnam. The both of us caught up in the chaos of combat, a friendship of two adrenaline-charged boys trying to stay alive, pretending that we were much tougher than we really were. Using bravado like a shield to prevent others from seeing our fear.

Television on a rainy Saturday afternoon is a great way to spend a little time with teenaged daughters. Alanna, 16, is my buddy today, which isn't always the case with dads and daughters. I flip channels, stopping at the Learning Channel because it is airing a documentary on Vietnam, on the battle of the *Ia Drang Valley*. That is the first half of the program. At the midpoint of the program the emphasis changes. A different commentator is talking about a secret war in Laos, and now I am really focused. The TV screen is filled with a familiar face. An older face from almost thirty years ago. The mustache is still big and bushy. The top of the head has lost its hair. But the eyes still smile the same way they did over thirty years ago. I look at Alanna and laugh.

"'The Plastic Man.' John Plaster. Let's see if he tells the story about the air horn."

Her eyes narrow. She always narrows her eyes at me when she disapproves of something I have done.

"You know about this? Were you there? Are you going to say anything?"

John Plaster didn't tell any stories. He talked about the SOG mission, the casualties, the wounded, and the dead. He talked about his fatalism, and the fatalism of everyone else. About death as an inevitable consequence of "running recon" across the border. How acceptance of death "freed" him to function in the face of it. Then the program ended.

Alanna's questions, however, have just begun. She repeats her challenge,

"You know about this? Were you there? Are you going to say anything?"

I open the door to the little deck off the kitchen and step out. Alanna follows me, her question suspended in the damp air. The rain has stopped but the sky is still solid clouds, and the breeze is quick off the Strait of Juan de Fuca. I look into Alanna's very brown eyes and plead.

"I'm not going to tell you something that isn't true. I know who John Plaster is. I know most of the people John spoke about because a long time ago I worked with them. Someday I'll tell you about what I did. Maybe all at once, maybe a little bit at a time. But I promise, someday I will tell you."

"You didn't go on those patrols in the jungle, did you?"

Her eyes are wet.

"No, I was always in the airplane. But I worked for those people."

"It was dangerous, wasn't it?"

I tell her the truth. It was very dangerous.

"Why did you do it?"

Did she really want an answer to this?

"Because somebody had to, and I volunteered."

That, at that moment, was the best that I could do. Alanna looks at me, the expression on her face hard to read. Is she angry? Disappointed? Is she thinking that had I been killed she wouldn't be here? I continue for a little while longer, trying to sound more dad-like, trying to let the love I feel for her touch her through my words.

"I could say that I was being careful, and I was. But being careful really didn't matter so much. I think that, more than anything, I was lucky, and that I survived so that you could be here. What matters is that you are here."

She hugged me and I hugged her back, keeping my arms around her to protect her as much as to keep her warm. It was still wet and cold. We stood there a few minutes more, looking out at the charcoal-gray water. It was clear enough below the overcast sky to see Vancouver Island. Beyond was the Pacific, and further on, Asia. In Asia is a year of my life, a year full of memories. I am still afraid to talk about some of them.

What Plaster didn't say in that documentary was that something as simple as an airhorn saved his team from what could have been a lethal ambush.

I'd been up since God only knew how early and had already flown four hours over southern Laos, looking at the result of overnight bombing raids. That morning it finally dawned on me that I had to stop looking for things the bombing had destroyed, like burned-out trucks or random bodies. I mean, I still needed to look for that, but I had to look to the edges of the area, to where the bombs didn't impact. If the area our B-52s had hit was known ahead of time, if the North Vietnamese had been tipped off prior to the strike, then they could hang around just outside the target area and move back just after the bombing ended. Because they knew that a Bird Dog, with a photographer in its back seat, might low-level over the area doing the same thing, bomb-damage assessment. In the span of a few hours the NVA could move a company of troops right up to the perimeter of a strike, dig and camouflage fox holes and gun positions, then wait for us to show up. And that was exactly what they did. I hated this mission because it seemed like we were always taking ground-fire. The NVA had to have been tipped off. By whom? Russian trawlers or submarines off the coast of Guam? A mole in MACV headquarters in Saigon? Because it seemed like they were always waiting. I was sure that if I got killed it would be flying a goddamned bomb-damage assessment.

No breakfast, as usual. Now, lunch for me, C-Rations. Franks and beans. I wished these C-Rats had cookies in them. It wouldn't matter how stale they were. Then I rearmed the Bird Dog's rocket tubes with white phosphorus warheads in the two outboards and high explosive warheads in the two inboards. Finally, I filled the gas tanks from the big, gray gas bladders. The refueling and rearming were jobs I always loved doing. I had no idea why. I just did. The rockets weren't too heavy and slid right into the underwing tubes. There was a step on the wing strut close to the cowl that let me bring the fuel hose to the top of the wing. I undid the gas cap and shoved the nozzle into the tank, squeezed the handle, and avgas flowed.

"Fill 'er up, wash the windows, and while you're at it, give me something that explodes." I announced this to no one in particular. I was the fueler and the armorer and the driver. It was me who filled the gas tanks, and the rocket tubes, and then washed the windows. A normal Bird Dog pit stop.

In a few minutes a SOG recon man was sticking his hand out for me to shake.

"I'm Frank Doherty."

"I'm Plastic man."

"Okay. But who are you, really, sergeant?"

"John Plaster."

"Good, because if you were going to stick to 'Plastic man' I would have to change my name to 'Captain Kangaroo.' Where are we going?"

John was scheduled to be inserted into an area in the extreme northwest of SOG's Laotian operating area. This was not a good place. He could tell by the expression on my face that we were going to be aerial reconning a nasty place. Sergeant Plaster's expression, on the other hand, gave away nothing.

Its distance from *Dak To* made this area risky. If John ran into trouble on his mission, he'd need helicopters as fast as he could get them to extract his team safely. Distance made fuel an issue. The longer the distance the less time the Hueys had to get the team on board before gas became critical. We called it "stay time," how long the Hueys and the Cobra gunships were able to remain on station until they declared "bingo." "Bingo" meant they had just enough gas to get home, but that they had to leave right away.

The area we reconned looked a lot like other areas we had reconned. Except that we got an occasional peek at a trail that was "elephant" wide. Apparently, trucks were being supplemented by elephants. I didn't ask what the SOG Operations Officer setting up John's mission intended, but I guessed that the destruction of transports, both trucks and elephants, was going to be involved. I didn't give a damn about the trucks or the people driving them. The elephants were another issue altogether.

As we bobbed and weaved just above the treetops, I heard a muffled ka-chunka noise. Ka-chunkachunkachunkachunka.

"Are you jiggling your knee?"

"Not me, Frank. Are you?"

Jesus, Mary, and Holy St. Joseph! A 12.7 anti-aircraft gun was shooting at us. It had to be ahead of me and off to my left, I thought. The airplane was almost dragging its wheels through the treetops to avoid the gun's extra-big bullets. If we stayed down, I hoped the gun crew would not be able to lower, or depress, the gun's barrel enough to hit us. If I could have flown through the trees, I would have. Because climbing now was suicide. The airplane would slow down in a climb, even at max power, the engine RPM red-lined. We'd be target practice. I got us heading east by using only the rudder, so we skidded around to a heading of ninety degrees. Aileron would have made the airplane bank in a turn, dropping a wingtip into the treetops, and maybe hitting a big branch, which could have smashed the wing and killed us. We stayed down on the treetops until we didn't hear the gun anymore. I had thought this little corner of Laos was evil, and I was right.

We flew away from the 12.7, a big Chinese machine gun with an easily recognizable, very slow rate of fire. Ka-chunkachunkachunkachunka. I can't believe that I had internalized the rate of fire of a Chinese gun. Of course, I had. I chalked this up to the price of staying alive. Once clear of its bullets I climbed my Bird Dog up to an altitude unreachable by small arms fire and not-so-small machine-gun fire, and we both relaxed a little.

John spoke over the intercom.

"I asked my father to send me a bugle."

Okay, this is apropos of what?

"Why?" I asked.

"Well, he couldn't find a bugle, so he sent me an air-horn. All I need to do is yank on this lever and it makes a very loud noise."

I looked out the window at the scenery passing beneath the wings. It was just beautiful below us. Lush and green, small rivers and waterfalls, a bazillion birds. How could it be so peaceful? It was a war zone. I didn't care. I would have rather accepted the grace of better angels than be shot at. And I was enjoying this whacko conversation.

"I give up. What's your plan with the air-horn?"

"Well, if we're being tracked, I know that they [North Vietnamese] are going to hit us, probably with an ambush." The NVA trackers usually tried to maneuver a recon team into a very difficult area to defend, and either race ahead to set up an ambush, or, if they outnumbered the SOG recon team, assault them, try to outflank them, and annihilate them. Plaster decided that an air-horn's loud blast was something that the North Vietnamese had probably never heard. He was right.

On his team's insertion a few days after his recon flight with me, John, his second in command Fritz Krupa, and the rest of his team were engaged by a slightly larger NVA force. John was on one side of a depression, moving along the spine of a ridge. His *Montagnard* point man at first thought he heard a monkey. Until the "monkey" began firing an AK. RPGs (rocket-propelled grenades) started pounding the terrain around RT California. If the team moved uphill, they would expose themselves to the NVA's guns. John's hand found the air horn attached to his web belt and he yanked the $CO_2$ lanyard that made the air horn howl. It roared. And then it was totally quiet because the NVA ran away. Mission accomplished without a shot being fired, without a casualty. All because of an air horn!

After our single morning reconnaissance mission, John Plaster disappeared from in front of my nose. He was still at CCC, but like Glashauser, I never flew with him again. I never saw him again, because our SPAF mission had changed dramatically over the last several months. Teams were still being inserted into Laos, but we had no role in those operations. From the end of March until I left *Kontum* in July, I flew photo missions, bomb-damage assessment, and area reconnaissance. Low-level always, at about 500 ft above the ground for the photo Bird Dog, and 800 ft for the cover Bird Dog. The perfect altitudes for the NVA to launch a gazillion bullets at me, and the second Bird Dog, if there was one. Sometimes it was me and the photographer, by ourselves. And not one mission a day. Oh no. Usually two. Which amounted to over a hundred hours a month. I think my logbook was now reflecting 135 hours a month for the months of March and April. Taking off before the sun streaked the sky and landing just as dusk turned to almost dark. And for a little extra jolt of adrenaline, our jeep sped by that damn cemetery twice, in the dark of pre-dawn or in the dark of just past dusk, with its headlights off. Spending time with anyone other than my flying partners Phil Phillips or Doug Krout, Mike Buckland the photographer, the Bird Dog, or my bunk, was unlikely. Maybe Glashauser and Plaster didn't really disappear. Maybe Doug, Phil, and I did. Flying an airplane that we loved. Flying our asses off. And somehow, not getting killed.

Sergeant Michael Buckland became a regular in our backseats. He was on his third tour in Vietnam, all in the Central Highlands, and all with SOG. The first time we flew together I confessed that if we got shot down, I was following him, because I was sure that he knew what he was doing in the mountainy jungles we flew over. I'd be lucky to know right from left on the ground. Michael "ran recon," served in CCC's "Hatchet Force" quick reaction company, which went to the aid of recon teams in trouble "over the fence." He was now in charge of CCC's photography shop. His cubbyhole darkroom office was a favorite hangout of mine. Midway through our first conversation I realized that I was looking at one of the smartest people I had ever met.

Dawn was a faint glow this morning, the light announcing its almost arrival. And I needed to remember the light. So beautiful at daybreak, even though I was moving away from the sun. Gold streaked the horizon and illuminated my way. I was in a race westward with the sunrise, a race the sunrise always won. I loved the light at this hour of the morning, my quiet time that I could slow-dance through, time when I could listen to the throb of the song the engine sang. I was free, free to be cooled by the wind that rushed past the Bird Dog's big side window.

Racing the sunrise was a made-up game I played. I spent no time thinking about it. Overthinking anything was like chewing too long before swallowing. What was the fun of eating if all I got to take was one bite, and chew and chew and chew? What was much more fun was another bite and another bite and another bite until the bites were gone. I didn't want to think. I wanted to beat the sunrise.

The radio was quiet now. It wasn't going to be too much longer, but for now the only noise in my ears was static. I couldn't turn the volume down. But I was able to tune it down. I'd learned how to hear without listening. Voices were not static. I knew how to respond to voices.

Bucky was asleep in my Bird Dog's back seat, a big camera cradled on his lap. He wasn't moving. I was able to see his face in the rear-view mirror on the left side of the glare shield. He had his visor up. My friend's eyes were closed. I was glad he was asleep. That meant I didn't have to talk to him. Yet. He could sleep and I could dream. We would talk in a little while. Maybe even yell at one another over the intercom. Right now, it was quiet. And I was busy. I needed to remember the beauty of the sunrise that I was racing to the west. The sunrise always won. It always got to Laos before I did. But the rest of the morning was still sleeping. The North Vietnamese, Buckland, everyone was still sleeping. The NVA needed to stay asleep so that Bucky and I could get down onto the treetops before the North Vietnamese knew that we were here. Let me drag the Bird Dog's wheels through the canopy, get past the soldiers on the ground before they saw us, aimed their weapons at us, shot at us, and tried to kill us.

We were where we were supposed to be now. No more time for thoughts to wander. Now it was time to concentrate. To listen. Then act. My backseat was awake. I saw his eyes open as we rolled inverted and spun toward the green roof of tree leaves. I let go of the stick and the spin stopped. My right hand eased the stick back, pulling the Bird Dog out of the dive. My left hand eased the throttle forward. The engine came out of idle and hummed up to about three-quarter power. I reached above my head and flipped four red toggle caps forward, then pushed four toggle switches forward too. My white phosphorus rockets were armed.

We could see through the leafy branches. The sun behind me lit the way, its rays' slanted beams illuminating the jungle floor. I heard the rapid click of the camera's motorized shutter. I didn't need to tell Sergeant Buckland what to do. Bucky was an old hand with SOG, and we have done this together a few times before. He balanced the long lens on the rear windowsill, the lens sticking out into the onrush of air. The camera whirred through film, taking hundreds of photographs, all of them of the Trail, and of what we've found.

I had my right foot pushing the right rudder about halfway in, telling the rudder to turn us to the right. My right hand had the stick over slightly to the left, telling the ailerons we were going to turn left. I was lying to the rudder and the ailerons. We were not turning. We were just flying sideways. Just like always.

I was sure that the shooting was about to start any second now, so it was time to really focus. Several trucks were stopped here. This had to be a transfer point. A small one. Drivers traded cargos. Those who drove north now drove back to the south. They had supplies and ammunition for the North Vietnamese Army. Those who drove south now turned around and took wounded north. I found their trucks a little after the sun found them. I raised the volume on my radio. There was an airplane above me. A big, four-engine radio relay C-130. At least 20,000 ft. Hillsboro. He was able to hear me, and I could hear him. Hillsboro could get me what I needed. I needed fighter-bombers. But not right now. Nothing more than reporting what we found today. Intel would decide what was to be done. I already knew what that would be. I'd be back, maybe in a couple of hours, maybe toward the end of the day, or maybe with tomorrow's sunrise, with A1s or Cobra gunships. We'd come loaded for bear and obliterate this place. And then the NVA would come back and after dark put everything back together.

What I needed to do right now was to remember what Bucky and I saw here. We called a turn-around like this a truck-park, but it was really a chokepoint. Traffic backed up here. We needed to photograph it quickly, to mark its coordinates on our maps, put them into today's code, and call in the coded location to SOG ops through Hillsboro. We would do this while we flew away from this traffic jam, flew away before the NVA saw us, before they started shooting, before we died here.

Bucky said,

"Got what we need. Let's go!"

The Bird Dog pivoted around the wing tip that pointed at the ground and headed East toward the Vietnamese border. We stayed close to the treetops. It was still quiet. No banging from a .51, no staccato rattle from AK-47s? How could that be? This was Laos. Flying recon over Laos always sucked. I worried that I'd overextended my ration of luck.

"Hey, Frank, I think we've just crossed the fence."

Bucky meant we were probably over the border into Vietnam. I started the Bird Dog climbing to gain altitude as we flew back to *Dak To*. A thousand feet above the ground was high enough. I could just about see *Dak To* from the Laotian border. After landing we parked the Bird Dog and disarmed the rockets. Bucky headed off to leave his film wherever he left it while I began to rummage through the cartons of C-Rations, hoping as always for spaghetti and meatballs or franks and beans.

"Please, God, don't let pork loaf and lima beans be the only C-Rats here."

Whoever thought pork loaf and lima beans was a good idea never had to eat this stuff. Today God liked us. Spaghetti and meatballs and franks and beans. I held both boxes out to Sergeant Buckland and asked him to take his pick.

"You pick first, *Dai uy*."

"No, you get first choice, *Trung si* (sergeant)."

"No, really, Frank, you pick first."

Ah, Alphonse and Gaston. After you. No, no. After you.

"You're sure, Michael? Okay, franks and beans."

Bucky looked a little disappointed, so I extended the franks and beans to him, which brought a smile. This was what officers were supposed to do for their subordinates. Michael Buckland was not my subordinate. He was my friend. Wasn't this what one friend was supposed to do for another?

There was a quality that was common to those of us who were involved with this covert Bird Dog operation, Operation Ford Drum the Pentagon called it. It wasn't only that our war was fought in Laos, in Cambodia, along infiltration routes, along the Trail. Or that the recon teams we supported operated there in "sterile" uniforms with no Dog Tags. Or that our excuse, were we to be shot down and captured, was that we were looking for a downed pilot. This quality reached far beyond place, identification, excuse. Deeper than the adrenaline rush, the mental cat and mouse, the physical and emotional endurance. I think what we all had in common was the ability to shut death out. It took me no time at all to realize that I could die flying for SOG. The Green Berets running recon all knew this. I can't imagine that the SPAF pilots who preceded me didn't consider the probability of death either. That was why we were all volunteers. Nobody was assigned. All of us asked to fly this mission, or were asked to fly this mission, and said "Yes." So that once dying was accepted as possible, as probable, as maybe inevitable, we stopped thinking about dying. Our focus homed in on our mission, and by extension, friends involved in our mission.

I was afraid. I absolutely was. But that fear had to do with not protecting my friends, with not being the SPAF pilot who let them down. Fear in combat had nothing to do with me. It had everything to do with not being there for Deaton or Phillips or Krout or Meyers or Ford or Glashauser or Plaster or

Buckland. Was I fatalistic? You bet. My willingness to not consider myself first allowed me to fly through fear, to fly to a more perfect, altruistic place. The mission flown with a singular focus on execution would keep me alive, but it was also the place where I forgot me, where the individual disappeared, and only the lives of the crew chiefs and the recon men and the other pilots and the cooks and the clerks and the grunts mattered. The war? The war for this country belonged to the South Vietnamese. They would have to figure out if all of Vietnam was worth fighting for or not. The North already knew. My war was not being fought for the Vietnamese. I was flying through my war for men I knew, people for whom I worked, boys for whom I would give up my life to keep safe. What I know to be true, at least true for me, is that Vietnam will never be about a place. I remember places. How could I forget? But my year revolved around the faces of friends, of boys trying to be men, who became so much more than colleagues or wing men or crew chiefs. More than brothers even. When I eventually screw up the courage to tell my children who I was and what I did, I think that my words will most certainly describe the faces of the men with whom I served, and events will fill in the spaces around my friends. I think of their faces, faces from Vietnam, faces that always make me cry.

# Chapter 8

# Our Bloody Spring

**March 1970, Seventh Month**

Prince Norodom Sihanouk, the ruler of Cambodia, ran away. A group of right-wing generals staged a coup and relieved the prince of his crown, his throne, his palace, and quite a bit of his money. He hightailed it to Peking, which hadn't become Beijing yet. He ran away before the generals could hang him.

On 18 March, we were told to "stand down." We got a whole two days off while Cambodia's new government was being sorted out. I had been flying the SOG mission every day since December. The SOG operations officer arranged with the flight surgeons at Camp Holloway to give us waivers on the number of hours we could fly without a break. I am convinced he was trying to fly us to death. And to tell the truth, I had no idea that there were limitations on the hours we could fly. Major Smithwick, the S3 (Ops Officer), wasn't about to let the cat out of that bag.

The overthrow of Sihanouk changed everything. Cambodia was thrown wide open. Two days prior we couldn't use Air Force fighters as close air support for teams on the ground. Now, if anything moved, we could blow whatever anything was to kingdom-come. Nothing was off limits. And the North Vietnamese, who for so long used Cambodia as a sanctuary, fought tooth and nail to protect that sanctuary.

The NVA built the Ho Chi Minh Trail, a leaf-shrouded super-highway that ran down from the Communist north, through Laos and Cambodia, into South Vietnam. During the year prior to Sihanouk's overthrow, March 1969 through March 1970, they sent over 250,000 men and drove who knows how many trucks, elephants, and bicycles over the Trail through Cambodia and into the South. They had also carved out an enclave the size of Massachusetts in Laos to train and rest their troops, and to stage attacks.

The Studies and Observations Group used their recon teams to upset the flow of men and materials along these infiltration routes. The North Vietnamese couldn't complain to anyone about SOG conducting operations across the border because the NVA wasn't supposed to be in Laos or Cambodia either. A deadly game of cat and mouse ensued and the body count for both sides climbed and climbed and climbed.

I'm pretty sure John Plaster was the last CCC one-zero I took on an aerial recon because we were now flying photo missions exclusively. Sometimes the flying required a high cover-ship Bird Dog and a low, on-the-treetops Bird Dog with a photographer in the back seat, flying bomb-damage assessments (BDA) seconds after a B-52 strike, arriving on station while the bombs were still falling. The fumes from the explosions were so new they burned my eyes. And other times it was just one airplane with a photographer in the backseat, doing what the Operations Officer demanded, to "just go find something." Never mind getting shot down when nobody knew where I was. A jungle-covered mountain looked like every other jungle-covered mountain. And it didn't matter what kind of a photo mission we were flying. The groundfire never stopped. Sometimes it was incredibly intense. Other times not so much. But groundfire always announced the possibility of death.

St. Patrick's Day, 17 March, the day before Sihanouk was pushed out of Cambodia, marked the beginning of my third year of active duty. I was about to be promoted to captain. Two years before this St. Patrick's Day I had been thinking of Finnegan's while reporting to Fort Knox. Now it was 1970, and I was not in Finnegan's on this St. Patrick's Day either. I was in the SOG bar at FOB 2, and the crowd here wasn't singing "There's Whiskey in a Jar" at the tops of their lungs. No, it was some Country and Western song. It was always Country and Western. On this St. Patrick's Day Colonel Abt had taken my new silver captain's bars and dropped them into a beer mug filled with a splash from every bottle of booze on the shelves behind *TiTi,* who was tending bar. I had to drink the mug empty, catch the captain's bars in my teeth, hand them to the colonel, who then pinned them on my flight suit collar. We exchanged salutes and handshakes. Then I executed a very smart about-face, walked out to the shrubbery, and exchanged the booze for a few very large gulps of humid air.

Lieutenant Jerry Poole followed me out. I stuck my finger down my throat, and after the alcohol came blasting out of my stomach, he handed me a canteen full of water. I poured some water into my cupped, impeccably clean hands, rinsed my mouth out, and thanked him profusely. Jerry was in the throes of adrenalin overdrive, and I was probably the only person on the compound who would put up with his jitterbug routine anymore. He had been training for an insertion, his first I think, into Cambodia, that would take place in six days. He was so nervous.

The young woman who cleaned our hooch and did our laundry had taken my two additional flight suits to her friend, a seamstress, who sewed my railroad tracks, my black captain's bars, on my olive drab flight suit shirt. So, on 17 March I was promoted by Colonel Abt's glass of booze and my hooch maid's seamstress. The entire CCC bar was neck-deep in alcohol, Colonel Abt probably had no recollection of promoting me, and I'm sure that my new cloth rank made absolutely no impression on the seamstress, provided she got paid. So essentially, I promoted myself.

Three days later, on the 20th, when Phil and I got back from flying we found Lieutenant Poole waiting for us. If Jerry was jittery in the bar a few days earlier, he was moving at 500 miles an hour now. With his insertion set for four days from today his words had almost no separation between them and he couldn't hold still. Jerry paced and jabbered, then paced and jabbered some more. He gave each of us a "short-timer's calendar." A drawing of a naked woman wearing only a green beret. Her body was divided into 365 numbered sections. A section was colored daily to indicate how many days the calendar's owner had left on his tour.

Recon Team Pennsylvania was inserted into Cambodia on 23 March. Three Green Berets and five *Montagnards*. The North Vietnamese had trackers on them almost immediately. Running and ambushing, hiding in dense jungle, then running and ambushing and then hiding through the night, Poole's team called for an extraction the next morning. The Covey Rider directed them toward a landing zone and readied helicopters for the extraction. Lieutenant Poole had injured his ankle, the team had slowed down, and the NVA trackers were right on top of them, so close to Lieutenant Poole that A-1 Skyraiders which were called in for close air support couldn't help. The team had to get out right then or die.

A Huey dove for the LZ, flared a few feet above the ground, and hovered there while the eight-man team scrambled aboard. The pilot radioed that despite the fusillade of bullets fired at them, he had gotten them all and started the Huey climbing. At 300 ft above the jungle the Huey exploded. Witnesses in the other helicopter said that they saw pieces of bodies flying through the air. They tried to see if there were any survivors, but the ground fire was so intense that they had to abort their attempt. Everybody, the three SOG men, the five *Montagnards*, and the four Huey crewmembers, twelve men, everybody, all dead. In the bar that night the SOG men sang *Hey Blue*. The lyrics included a litany of names, from Larry Thorne, the first SOG man killed in Vietnam to the most recent, Jerry Poole. And all the names in between. Our bloody spring had begun.

It is cool this Sunday afternoon, 12 October 2012, the day of John Pappas's funeral. The breeze scoots up from the Hudson River, chilling the autumn air. The cemetery at West Point is a somber place despite the golds and reds that set the neighboring oaks and maples ablaze. My friend John Pappas is buried here. John is listening to memorial words the Greek Orthodox priest speaks. The words bless him.

The monuments here announce a sacred place because fathers and sons lie side by side here. Heritage, a tradition of service passed as legacy from one generation to another. West Point is a celebration of loyalty, of selflessness, of devotion, of altruism. John Glimis Pappas, a member of the class of 1966, will rest in this special place. I will remember him here, and I will remember him from another time, from when we went flying my last month in Vietnam's Central Highlands.

My wife Katie and I place a white rose on John's coffin. Here, at his graveside, I realize that I cannot hide from that year, a war year that I have kept buried for over forty years. A war year that has been so difficult for me to confront. A war year that makes me ask if that boy was really me, who knows I did things I don't want to remember. I still never talk about those things. I don't think many of us do. I am afraid of my memories. Not even when Meighan or Alanna asks me, my two daughters to whom I would give anything. I cannot give them answers. Because I think that I have nowhere to go with the memories. Katie gently holds my hand. We watch as four other pilots, friends of John, and friends of mine, with their wives at their sides, place white roses on John's casket. Tears start, finally.

I don't know why, as I stand at John's graveside, I now feel that I can revisit painful hours, painful days, painful memories. By hearing myself say the words that explain that year I hope I might find solace in them. Maybe I understand that John is giving me permission to go back. And maybe the caress of Katie's hand is an unspoken question, signaling that she wants to know what I have not said. I know I must tell her. I realize that I want to. I cry this funeral day as I have not cried in four decades, and tell myself that it's okay to look back, that I need to remember with words, before the memories fade like old shirts with frayed cuffs and collars.

After John's funeral I take my Army Aviator Wings and three medals from the back of a drawer and show them to Katie. Her finger touches the navy blue ribboned Distinguished Flying Cross, the DFC.

"What is this one for? What did you do to get it?"

I tell her what the medal is and why I have it. I tell her about April mornings. I tell her about the war and the boy who was me. The words come tumbling out.

That medal reminds me of who I tried to be as well as what I tried to do. It says I am a hero, but I don't feel that way, because it takes me to what I failed to do. I tell her about 1 April, in 1970, a day I have been unable to talk about for more than half my life. I tell Katie about the sapper I found. I tell her about death.

Late March, my seventh month in country, had turned into a bloodbath along the borders of Laos, Cambodia, and Vietnam. Twelve men in one day. On one mission. We began to lose recon team members on every mission, usually more than one. And sometimes a whole team. Special Forces troopers, *Montagnard* or *Nung* (ethnic Chinese), mercenaries, it didn't matter. Chaos was every day, and it did not discriminate.

Mid-morning, April Fool's Day, a gray, wet-cold, windy morning, a morning that made me not me anymore. I became a different me because I killed a man. I saw him as I killed him. I was 24 years old. A boy no longer. I saw the sapper's face. It stared up at the sky. His head was thrown back, his eyes were open, his mouth too. The satchel charge and the AK-47 he was carrying lay on the ground beneath him. That ground was darker than the rest of the ground near him. His arms were tangled in the razor wire. He was stuck there because he never had a chance to use the satchel charge, to blow a hole in *Dak Seang*'s razor wire so that his squad of NVA could race through.

I caught him running from a trench his men had dug. It got them close enough to breach *Dak Seang*'s perimeter. The sapper's job was to use his bomb to blow open a passageway through the razor wire. As his arm stretched rearward to fling his bomb, I fired a flechette rocket. A lucky shot. It hit him at his waist. I was far enough away from him so that the rocket armed, but close enough so that the little darts, still tightly packed like a swarm of bees, cut him in half. His pelvis, his legs, his feet, stretched out behind him; his torso tangled in the wire's barbs. The sapper's satchel charge unexploded, his AK silenced. I threw up out of the Bird Dog's window. I hadn't eaten anything since the night before. I threw up anyway. Stomach acid burned my throat.

I had spent the early hours of 1 April alone above the Ho Chi Minh Trail looking for the NVA. When I landed at *Dak To* for fuel two Huey gunship pilots asked if I could help them. The Special Forces camp at *Dak Seang* was being overrun, they said. Maybe I could get fighters released to provide air support for the Green Berets on the ground. Air support, a euphemism for "bring lots of bombs." No time for breakfast now. While the UH1-C gunships were being rearmed I refueled my Bird Dog, filled my helmet bag with smoke grenades, and loaded rockets into their under-wing tubes. White phosphorus for marking targets in the two outboard tubes and flechettes (we called flechettes nails) for killing people in the two inboards.

I flew over *Dak Seang* from the west at about 500 ft above the ground. As I steep-turned back to the east I saw the trench. Then I saw the sapper. I fired the rocket which turned his midsection into a spray of red, and then I threw up. I knew that I had killed people before. Until now I was always a step removed from the act. I hadn't toggled the napalm or the high-explosive bombs. My finger hadn't been on the triggers of 20-millimeter cannons. But I said "there" with my smoke rockets. I said "there" with my smoke grenades. I had never ever seen someone die that I helped kill. Until the first day of April, when I cut the sapper in half. When I killed him.

It got wet-cold in the mountains during the monsoon season. *Kontum* was in the mountains. No rain on this early April Sunday morning only days after *Dak Seang*. Waterlogged clouds almost touched the ground, so no flying until they lifted a little. I'd go flying again as soon as the colonel could see from one end of the compound to the other. A chaplain had a folding table set up to serve as an altar; a Catholic chaplain was going to say Mass. The altar was covered with a purple cloth. It was Lent, a time of repentance. The wind kept trying to lift the cloth away. Maybe the wind could blow my sins away.

Before communion the chaplain gave us all absolution. Tell God you're sorry for whatever is turning your guts inside out. Jesus and the wind will make your heart feel okay again. Jesus was well-intentioned, I'm sure. And the breeze on wet spring monsoon mornings was almost always present. It made the rain fly sideways, but the breeze was never able to blow the heartache away.

Almost fifty years later I was still able to see him, and what happened at a Special Forces camp near the *Montagnard* village of *Dak Seang* would always come back again.

My daughters, two little blond girls, saw my medals once, a long time ago, just before I hid them in a drawer, before I showed them to Katie. As if by not seeing them I believed I could somehow erase memories that the cold, wet winds of *Kontum* had not blown away. The war receded into the depths of time, replaced by the busyness of raising children. Vietnam was hardly mentioned. Then schoolbooks and television shows brought questions, and memories grew large again. Blue eyes and brown eyes searched mine. My girls looked, trying to see if I told them everything, or only part of everything. They were able to see the pain on my face, and I was sure that they knew there were things I could not say. I kept those awful things to myself.

The war was more than fifteen years in someone else's rearview mirror, but never in mine. I had moved our family from the craziness of Venice Beach to the Pacific Northwest in 1985. We lived in Spokane, in a big Queen Anne Victorian on Cannon Hill Park, which overlooked the city. Meighan and Alanna, 6 and 5, were able to walk to school in their red and blue plaid uniform jumpers. I was a B-737 First Officer, commuting to Western's hub in Salt Lake City to fly my trips. I saw the sapper's face almost every night. The nightmares were at their worst. I had no name for what was eating away at me. Whatever it was, I left it unsaid.

Spokane spread out from its river, which ran through downtown, a cascade of almost 100 ft at 31,000 cu ft of water a second. The roar of the river's waterfall was this little city's background music. The Menock Bridge spanned the river. An old, Depression-era bridge, its edges protected by low block walls, which were not much defense against black ice on a cold, snowy morning. I crossed that bridge every time I drove to the airport. A choice of life or not, made 520 times between 1985 and 1990.

It would have been easy to send my blue Jeep into the river. A plan to commute to Salt Lake on the early morning flight but never get to the airfield. Look to see that no other cars were around, then go like hell to midway on the bridge and steer at the guardrail. Black ice. Because something, for which I had no name, was tearing at my heart.

Those days, over thirty years ago, on the walk to Cataldo Catholic School across Cannon Hill Park, which overlooked the city of Spokane, I held little hands tightly in mine. To keep my daughters safe. Meighan and Alanna held mine as tight as little girls could. To keep me here. To keep their father from blowing away.

Their little faces smiled up at mine. I could not leave them, abandon them, desert them. I brought Meighan and Alanna into the world. I owed them life. I owed them me. The bridge was crossed, then again and again. The notion didn't disappear, but the act of selfish death became impossible. Laos, Cambodia, and Vietnam would always be in my dreams. Sometimes fragments of pain, sometimes all the pain, played out over a week or a month or a year. Or even forever. A war, decades ago, again in the dark, where nightmares are made.

My grandsons look at the now framed medals sometimes. Especially the one Katie first pointed to. The navy ribboned one, the Flying Cross.

"What is this, Cappy?"

They have begun to ask questions about war. About what it is like. They have seen pictures of me, of my Bird Dog, of the mountains in Laos. They have asked me if I had a gun. Did I shoot it? Did I kill anyone? I look at those little-boy faces and realize that they see war through little-boy eyes. Tree forts and pinecone hand grenades. Young lives with endless horizons. I only tell them that I shot my rifle. I only tell them that I fired my rockets. I cannot say more than that. I don't have the courage. I found some of the words for Katie, but the words for my daughters and grandsons are just not here yet.

Sometimes questions demand answers because the questions are inescapable, and the answers are owed. The stories are told, some are easier than others to tell, and some unbearably painful to tell. Then, because of the pain, the whole story becomes some of the story. Not untrue, just not all there. Sometimes all the truth is a painful thing.

The sun is just barely up in the early morning of 28 August, 2019. Only Lucy, my dachshund, and I are awake. Lucy is on my lap, a cup of coffee steams on the table next to my laptop. A photograph of a gravestone appears on the computer's screen, on Facebook, on the MACVSOG page. There are so many of these sites now. I belong to a few. On several occasions I have seen names I recognize, people I once knew, some living and some dead. The photo of this gravestone announces a name I instantly recognize, and the person who posted it writes that the Green Beret buried beneath this gravestone died in a plane crash. I look at the name, I look at the date, 2 April 1970, and that awful moment comes up from my basement of bad dreams. The name I read is one that I will never forget. The date of death as well. I know the name and I know the date, because I was there the day this man died. The person who posted this is wrong, though, on how this life was lost, and where this life was taken away. There was no crash, and the place was not where the writer said it was. I saw it all.

This is how Don Armstrong died. What happened, on this day after April Fool's morning in 1970, still hurts my heart. Why Captain Phil Phillips and I survived I have never understood. Only Sergeant Donald Armstrong died, and I have never been able to escape blaming myself for his death.

We were flying a two-airplane photo-reconnaissance mission over southern Laos very close to the Cambodian border. Sergeant Armstrong and his giant Pentax camera were in Phil's backseat. Phil was flying as the low ship. He skimmed about 100 ft above the jungle's bright green canopy. I was Phil's cover ship, with no observer in my backseat, flying several hundred feet above Phil, watching him, and watching out for him. Phil's Bird Dog was at the low edge of ground fire's kill zone. At my altitude I thought I was a perfect target.

It was just after dawn. Sunlight poured through the trees at a perfect angle, exposing a big NVA base camp. The huts and bunkers were bathed in gold. Dew sparkled on a million leaves, flashing prisms. No smoke from their breakfast fires yet, but they would wake up as soon as they heard us. They would grab their rifles, man their anti-aircraft guns, and wait, hoping we would come back.

We came back. How many times had we admonished one another with the one rule we always stuck by? One pass and haul ass. Never, ever, ever, do "seconds!" But Armstrong was zooming on adrenalin; this was his first photo mission. Phil surprised me by changing direction.

"Oh, don't do this!" I yelled to no one. Phil slid the Bird Dog up a parallel valley, then eased over an adjacent ridge line and approached the camp from a different direction. Hanging halfway out of my airplane's big side window, I searched for the anti-aircraft gun that I knew had to be here somewhere, but I couldn't find it. Absolutely sure that it had to be lining us up, my eyeballs strained to find its muzzle-flash. I knew that if I heard the gun first then the gunner would have us zeroed in, would be able to shoot us down, and kill us. The Chinese anti-aircraft gun's muzzle flashes lit up a tiny clearing right where I thought the gun had to be. Except that I heard the gun banging away first. Just a heartbeat before I saw its tongue of flame. Somehow Phil and I escaped the trap. The airplanes took bullets that just missed Phil, and just missed me. One bullet connected. The one we couldn't dodge, the one that found its way to Don Armstrong. The one that killed him.

Phil and I buried this bad dream for decades. We stuffed it down into the dark place of terrible times that we couldn't bear to remember, that we never wanted to drag out into the light. About which we didn't want to talk or be surprised by if asked. And then, because of some person or because of some reason, totally unexpected, this awful moment said, "remember me?"

A man with the same family name replies to the photograph and to the post, asking if anyone knows anything more about this death. The headstone bears his father's name. It is his son asking. The son says that for almost fifty years he has not wanted to know. But now he does. I read his request, written below the photograph, several times. I can feel the sorrow in the son's request.

My eyes search the corners of my kitchen, looking for an escape route in the early morning light. There is no place to go. Looking again at the photo of the tombstone, I realize that history has come calling. The name on the tombstone becomes a vaguely recognizable face. The face becomes a man I met in that long-ago morning's dark pre-dawn, a man with whom I had spoken not a dozen words, words I can't even remember. A man wearing metal-framed glasses with round lenses that reflected the moonlight. A man in adrenaline overdrive, his body almost frantic, his hands never still, fussing with his camera's enormous telephoto lens. Every action done in triple-time. A man about whom I knew almost nothing. I have always hoped that no one would ever come asking about him. But someone has.

Lucy, in the crook of my elbow, is quiet. She has buried her head under my bathrobe. I wonder out loud,

"Do I want to go there? Do I need to drag this up again?"

I feel that I should. No. I know that I must. The son has a right to ask, and I think that I am honor-bound to respond. It's time to consider an answer to whatever questions the son might ask.

"There was no crash, and this didn't occur where the report says it occurred."

I write this as a comment beneath the headstone photo. He messages me almost immediately; only I can read the message.

"I'm Kenji Armstrong. Please tell me whatever you can about my dad."

He gives me his email address.

Phil and I had not spoken about this day to one another for over forty years. I don't know if Phil ever related the story to anyone else. I told my father and my brother on a rainy morning in Alaska, and, after John Pappas's funeral at West Point, I told Katie.

Several years ago, when Phil called to get the details of what had occurred at West Point, at John's burial, he asked me an odd question.

"How did we get to *Kontum* from *Dak To*?"

This had nothing to do with that autumn day at West Point, and he didn't need to put the question into context. A scene didn't need to be set, and a name didn't need to be mentioned. I knew exactly what Phil was asking and I didn't try to guess an answer. He was asking about that terrible second of April morning, the day after the sapper at *Dak Seang*. He couldn't remember how we got from the Special Forces camp at *Dak To*, which was our mission launch / recovery airfield, back to our home airfield at *Kontum*. I had to think about this for a minute. Not because his question took me by surprise. No. I couldn't remember either. Who flew back?

Phil asked me if I could fill in this blank space in his memory.

"Your airplane was too full of bullet-holes and severed control cables to be flyable. My Bird Dog had its share of holes too, but everything in it worked. You know, it's amazing that we both blanked on this. I just don't remember doing it, but I had to fly us. I had to, don't you think?"

It must have been me because Phil's Bird Dog really was shot up like Swiss cheese. No ailerons and no tail wheel steering cable. We didn't get a ride back in a Huey. I would have remembered that because I really hated riding in helicopters. And, in our phone conversation, Phil and I didn't say the name. We didn't say "Armstrong."

I knew that Phil wouldn't want to go through this again after all this time. But I also knew that I had to talk to him. I waited until mid-morning, and then called. As I explained what happened, the photo on the MACVSOG page, the incorrect place and circumstance of Don Armstrong's death, and the contact with Kenji Armstrong, Phil said not one word. I kept talking. I told him that I'd deal with explaining to Kenji, and that before I related anything that happened almost fifty years ago, I would run it by him (Phil) first.

"You don't need to get involved, Buddy. I'll handle it for the both of us."
He referred to me by our old call-sign.
"Thanks, SPAF. Let me know what you decide to say."
Now I needed to figure out how much of the story to tell.

The sky around us that morning became a blur of green "tracer" bullets, making snapping sounds as they went by me, my Bird Dog vibrating when they hit it. The anti-aircraft gun was ka-chunking more slowly than the AK-47s but firing bigger bullets. Phil was yelling over the radio, a yell measured not in volume but in octaves. His voice now almost gasping.

"My ailerons are shot out and there's blood and brains all over the cockpit!"

I yelled back at him to turn east, run for the border, and not climb.

My Bird Dog pointed almost straight up, and then I pushed the right rudder pedal hard to its limit. The airplane flipped over on its back and changed direction. We were pointed straight at the ground. The big gun's muzzle flashes were now directed at me.

"Do I die here?"

I fired all four of my white phosphorus rockets one right after the other. The Bird Dog and I twisted and turned until we were almost in the trees, then I wrenched my little airplane out of our dive and stood it on its wingtip to turn east.

Phil was up ahead of me, in some numb and hazy space. He was flying straight, bobbing up and down a little but flying straight, hugging the treetops. I remembered that his ailerons had been damaged so he couldn't juke and jink his airplane. He was only able to fly straight ahead. I felt the absence of ground fire, I didn't see tracers or hear the pop of bullets or the banging of the machine gun anymore. My ears were ringing though. Everything sounded muffled, everything seemed foggy. I radioed ahead to have a Medevac helicopter ready and get Huey gunships released. The gunships escorted Phil back to the airstrip at *Dak To*.

All of this, Armstrong, the Chinese anti-aircraft gun, yelling over the radio, all of this took a heartbeat, a deep breath, a curse word. No more than a one-potato from the counting game. Once the anti-aircraft gun opened up on us I don't remember thinking about anything. Cover Phil. Roll in on the gun so that Phil can get away. I've always wondered about the "automatic" of me, about the "why did I do this" and the "how did I do this" of me. Where does thoughtless reaction come from?

The everyday of dying? I don't know. Dying was something seen all the time in this gory little war along the Ho Chi Minh Trail, but death can never really be casual, or matter of fact. I don't think someone becomes inured to death just because the catastrophic becomes commonplace. What touched me so deeply was that the body bags were every day. If I tried not to look too long maybe the image would go away. I never got used to dead friends.

Phil landed and managed to keep his Bird Dog on the runway. A round severed one of the cables that controlled the tail wheel, so he had no way to steer. I could see the cable trailing from its tail wheel connection and warned him. He used his brakes to keep the Bird Dog going straight, to keep it from swerving into the dirt. An ambulance jeep was quickly alongside him. I landed a little behind Phil, taxied clear of him, shut down, and ran. I got to the ambulance just as Sergeant Armstrong was being lifted from Phil's backseat. He still had his flight helmet on; it held his head together. There was a big hole in the top of it. He had no face.

Don Armstrong allowed the ballistic missile of his adrenaline rush to snatch away his life. Did his son really need to know that? I asked myself if it was necessary for me to go back again to everything that happened? To explain that Sergeant Armstrong's insistence on a second pass over the camp was an invitation to have a bullet slam into his head. That when it exited through the top of his helmet, blood and brains sprayed all over the airplane's cockpit. Sergeant Armstrong's wound was gruesome, and his death had to have been instantaneous. How much about this terrible morning do I need to tell his son?

Phil should have refused Sergeant Armstrong's pleading to make a second pass. He could have told Armstrong no. Phil was a captain. He could have pulled rank on the sergeant and ordered Armstrong to shut up. But he let himself be persuaded. He gave in to the pleading and went back for more photos. And me? I should have refused to let Phil make that second pass. We had that rule! And we both knew better than to break it. I should have blown his eardrums out with my yelling over the radio when I saw Phil slip his airplane over the adjacent ridgeline so that he and Armstrong could come back again, even from a different direction. I should have reached through the radio transmission and grabbed them both by their collars, and shook them, and cursed at them. Why didn't I? I swore out loud.

"Oh, don't do this. Oh, please Jesus, no."

I said all this at the top of my lungs, but only to myself, my protests banging around inside my own cockpit, my words streaming out the open side windows of my Bird Dog and racing unheard into the air that sped by my airplane. I stayed with Phil because I was the cover ship. I stayed above him because that was where I was supposed to be. I stayed with Phil because he was my friend.

Phil's airplane rocked as rounds impacted it. I heard the bullets crack as they swarmed by me. I felt my airplane shudder as they hit it. Then Phil was yelling about blood, brains and shot-out ailerons. I was certain that Phil's bullet-spiked adrenaline had to be roaring now, because mine was through my cockpit's roof. The green streaking tracer rounds whizzed by, as if every AK-47 in the world had begun shooting at us. And Armstrong was dead.

Telling some of the truth doesn't make the truth less true, I decided. There is nothing to be served by sifting through every detail, parsing every sentence, defining every word of this April morning's story. It had taken almost fifty years for Don Armstrong's son to ask his question,

"I'm Kenji Armstrong. Please tell me whatever you can about my dad."

I decided to tell him as much as I was able. I also decided that I didn't have the right, after all these years, to diminish the image of a father, seen through the eyes of a little boy. I was not going to do that. He asked me to tell him whatever I could about his father. And that, I decided, was what I was going to do. To tell him whatever I could.

I explained to Kenji the mission his dad flew with us that barely daylight morning. That the other pilot will never speak about it. That his father showed great courage in volunteering to fly over the border into Southeast Laos, to fly over the Ho Chi Minh Trail. To hang out of a Bird Dog's back window, to fly in an unarmed airplane dragging its wheels almost across the jungle canopy, to take photographs of a very big NVA camp. I told Kenji Armstrong that we encountered more groundfire than I had ever experienced. That the AK-47 round that hit his father must have killed him instantly but that we weren't sure. And that is why we flew back to *Dak To* with our airplanes' engines "red lined" at their maximum power, hoping that we could save his father's life. That is why we radioed ahead to have a Medevac helicopter ready to take Sergeant Armstrong back to the big hospital in *Pleiku*. And that we found out, as he was removed from Phil's back seat, that Kenji's father had died.

I think about the time in between this man's email to me and his father's death, when this man was just a boy of 9. All those years of not knowing about his father. Of not wanting to know. Of anger because a dad was sacrificed to a war conceded as lost by old men half a world away, old men who would not admit that it was futile to continue to send boys to die, old men who could not say "stop."

The war keeps coming around, again and again. Always taking a piece, if not all, of someone's heart. Years ago, on 2 April in 1970, the war took a piece of a little boy's heart from him. It took his father from him, and left this boy blinded by grief. Now grown, the son reaches out.

"I'm Kenji Armstrong. Please tell me whatever you can about my dad."

I do. Carefully. Gently. But not everything. Because I am not going to give Vietnam the chance to come back around on a second pass again. I hope that what Kenji Armstrong isn't told spares him from pain I truly believe he doesn't need to feel. I hope that what he does hear from me convinces him that Donald Glenn Armstrong was a brave man, a man of whom he should be proud. A hero.

Phil and I found our way to the enlisted men's little bar the night of Don Armstrong's death, to join with everyone in the singing of *Hey Blue*. We didn't know the names of most of the SOG men who were memorialized in that song, but we knew John Boronsky's name and Gary Harned's name and Jerry Poole's name. They were recon team Pennsylvania. Armstrong's name was the last one sung. We knew that name.

# Chapter 9

# Arlie Deaton

In mid-April 1970 I flew down to Holloway from *Kontum* and was asked to take an airplane to Battalion Headquarters at *Qui Nhon* for maintenance, and then fly our company Beaver, its maintenance finished, back to Holloway. Bigger than a Bird Dog but smaller than an Otter, the Beaver, also made by *De Havilland*, was great fun to fly. It had a tail wheel, a big radial engine, and hydraulic flaps that you pumped up or down with a lever. On take-off I could leave the wing flaps up, and with the Beaver going as fast as it would go, pump the flaps down to the take-off position. The airplane would hop off the runway like a terrified frog. Just hop off the ground, settle a little like it was surprised to be airborne, then start climbing. I loved to do that. This was a great way to spend part of a day, flying a Bird Dog for CCC on an early morning photo mission along the Cambodian portion of the Ho Chi Minh Trail, then fly down to *Qui Nhon* to deliver that airplane for a maintenance inspection, and then get to fly the Beaver back, terrified-frog takeoff – you bet.

I walked into Battalion HQ, planning to get the Beaver's maintenance log and then return to Holloway. The operations officer said that the airplane was on the ramp, fueled and ready to go, handed me the logbook, then turned to a man I didn't see right away. But he saw me.

"Captain, this is your new Company Commander, Major Arlie Deaton."

Nobody told me I'd have a passenger, or a new company commander. The ops officer was gesturing toward Deaton, and Deaton was smiling. He extended his hand, and as he tried to crush my knuckles, he looked at me, then at the Ops officer, then back at me. If somebody had to be the boss, and in the Army there always had to be a boss, I knew I could not have asked for a better one.

"I remember you, captain. Yes, I do. Show me what you've learned about flying." Deaton teased me now, and he would spend the next four months teasing me.

At that moment I wasn't sure if I'd ever be able to move the fingers on my right hand again let alone handle the Beaver's controls. And I had the feeling that our flight back to Holloway was going to be the check ride revisited. As it turned out, we flew a practice instrument approach into *Qui Nhon*, made a practice missed approach, then headed west for Holloway. Deaton never once touched the controls. I did all the flying, and he did all the watching. Deaton was the same Deaton who flew with me back at Fort Stewart. The same Deaton who explained *Chandelles* and Lazy Eights. The same Deaton who flunked me but got me recycled back so I could learn what I was never taught. I owed him whatever he asked, and I would have given him whatever that was even if I didn't owe him anything at all. Arlie Deaton was the best commanding officer I had ever had.

Two weeks before Arlie arrived, Phil and I flew back to *Kontum* from *Dak To* in my airplane after Don Armstrong's body was removed from the back of Phil's Bird Dog. Phil's flight suit was sticky with blood. As we stowed our flight helmets and survival vests in the little flight-ops room Ben Brown, one of our crew chiefs, leaned into the room through the door and announced that our platoon leader, Captain Willie Ridgeway, had died there earlier in the morning when he crashed on takeoff. I remembered being told by Ben about Willie's death, but it just didn't register with either Phil or me. Maybe Willie's crash was too much for the two of us to confront. *Dak Seang* the day before, then Don Armstrong on this second of April morning over Laos, and now Ridgeway? Too overwhelming to sort out. We climbed into our black SPAF jeep, drove to the Special Forces compound, grabbed our soap and towels, and walked to the showers. The water was on. We took off our leather boots. I started to unzip my flight suit, but Phil walked straight under the shower head, turned on the water, and started methodically scrubbing Armstrong from his clothes. And I did the same. I thought Phil smelled like blood. Everything smelled sticky sweet. Like blood. My stomach was churning. We scrubbed one article of clothing on our bodies at a time, removed it, and started on the next, scrubbing until we were naked, and couldn't smell the stink of us anymore. No talking. We kept scrubbing even after we used up all the not-quite hot water.

Phil and I met Major Smithwick, the SOG S3, the operations officer, in the mess hall later that afternoon. He needed to de-brief us about what had happened. Major Smithwick launched into a barrage of questions. Yes, we got nailed in a "fifty trap," which meant that we were caught in a .50-caliber machine-gun crossfire. Yes, Don Armstrong died because of groundfire from the encampment we found. Yes, Phil's airplane got shot to shit, and yes, we could find the camp again. Major Smithwick stood up.

"Tomorrow morning, captains?"

I responded, "Before or after breakfast?"

Smithwick glared at me, so Phil and I saluted. He returned our salute.

"Take-off at 5am."

Then he walked out. Why did this guy hate us, I wondered?

"Fucking asshole." Phil was furious. Me too.

The tension between Phil and Major Smithwick got worse. About three weeks after Smithwick's Armstrong debriefing I came back to FOB 2 after flying most of the day and found that Phil was gone. Gone from our hooch and gone from the Special Forces compound. Banished to the MACV compound, closer to the center of *Kontum City*. A few hours earlier, at *Dak To*, Phil and Major Smithwick had engaged in a shouting match over how much we were flying. Since Sihanouk's overthrow we had been airborne all day, every day, from before dawn until almost dark. We always took fire from AK-47s. Sometimes .51 caliber machine guns fired at us too. But there was always someone firing something at us. Our airplanes were beginning to look like a crazy-quilt of sheet-metal patches. The stress was beating us up. Phil tried to explain to Major Smithwick that we were worn out. That we needed a break. One day, maybe, or just an afternoon. Phil said the major told him, "Stop whining, captain."

Phil sneered back, "Whining, major? Whining? At home we shoot people for less than that!"

Mike Buckland let me use the radio telephone in the photo shop to contact Arlie at Holloway. I pleaded,

"You need to get up here right away. Like first thing in the morning, tomorrow."

Major Smithwick wanted Phil in jail for threatening him, a senior officer, and was planning to court-martial him. I asked Arlie to arrange a meeting for the next day. Because without our company commander's intervention, the charges against Phil would surely stick, and Phil would be in the stockade.

We met Arlie and Major Smithwick in the mess hall. It wasn't morning. We were airborne long before morning. It was mid-afternoon. Smithwick made sure Phil and I were flying before dawn again. Phil still worked the SOG mission but how he was able to maintain his focus with the threat of a court-martial hanging over his head was beyond me. Phil drove to the airfield from the MACV compound, and I briefed him on what we were supposed to do when I met him at our flightline.

At his meeting with Major Smithwick, Arlie was able to pacify the sorry bastard. He told Major Smithwick that we could fly as much as he needed us to fly provided no charges were brought against Phil. The major agreed. I guess he thought flying us both to death was better than locking just one of us up. Then Arlie asked if we had eaten anything since breakfast. Breakfast? We were always airborne before the mess halls here and at the MACV compound opened for breakfast. We never got breakfast! Major Smithwick grudgingly made peanut butter sandwiches and beers appear, along with a "get out of jail" card for Phil.

Did I mention that I hate peanut butter? I have always hated peanut butter. But that afternoon, in the mess hall with Arlie and Phil and the major, was the one time in my life when I ate peanut butter. Because I was starving, because I could wash the peanut butter down with the beer, and because I didn't want to give an inch to this condescending jerk by choosing not to dine. Major Smithwick repeated his order from two weeks ago.

"Tomorrow morning, captains."

Smithwick stood up, and so just like two weeks ago, Phil and I rose and saluted. He returned our salute.

"Take off at 5 am, captains."

Before breakfast, of course.

Then Arlie started talking. His voice was soft and calming. He talked us down from the hangover of Armstrong and Ridgeway, from the condescension of Smithwick. Arlie passed around beers from the six-pack. He nursed one while Phil and I drank the rest. We sat talking until the afternoon faded into twilight. Phil had to drive the jeep he stole several months ago back to the MACV compound, and Arlie had to fly back to Holloway before nightfall, but Arlie stayed with us long enough to be sure we were as emotionally settled as we were ever going to be. So settled that four decades later neither Phil nor I could remember who flew back to *Kontum* from *Dak To*, from Phil's shot-up airplane, from Armstrong's lifeless body. The day after our meeting with Major Smithwick, Arlie Deaton submitted the paperwork for two Distinguished Flying Crosses. For extreme heroism in aerial combat. One for Phil, and one for me.

Smithwick was determined to have the last word. As the last days of April began to bump into May, the rain clouds moved closer and closer to the treetops. Monsoon season was approaching. When the rain increased, the visibility decreased. Then flying anywhere couldn't be in a straight line because we couldn't get above the cloud-shrouded mountains. Weaving through narrow valleys to avoid hitting the side of a hill meant a longer flight to the objective, but more importantly, zigzagging ate more fuel. As we made our way west toward the Thai border, toward the *Mekong River*, the possibility of having the weather go down behind us was frighteningly real. And then what? Where do we go if we can't get back to *Dak To*? I decided to ask him.

I took the SPAF jeep back to FOB 2 at dusk. It had been a long day. Almost ten hours of flying. I was tired, grouchy, hungry, and I smelled like an airless gymnasium. I found Major Smithwick in the office he shared with the S2, the intel officer, and started to explain about the weather. He stopped me when I got to the part about not being able to get back.

"Captain, do you have your map with you?"

I did. It was a big map, folded and stuffed in the zippered map pocket of my flight suit. I took it out and handed it to him. He opened it up and took out a pair of scissors from his desk.

"Don't even think about going to Thailand, captain."

Then he cut my map at the *Mekong*, and Thailand went into the empty grenade crate trash can next to his desk. I was absolutely stunned. Chopping Thailand from my map? Was this clown trying to get me killed? I looked at him in disbelief, saluted and not waiting for him to return it, I left without a word. I walked back to our hooch, opened a beer, boiled some water for rice, and sat quietly for a minute to calm down. How do people get to be such jackasses? Then I laughed. The big map at our Ops hooch at *Kontum*'s airfield showed all of Vietnam, all of Cambodia, and all of Laos. And it showed a big chunk of eastern Thailand. Our air base at *Ubon,* Thailand, was on that map, northwest of *Dak To*. If I was near the Cambodian-Thai border, I was pretty sure that flying a heading of three-three zero would get me close to the airfield. I could broadcast a "Mayday" on my airplane's radio, be located on *Ubon*'s radar, be given a "radar steer" to the runway, and land. Then find a radio telephone, get patched through to SOG Ops at FOB 2, ask to speak to Major Smithwick, tell him where I was, and then end the call with a "Hey, major. Wish you were here!"

It would be worth dodging rain squalls to get to *Ubon* just to make that phone call.

Near the end of April, I took an airplane down to Holloway. I don't remember the reason why. I just remember having to do it. The day started in the dark, just like it always did, flying over Laos. After refueling at *Dak To* I arrived at Holloway just before lunch. I parked on the ramp, took off my flight helmet and unstrapped my shoulder harnesses. And as I climbed out of the Bird Dog, I realized that I had left my hat in the flight line locker, back in *Kontum.* I was hatless. Deaton was death on hatless people. Don't leave home without one and have it on your head when you're outside. Army regulation, a soldier was "covered" when not in a building. I looked around the maintenance office for a stray baseball-style hat or a floppy "bush" hat but couldn't find either. All the crew chiefs and their hats were already dining on something other than, and therefore much better than, C-Rations. Especially not the pork loaf in aspic with lima beans. There was only one option left, because I had to have a hat, because I had to walk up to the Company Orderly Room. Arlie would surely be there, or in the mess hall.

My only choice was to retrieve my flight helmet from the Bird Dog and put it on. The 3ft-long commo cord dangling from the right earpiece made my helmet and me look especially ridiculous. I laughed as I put my flight helmet on my head and tucked the plug end of the commo cord into the pocket of my flight suit, and "covered," headed for wherever Deaton might be. I only made it half-way, before I realized that Deaton was in front of me. I stood at attention, very stiff and very still.

Arlie eyed the flight helmet on my head. He was smiling but he wasn't laughing.

"Are you making fun of me, Dawtry?"

He never did pronounce my family name correctly. Arlie was from Alabama, which in some ways still lingered in the nineteenth century. Dawtry was nineteenth-century Alabamian for Doherty. And he never called me captain or Frank. Always Dawtry, always on purpose, because I had the nerve to tell him how to pronounce my name months ago, in flight school, when he gave me the check ride that I failed.

I followed him into the Orderly Room. Arlie called me to Holloway that day to try to convince me to apply for a Regular Army Commission. He told me I couldn't be a general if I stayed as a reserve officer. And he tried to convince me to extend my tour for an additional six months. He said that I could have a great career in the Army, rise to colonel at the very least, and that I was needed for the SOG mission. I thanked him for the encouragement and said I'd think about what he said. There was no way I was going to be disrespectful to him by dismissing him out of hand. An "I'll

Arlie Deaton, 219th Aviation Company Commander, 4/1970.

*Above*: 1st Lieutenant Francis A. Doherty & U-1 Otter, 18th Aviation Company ramp, Da Nang 9/1969.

*Below*: 1st Lieutenant Francis A. Doherty and Sister Angela, Orphanage, Da Nang 10/1969.

Death's Head Patch, Military Advisory Command Vietnam Studies and Observation Group, Command and Control Central (MACVSOG, CCC).

1st Lieutenant Francis
J. Doherty, Aviation Cadet,
1942.

Captain Francis A. Doherty, 2nd Platoon Ready Room, Camp Holloway 8/1970.

Mother and Father, Tucson Arizona, c.1942.

A-1 Skyraider, rolling in on a target I had just marked, about 500', 7/1970.

Captain Doherty rolling in to mark a target, Polei Kleng Vietnam, 8/1970.

Captain Doherty and Sergeant Buckland returning from mission over Laos, 3/1970.

Katie's Debutante photo, New York City, 12/1965.

Lloyd Harbor / Lloyd Neck.

Laos Mountains, Me & Buckland, 2/1970.

Bombing bridges on H. C. M. Trail, 6/1970.

Bunker, Dak To.

Bunker, FOB-2, Kontum.

219th Reunion, Annapolis Maryland, 1999, Vietnam Memorial Back: R. Kane, C. Slimowicz, J. Meyers, A. Deaton, D. Shipp, C. Phillips, F. Doherty, G. Savani. Front: B. Bernhardson, John Pappas, John Estill.

Katie and Francis, Biltmore Mansion, Ashville North Carolina 8/2013.

My father (Francis J. Doherty) and me, Lloyd Neck, 9/1979.

Headhunters Patch, 219th Aviation Company.

Mom (Celestina Paulina DeGuira) 1939.

Delta Airlines, Captain Doherty, B767ER, Dublin Ireland, 2001.

*Above*: Sgt. Michael Buckland & O-1 #001534, Kontum Airfield 1970.

*Below*: Katie, (Catherine Grace) Women's March 1/2017.

*Above*: O-1 Bird Dog, Smithsonian Annex, Chantilly Virginia, 4/2018.

*Below*: Head Shot 11/24/2022 for book jacket.

think about it," would have to do. I did end up thinking about it. For about two seconds.

"Let's have some lunch."

I followed Arlie out the door with my flight helmet on. He looked at me, laughed, and shoved his hat in his back pocket. I took the flight helmet off and walked alongside him to the mess hall. It took one to know one.

It is almost the end of April, and I am alone over Western Laos. Only the hum of the engine keeps me company, keeps me focused, keeps me alert. I need to pay attention. Because I am by myself. Nobody in the back seat, nobody to talk to, nobody to worry about or for whom to feel responsible. On misty days the tops of the mountains I am flying around are obscured by clouds. It takes all my concentration to not fly into one of them. I am looking for people, and I need to avoid the jagged fingers of rock that would crush my little airplane like a paper cup. I forget about the empty back seat. I usually talk out loud about what and who I see. My voice keeps me company. It keeps me where I need to be.

On sunny days I can see these same mountain tops. They go on and on to the edge of my horizon. Most are covered with vegetation. Soft green shrouds their hard skin. Little valleys between the peaks are places where people live in houses on stilts with walls made of bamboo and roofs laced together from thatch. Grouped together, the houses make up villages, connected by paths through the foliage to other clusters of houses. These groupings of little villages are not called towns. They are called hamlets, and the people in the hamlets are almost all farmers. The land they farm has been in their families for generations. It is sacred, tied to their religion, connected to their ancestors, whom they revere. These people are indifferent to a war that happens far from them, that seldom touches them. Indifference goes away when war touches them. If this war finds them, it usually means that some of them will die.

Sometimes the North Vietnamese kill a few villagers to spread fear among them, so that they don't help the South Vietnamese Army. I help the South Vietnamese Army. I bring the war to these farmers. When they see me, they know that death usually follows right behind. They see me now. I am flying in circles above them. Climbing and descending, twisting, and turning, trying to see through the layers of leafy tree limbs. Looking for

119

people who look like them. Looking for the guns that will be used to try to kill people who look like me. The guns, if they have any, are well hidden. They must be, if the farmers really have them. If they do.

I fly up and down these skinny valleys, studying the villages and the dirt paths and the hamlets and the people. Almost always the people look up at me. I have never spoken to any of these people, but I am pretty sure I know what they are thinking when they see me. I know what I would be thinking if I changed places with one of them.

And I am also thinking that I don't want the Bird Dog's engine to quit. Because if it fails I have nowhere safe to go. I will have to put my plane down in one of these little valleys. I am very far from the Vietnamese border. Which means I will have to find my way to Thailand even though Major Smithwick chopped Thailand off my map. If the farmers or the North Vietnamese or the *Pathet Lao* (Laotian Communist Army) don't find me first, that is. I keep a few extra rounds for my pistol in the breast pocket of my flight suit. Just in case I don't get to Thailand. There is a reward given by the North Vietnamese to anyone who turns me over to my enemies. My captors will torture me before they kill me. I keep bullets in my pocket. I am 24 years old, and have planned my own death, all by myself.

I think about other things too, sometimes while I'm out here looking, so close to Thailand and so far from our staging airfield at *Dak To*. I think about the notion of calling these people "my enemies." I think that this is just nuts. How can people to whom I've never been introduced, either formally or informally, be my enemies? Sometimes when I fly over these little villages, I see women holding babies. They are looking at me and I am looking at them. They hold no weapon aimed at me. My enemies? I am the person who is armed. I am flying the airplane that can command bomb-laden jets to kill these women holding these children. I finally realize is that mine is a very little picture, a very personal picture of my very tiny place in an otherwise giant conflict.

When I first got to the 219th Reconnaissance Airplane Company I thought I knew what Vietnam was all about. But as I became immersed in the covert mission I was flying, my big picture kept getting smaller and smaller. Because I worked alone most of the time. Because when I worked with others, the "others" never amounted to more than ten men. Reconnaissance teams sneaking around in the little valleys, their casualties a constant. I didn't see bodies stacked like firewood along the sides of the runway at *Dak To*. Our casualties numbered in twos and threes. For most of our missions, body bags, in twos and threes, were placed alongside one another, by the runway. Every mission.

Except for one time, I never knew what happened to the intelligence I gathered. If I had a photographer along in the back seat, he would take rolls and rolls of film. His camera had an automatic shutter. He pushed the button and took a dozen portraits. Of men who were farmers, of women holding babies. I seldom knew where the film went. If I was alone, then I was debriefed after returning to our base in *Kontum* by the S2, the Intelligence Officer. I told him what I saw and where I saw whatever it was that I saw, and provided him with map coordinates to pinpoint locations. It was usually dark by this time, and the mess hall was closed. Then dinner was my usual. Rice, dehydrated vegetables, hot sauce, and beer.

I had concluded months ago that we weren't going to win this thing. I wondered now about the point of what I was doing. I still didn't think about the war in larger terms. Alone in an unarmed airplane miles and miles away from a friendly airfield, my war, my world, remained little. And in this little world I became more determined than ever to survive. One mission at a time. Concentrate on what I was tasked to do. Find their guns. I had to find them first. If I just heard them, I was probably going to have a few bullet holes in the Bird Dog's sheet metal skin. Maybe my skin as well.

The information I gave after one of my very first missions so close to the Thai border surprised me. It became something. It led to an airstrike on a village. A village where the men who were farmers and the women who held babies looked up at me. I didn't see any guns, or gun emplacements, or anything that looked bad. That didn't mean that guns and ammunition or anything that looked bad wasn't there. It meant that I didn't see them. There were probably tunnels; all the villages had tunnels. So that the people could hide from the bullets that both sides in this war might aim at them. No one shot at me when I found this place. They only looked.

In my debriefing with the Intelligence Officer, when I described in detail what I saw in that village, I made a point of telling him, with as much passion and insistence that a captain can express to a major, that the village was quiet, that I had taken no ground fire, and that I had not seen anything worth noting. But I was only a captain, and maybe I didn't know what he knew. The major said very deliberately that the villagers were *Pathet Lao*.

"But they never fired at me," I protested.

"Captain, you just need to trust me. They are *Pathet Lao,* Frank. I am sure," the major promised.

I received my mission order. To me it was so sad. I was a single airplane / single pilot tasked to orchestrate an air strike on that village. I begged the Intelligence Officer to reconsider. But he was a major, and I was merely a captain. Majors operate on a grander scale, and I didn't know what he might know. His world was far bigger than my little one, I guessed. The major reassured me, again, that these people were *Pathet Lao*, Laotian communist troops, allied with the North Vietnamese, and they would kill me without hesitation. He told me that he understood my disbelief, but that he is positive of his information.

"Frank, I am sure," he said again.

My memory of this morning has never been a coherent one. A morning with morality doubted, humanity tested, and conscience shaken, a morning with splashes of color. The orange of the napalm and the yellow of the bomb-flash and red of the tracer rounds. The point of this morning's air strike was never explained to me, was never understood by me, and was never forgotten by me.

You know what I hope? I hope that when the farmers and the women woke up to the sound of airplanes, they didn't see me. When they looked up at the morning sky belching bullets and bombs, they didn't see me. But I saw me. I still do. And God saw me.

"They are *Pathet Lao*, Frank."

I want to believe that. Do I need to be forgiven? If I need forgiveness, then I hope God does forgive me. That God then tells me that they are who the Intelligence Officer says they are, *Pathet Lao*. And that it's okay to forgive myself. That's what I hope.

When I returned to *Kontum* after this mission I was informed by Major Smithwick that we were being moved from FOB 2 and relocated to the MACV compound, which was closer to *Kontum City*. Packing wasn't going to take too long because I had almost nothing in the way of personal possessions. Phil had cleared everything out when Major Smithwick gave him the boot a few weeks earlier. He was already established at MACV, and his poster of Naked Sandy was the first thing he thumb-tacked to the wall of his new hooch. Getting away from Smithwick was a real plus for me too, but I was annoyed that I was being so casually drummed off the Special Forces compound. I didn't expect a parade and I was still flying for SOG. But there was something petty and mean about the way Smithwick handled this. We worked our tails off at Smithwick's insistence and the best we got was his ever-present sneer. That evening I thought it was just as well that, except for mission assignments, we no longer would have much to do with this pompous dope. Our lives would be free of a world-class jerk. I was so wrong. Because the very next day his even more-evil twin arrived. Gutz.

I think it was the last day in May, nine months into my year, when Captain Edwin C. Guttrobb replaced Captain Bob Segal, taking over command of the Second Platoon. Guttrobb jumped out of the jeep that delivered him to the MACV compound and motioned for the jeep's driver to carry his duffle into his hooch. The private looked questioningly at me and I shrugged.

"Captain, maybe you should hump your own gear."

He looked at me, eyes wide with surprise, then turned to the driver and told him to bring the duffle into his quarters. As soon as Captain Guttrobb turned his back the driver flipped him the bird.

Guttrobb said, "Call me Gutz."

He looked at me expectantly, his right hand extended to me. I didn't shake his hand this day, and I don't think I shook his hand any other day either. You treat one of our enlisted men like that and you think I'm going to like you?

"Call me captain, or Doherty, or better yet, call me Captain Doherty."

Glowering now, he told me that he was the ranking officer, and I was required to salute him when appropriate. I told him that we were both captains and that I thought a simple hello would suffice. His tall, awkward self visibly stiffened.

"You will salute, Doherty. Please tell me what the nature of your mission was that you flew today. You did fly today, did you not?"

Did I not? I told him that I did indeed fly today but that I could not tell him what I did because it was a secret. The word "secret" edged him to the verge of apoplexy.

"A secret?"

He was almost screeching. Better yet, his eyes were bugging out a little. Good. It took all of two minutes for me to realize that the North Vietnamese weren't my only enemy.

Phil, my flying partner for so many months, was getting ready to go home. He made the presentation of the keys to our SPAF jeep a big production. Gutz really wanted our jeep. It was too easy for us to get away from him if we had our own jeep. Phil stole this jeep fair and square several weeks ago from a MACV major. Taking care of something or other at MACV, Phil mistakenly parked a Special Forces jeep he was driving in the major's private parking space. The major flew into an unbelievable rage when he discovered a Special Forces jeep occupying his spot.

"The major had his face right up to mine, screaming at me. I was so soaked with spit that I almost asked him for a towel."

Thank God Phil didn't. The major's jeep magically showed up alongside our SOG compound hooch the following morning. Painted black. With SPAF stenciled on the front. The paint was still tacky.

Phil blamed the theft on Ben Brown and Bob Hall, two of our crew chiefs, and they gladly took credit for the heist. They have repeatedly sworn that they stole the jeep. None of us believed them. They may have helped, but we were sure Phil orchestrated the entire jeep-jacking. He has answered to the alias "Grand Theft Auto" ever since. And every time the parking space next to the major's parking spot was empty, we parked the SPAF jeep there. Just because we could.

Gutz repeatedly whined about not having the jeep's keys and I kept not remembering to give them to him. He was never going to get them. During his first week in *Kontum* Gutz met Phil and me at the airfield after we completed a Southern Laos recon mission. He demanded to know who we worked for and what we did. That he didn't know was really bugging him. So he made another try at getting the information from us. And brought up the jeep. Again.

"What is the nature of your job, captains?"

Phil looked at me and then back at Gutz. In his soft Tennessee drawl Phil answered.

"Can't tell you. Ask the Studies and Operations Group Ops Officer, our friend Major Keith Smithwick, what we do. Maybe he'll tell you. Right, Frank?"

"Frank? It says on your records folder that your name is Francis. Should I call you Francis?"

"No."

Gutz's face had gone from regular potato white to head-exploding beet-purple. No job description and no first name familiarity.

"Can you explain how you happened to come by your own personal black jeep, captains?" Gutz's eyes bugged. Phil laughed.

"Ask Major Smithwick."

Irrelevance was tough for Gutz to swallow.

Shortly before Phil left Lieutenant Charles Ford arrived to replace him. Gutz conducted a one-on-one interview with Charles on the evening of his arrival. Charles walked out of his meeting and came straight to my room. Gutz kept him through dinner, and as usual the mess hall was closed.

"Who is that asshole?"

Phil and I burst out laughing and Phil handed Charles a beer.

"Call me Jerry,"

Never, ever, have I referred to him as "Jerry." Absolutely always as "Charles." Just to tease him. He pretended that he didn't like to be called "Charles," and since that night has reminded me over and over and over again that his name was Jerry. And I have repeated for the thousandth time since that night, that I didn't care.

During his second week in *Kontum*, Gutz was at the airfield doing paperwork. Earlier Charles had taken the Second Platoon jeep back to the MACV compound, leaving Gutz to finish up whatever it was that he was doing. The afternoon wandered into the evening. Without a jeep of his very own, Gutz must have figured that he and the crew chiefs would catch a ride to MACV with me in the SPAF jeep. It was just barely dusk when I landed. I looked at my watch and then told the crew chiefs that I'd drive them to dinner before the mess hall closed.

"I'll be right back to get you, Gutz."

"No," he bellowed. "You wait until I'm finished!" So, we waited, and we waited, and we waited for Gutz, who fiddle-farted around forever. It had become so late that the mess hall at the MACV compound would finish serving dinner soon, and then none of the crew chiefs would be able to eat.

We continued to sit in the jeep in front of our operations hooch. It didn't matter to Guttrobb that these kids were missing chow. Whatever he was doing was obviously going to be a big help in winning the war, so nobody was going to go anywhere until Gutz was ready. I called, "Captain Guttrobb, the trip out and back will take less than twenty minutes, and it will still be daylight the whole time."

Guttrobb stepped out of the flight operations shack, glared at me, and said, "Captain Doherty, I am ordering you to remain where you are until I am ready."

I watched as a crew chief's fingers wrapped around the butt of his .45 and began to draw it from its holster. I could see the anger in that young man's eyes, the sneer on his lips, and shook my head "no." My heart was in my throat. I was scared beyond belief that he might draw and shoot before I could stop him. The gun slid back into its home. Thank you, thank you, thank you. In this beginning of the evening, this balmy night that smelled of jasmine, this gentle-breeze end of the day, I decided that I detested Guttrobb. For his arrogance, for his selfishness, but most of all, for his lack of caring for the men he was supposed to lead. I admit that I goaded him, I was disrespectful toward him because I ignored him, and on this night, I may have saved his life.

I seldom had to see Gutz. The SPAF pilots would leave for the airfield before dawn and seldom returned before just past dusk. The mess hall at MACV was closed in the early morning and by dark so we never had to make small talk with him. We had cases of dehydrated shrimp and vegetables with rice for dinner, which all of us, enlisted and officers alike, shared if we missed the chow line. We had C-Rations too, but rarely were we desperate enough to heat up those culinary travesties. Sometimes we were able to scrounge hot dogs or hamburgers, but only sometimes. And beer. We had a lot of beer, and a refrigerator that kept it cold. We shared the beer too. Had Gutz joined us I would have handed him a beer. I may have disliked him, but I would have handed him a beer. He never showed up. We never saw him. I wondered if he ever saw us.

Arlie Deaton advised SOG that he needed to see me. He didn't tell Gutz. I gassed up my Bird Dog at *Dak To* and flew to Camp Holloway after completing an almost five-hour (damned near ran out of gas) morning mission over the Trail, right where the three borders of Vietnam, Cambodia, and Laos, met. Calling this area a "Trail" was a joke. We often referred to it as the San Diego Freeway. I didn't need to look for trouble here. Trouble had taken up permanent residence in this place.

Arlie met me at the flight line. I shut down the Bird Dog and chocked its wheels. Arlie and I leaned against my airplane's fuselage under the shade of its right wing and talked about Gutz.

"How is he doing as a platoon leader? Is he easy to work for?"

I looked hard at Arlie. We had been friends for two years, and I was sure he wasn't baiting me.

"Honest answer?"

"Yeah, Dawtry, tell me the truth."

"Sir, nobody likes him. Not the pilots, not the enlisted guys, not the hooch maids. Nobody. We don't have a dog, but if we did, the dog wouldn't bite him, for fear of being poisoned. But the pooch might pee on his leg."

"Does Lieutenant Ford feel the same way?"

"You should probably ask him, sir, but I am guessing he will say the same thing."

Arlie smiled.

"What about the dog?"

Two weeks later in the half-light of pre-dawn, Gutz was pounding on my hooch's door. He was ecstatic, his smile that of a maniac.

"Get your things together, captain. You have forty-five minutes. It will be daylight then. I'm flying you to Holloway. Major Deaton is reassigning you."

It took me a minute to digest this, then a few deep breaths to settle myself down. I decided to say as little as possible. Charles rode shotgun out to the airfield with us. I drove, with Guttrobb exiled to the bumpy rear seat.

We pulled up to our little flight operations shed. I handed Charles the keys to our jeep. "You're the new jeep commander, lieutenant."

Gutz turned purple.

"Give me the goddamn keys, captain!"

"Not a chance, Gutz."

I very deliberately put the jeep keys in Charles's hand.

"You're on your own, Bunky."

The eastern sky was brightening. It was time to go. I thought that I would probably never see this airfield again. I loaded my duffle into the way-back of the Bird Dog, but bungeed my AR-15 to the cockpit door. I claimed the pilot seat, told Captain Guttrobb to get in the back seat and that I was flying the airplane to Holloway.

"Don't say anything else or I'll leave your miserable ass here, you prick."

After landing I parked the Bird Dog on our company ramp, unloaded my gear, shouldered it, and started toward our orderly room to look for Arlie. Gutz called after me.

"Captain Doherty!"

I half-turned to look at him. He smirked.

"Fuck you, captain."

I laughed in his face.

I found Arlie in the mess hall. It was open! It was breakfast! I wasn't flying over Laos before the sun came up! I had two soft-boiled eggs with grits! A little pepper, a splash of tabasco! And bacon. Bacon, bacon, bacon. I wondered about water in the showers. Maybe it was turned on! Maybe it was hot! So, this is how the rest of the 219th lived? None of these bastards better ever complain!

"I'm doing you a favor," Arlie said. Because I was too close to be going home. "No more SOG for the rest of your tour," he promised.

He needed Guttrobb to stay in *Kontum*. There was no one else with the rank required to command the platoon, and that as soon as a qualified officer came into the unit he planned to relieve Gutz. All of this sounded possible to me, but none of it ever occurred. I never believed any of this would happen because I suspected that Arlie had another, more personal motive for keeping Gutz at *Kontum*. Arlie wanted Guttrobb to be as far away from Holloway as he could. He probably couldn't stand Guttrobb either.

Arlie asked me to give my friend John Pappas some help at the first platoon. None of John's pilots had a lot of experience. All of them were relatively new. John introduced me to his crew, and one of them, a lieutenant, said that he was told that I was a real hard-boiled son of a bitch. John and I both laughed.

"Did Captain Pappas tell you to say that?

The "not having to fly the SOG mission" promise lasted less than a week. The "whoever those guys were" operation was still running from *Du Co* into Cambodia, and it took John just three days to corner me.

"I have a job you'll like, Frank. You know the mission, you've got the experience, and they need you."

I realized that this was not exactly a request. John was polite, but I knew that "no" wasn't going to work. Here I was, right back to where I started last November with the Studies and Observations Group, when I was trying to figure out how to fly sideways to make the bullets miss, trying to figure out how much of what I did was enough, and trying to figure out how to "fly and pee" at the same time. I felt like the dog who finally caught his own tail, surprised and wondering "now what?" Except for about three missions "in country," the next seven weeks were spent back over the border. Southeastern Laos, Northeastern Cambodia. I knew this area. I knew where I was.

SOG flying was no less dangerous than it had been the past nine months. But as it turned out, it was one of my rare "in country" missions that almost got me killed so late in the game. I teamed up with another first platoon pilot, Bob Jackson, on a two-ship recon east of Holloway, looking at a place we called VC Valley. This skinny slot between ridgelines ran north-south and was a designated free-fire zone. That really meant that if we found anyone or anything, we could kill anyone or blow up anything. We found "anyone." We found a guy. All by himself. In VC Valley, a place he shouldn't have been. There were no "good guys" in VC Valley.

I was about 100 ft above the ground with Bob about 300 ft above me. I passed over an abandoned paddy that was still filled with water. (The water really didn't mean much because it had rained a lot these last few days.) In the middle of the paddy was a brown lump. It wasn't a pile of mud. Every square inch of this paddy would have been crowded with rice shoots had it still been in use. It wasn't planted, but that didn't matter. Paddies never had piles of mud in them because dikes contained their water and soil, keeping the paddy bottoms flat and able to be planted. As I came around again the lump stood up. It had run out of breath. I drew my .38, held it in my left hand, and aimed it out the side window of the airplane. The lump raised its hands over its head and surrendered.

I flew left-hand circles around a soaking wet guy in an NVA uniform. I had no way to actually "capture" our prisoner. I couldn't land anywhere. And even if I could, with Bob covering me from above, I'd have to march the prisoner back to the airplane at gunpoint. Nobody on the ground had shot at us yet, but that didn't mean that nobody would. Once I got our guy to the airplane, I'd have to tie him up and stuff him in the Bird Dog's back seat. He'd be sitting behind me. What if he got loose?

My prisoner had no idea what a terrible shot I was. If he did, he could have waved bye-bye and simply walked away. Because I couldn't hit the broad side of a barn with anything. Even if I was standing directly alongside the barn. To tell the truth, I don't remember ever firing that .38 once, not even when I first got it, to see if it worked. I continued to orbit our captive while Bob called back to Holloway to see if anyone there had any ideas. After a few back and forth exchanges an almost recognizable voice came on the frequency.

During all the radio chatter our prisoner had taken a few sneaky steps rearward toward the paddy dike behind him. I fired a "quit that" round that missed him by a good 50 ft. The gun worked. He moved back to the center of the paddy. The "I think I know who that is" voice on the company frequency never identified himself. No name, obviously, but no call-sign either. I don't remember Bob's call-sign, but I would have been Headhunter One Two. First platoon, second in the platoon's hierarchy. Call signs were the same as a name. Our mystery assistant suggested that we plot our grid and use artillery.

"You want us to what?"

Bob and I were amazed. Nobody in their right mind would do something so idiotic. We were flying around one all-by-himself enemy soldier. In the first place, circling a guy in a rice paddy while waiting for rounds from a battery of Howitzers to rain down from above was suicidal. An artillery shell could hit one or both of us by mistake. Or fragments from the exploding shells could shred through our Bird Dogs. And second, because neither one of us was stupid enough to hang around on top of a target while shells were falling and exploding, our prisoner could just *di di mau* (Vietnamese slang for haul ass) as soon as we moved away from him. Bob then replied to the familiar voice with undisguised sarcasm.

"Thanks for all your help."

Holloway tower finally chimed in. Two UH1 Hueys were inbound to the airfield and on frequency. Bob called the flight leader and asked the two of them if they would help us out. Lead, the pilot in charge of the Hueys, wasn't laughing.

"Are you out of your goddam mind?"

Bob started to bargain, beg, plead, wheedle, and cajole. And he didn't stop until Lead finally relented.

"There's nobody else down there, right? No groundfire, right?"

I jumped in and explained.

"We've been flying circles around this guy for an hour and nobody else has shown up yet. Except for you guys."

"Oh, what the hell."

The helicopters gave our captive a ride to an interrogator.

Because I couldn't leave well enough alone, I called *Kontum* and had Jim Shelly, one of my old crew chiefs, check the second platoon's flight logs for the day. I knew I recognized the mystery voice that tried to kill us. I was right. Edwin C. Guttrobb. I hung up the receiver and stared out the door.

On an early evening a few days later, I landed at Holloway and was doing a post-flight check of my airplane. I looked over toward the maintenance revetments and saw Gutz. What the hell was he doing here? Guttrobb and our executive officer Don Shipp, the same Don Shipp who conned me into flying the SOG mission when I first arrived at the 219th, were following John Pappas, who was walking toward me. John stopped alongside the airplane and said, "Frank, I need you to fly a mission that might be on the risky side. These other guys aren't ready to fly this SOG stuff. I hate to ask."

Before I answered I looked to see Don Shipp and Guttrobb, now standing on the other side of my airplane, listening to John as he began to explain what we both knew I would volunteer to do. As soon as John finished what amounted to a mission briefing, I asked, "Before dawn?"

Ten months of this mission and I still hadn't realized that Bird Dogs could only take off or land in the dark or the almost dark. At least I could stay at Holloway.

The three of us turned to face Gutz, because he had jumped in on the end of John's request. He was lecturing me about something we all knew he'd never done.

"Remember never to fly a straight course. Always zig and zag, change altitude a lot. And cross-control so that the NVA miss when they aim off your nose. Never look back over your shoulder, and never make a second pass!"

What in God's name did he know about flying SOG, about the ways to make the bullets miss? He had no idea what was involved unless he had tortured Phil's replacement, Lieutenant Charles "call me Jerry" Ford, for information on this across the border mission.

I wondered why it was so important to Gutz to shoot his mouth off. Was it because he recognized the respect that John and I had for one another? Did he see in John the kind of leader that he would never be? Did Gutz realize that we saw him for the empty flight suit that he was? As I looked at John and Don, I could see the same "what the fuck" expressions on their faces that I was sure that I had on mine. What John described was the same mission I'd been flying for almost a year, a mission that Gutz was never going to be asked to fly. Not by John. Not by Arlie. Not by the operations officer at the Studies and Observations Group.

I was on the outraged side of angry. I poked my finger into Gutz's chest.

"You have no idea what this is about, so shut up, Guttrobb! Don't talk to me."

I should have walked away, but I didn't. I lowered my hand and rested it on the butt of my pistol. Gutz launched into a beet-red tirade, calling me every curse word he'd ever heard.

"I know what you're going to do. You're going to fake flying the mission, never get lower than 5,000 ft. I bet you land on a road next to a Special Forces Camp and goof off for a few hours. Then fly back to Holloway and make up a phony report."

Guttrobb didn't need to say "coward."

Up until this very second killing was never a matter of "wanting to." It was always a possibility, and for the most part a sad but impersonal collateral to a mission. But not today. Not after what Guttrobb said. Coward? After I put my life on the line every day for almost ten months? Rage was smothering my ability to reason. My right hand enveloped the .38's butt and my index finger slid through the trigger guard, cupping the pistol's trigger. All I had to do was just draw and shoot. He was much closer than the barn I couldn't hit. At this moment I wanted to kill him. But the .38 stayed in its holster. A slice of reason slipped between my temper and my gun. I couldn't make the .38 move.

John tugged on my sleeve, and we walked together with no words spoken, to our hooch. I took a shower, as much to think as to cool off. Is this what I've become, I wondered? What happened to the boy I used to be? Could I really have pulled that trigger? Did I hate Guttrobb that much? Or did I hate the place his words almost took me? The place to which I almost allowed myself to go.

I ate dinner alone in the Officers' Club. I needed to re-engage my conscience, to understand how I came so close to descending into a hell of my own making. No chance of seeing Guttrobb again today. I heard his airplane take off. I never saw him again. Ever. Later that night John and Don Shipp sat down on either side of me at the bar. I ordered all three of us double scotches. Don put his giant hand on my shoulder and said, "I knew you would walk away. You've done a great job, Frank. We've all got a little rearranging to do when we get home."

I thought I might cry.

# Chapter 10

# John Glimis Pappas

My year's tour was just about over. For so long I thought I might never live through it. And now I had just days to go before I left Holloway. I never said that I was leaving Vietnam though. I knew, the first time a bullet pierced the skin of my Bird Dog, that Vietnam would be part of me forever. I was coming to the end of a year that was never going to end.

It's August. The last month. And it's so hot! The monsoons of spring have ended and the mud that clogged Holloway has disappeared. But the humidity is sky high, so every movement I make sends rivers of sweat into my eyes. I can't wait to go flying, to get airborne. The big side windows on my Bird Dog, latched open under the wings, stream cooler air through the cockpit. The temperature is always cooler a couple of thousand feet above the ground. Unfortunately, I am seldom a couple of thousand feet above the ground for very long. The Bird Dog's war is still a treetops war. The outside air still zips through the big windows and over my sticky flight suit. It's just hotter down here, a few feet above the jungle canopy. And when somebody is shooting at me it gets hotter still.

Everything is baking. The hooch is like a rabbit-warren of little, windowless, smelly rooms. It's air-conditioned, thank God, but the air in this building is old. Old, like the locker-room smell of sweaty clothes old. Like the dive bar smell of stale beer and cigarette smoke and cheap scotch old that has permeated everything. The air doesn't move. We should open all the doors and let the outside in, then hope any breeze washes everything a little fresher. But the doors don't ever get opened, because of grenades and booby-traps, snakes and scorpions. And spiders. I hate peanut butter, hard-boiled eggs, and spiders.

John Pappas is banging on the door of my room. I open the door, already knowing what he wants. It's still dark but what else is new? I could get eggs and bacon or an omelet for breakfast if I was ever here for breakfast. But I'd rather get out of this stuffy hovel, go flying, and cool off. John doesn't try to come in. I don't blame him. It stinks in here. It stinks of me.

"Let's go over toward *Polei Kleng*. I bet we can find something going on in the *Plei Trap* Valley."

John, my platoon leader, always frames his orders as requests. Like I have an option. I don't even bother asking about eggs and bacon.

"Do I have time for a shower?"

"That can wait until we get back. It would be nice if you brushed your teeth though." Stale cigarette breath is not very attractive. I jog to the big latrine, scrub my face, hands, armpits and crotch, teeth and tongue. Spectacles, testicles, wallet, and watch! Ready, set, go.

Two airplanes sit on the ramp, waiting for us. John advised his platoon sergeant we'd be taking off, so our Bird Dogs are gassed up and inspected by our crew chiefs. Then we do our own "walk around inspection," making sure we've got Willie Petes (white phosphorus rockets) loaded in the four rocket tubes, putting our parachutes (I am never jumping) against the seat backs, stashing helmet-bags full of AR-15 clips under our seats, and strapping our rifles to the cockpit doors. The crew chiefs leave the big side windows open. Our back seats are empty. No observers. We are airborne in less than ten minutes, heading northwest toward *Kontum*, toward *Polei Kleng* Special Forces Camp, and the *Plei Trap* Valley. Intelligence reports say that the *Plei Trap* is heavily trafficked by North Vietnamese. How many NVA? Two regiments, it turns out. That's about 3,000 men. Some of them are going to be staring up at John's Bird Dog and at mine. And some of them will start trying to shoot us down.

John Pappas looks just like an altar boy, a Greek Orthodox altar boy, which is what he was once. His features are soft and smooth. His brown eyes and his voice are always smiling. John is a cherub in an Army flight suit. I have only seen him angry once. That was when he was easing me away from stupid Guttrobb. John is a great officer and a better man. He is what West Point means when the Academy defines an officer. This is our "Everyday John." The officer who puts the boys who work for him first. Who treats the boys who work for him with respect. Who seldom raises his voice to, or ever publicly reprimands, the boys who work for him.

Today I am dodging around the trees with "Combat John." So very different from "Everyday John." I hear the differences when I listen to his voice. "Combat John" is totally focused, flies the airplane without thinking about flying it, makes correct decisions, and stays three moves ahead in the chess game that is war. I am the low ship, poking around close to the ground, trying to look through the layers of green for the North Vietnamese we are told are here. John is above me, covering me. Because he is about 700 ft above the ground, he has a more panoramic view. And in his picture window of vision, out in front of him, he sees troops in brown uniforms. They are not our troops, and they are shooting at us while running away from us. We are in luck. Because we have UH-1C Hueys, helicopter gunships, close by.

The area the NVA are running through is open on their right and heavily wooded on their left. John sends several gunships up the left side of the NVA's path. That prevents the soldiers from disappearing into the tree line. He sends more gunships racing to get in front of the NVA so that they have to wheel to the right, keeping them in the open. All this maneuvering takes place in the time it would take John to tell me to get Tac air (fighters). Which is what I do. A quick radio call to DASC (Direct Air Support Center) gets me a flight of two A-1s, callsign Spad, out of *U Tapao*, Thailand, I think. They are full of fuel and loaded with ordnance. When they check on our radio frequency, I explain the tactical situation to the Spad "Lead" and he then gives me their "rundown," essentially an accounting of the types and amounts of whatever it is that the two Skyraiders are carrying. So many canisters of napalm, so many high explosive bombs, so many rockets, so many rounds for the miniguns. To me it seems like it takes forever. At the very end of all this, Spad Lead makes me laugh.

"And we've each got six rounds of .38 [their sidearms] if you need them."

I decide to run the first Skyraider over the tops of the UH-1Cs that are blocking the tree line, dropping napalm. This way Spad Lead is not coming close to the helicopters who have executed John's L-shaped blockade. I send the second Spad in behind the first, using napalm again, just beyond where the first nape canisters explode. On subsequent runs, always away from or parallel to the direction of the Huey gunships, I ask the Spads to use their miniguns to strafe anyone they see. And to expect ground fire, which has gotten ferocious as the fight evolves. More nape, more minigun, and finally, HE (high explosive bombs).

John is working at about 800 ft or so above the battlefield. He sees everything. He is still several moves ahead of everyone on the ground. John coordinates the positioning of the Huey gunships with the direction the A-1s fly on their runs-in over the NVA. He uses the gunships to prevent the North Vietnamese from melting away into the tree line, the jungle, the elephant grass. Like a shepherd would use a Border Collie to corral a flock of sheep. But we are not protecting these sheep. Not this morning.

And now the "brass" arrives. Another Huey. Not a stubby gunship Huey but a "slick," a station wagon Huey, a "command post" Huey. A colonel's private limo Huey. A new voice, his callsign "Six," is on the radio, cluttering up the frequency with a stream of questions that interrupt everything we are doing.

"What's our situation? Where are our guys? Where is the enemy? How many do you estimate there are? Do you have a body count? How many fast movers do you have on station? Any friendlies down there?"

Bosses use the designation "Six." This is a boss, and it is John's responsibility to deal with him. I need to stay ahead of the action on the ground, to talk to the gunships and the Spads, to try to keep John's plan moving. John tells Colonel Somebody to switch to a different frequency for an explanation of the engagement.

"You stupid motherfucker! Climb that fucking Huey now, Six! Are you trying to kill me? Get out of the way, goddammit!"

The "Command Post" almost slams into John's Bird Dog. They barely miss one another. "Six" is supposed to be higher, observing, letting the FACs (forward air controllers), that's us, do what we know how to do. The North Vietnamese are still running all over the place on the ground, except there are a lot fewer of them now than when the fight started. The ground fire is still intense but easing. I can tell by the sounds the bullets make as they go by. Not as many as before. And I can see bodies. In all this craziness, I wonder if this is my last morning as a pilot. Calling a colonel a stupid motherfucker is not something a captain does regularly. John and I are a team, so I think we might both be in trouble. I am so relieved because we don't hear anything further from the colonel.

An Air Force FAC in a Cessna Skymaster, a twin-engine spotter-plane, arrives. The UH-1C gunships are just about out of ammo and gas. They break off and head for *Dak To* for fuel, accompanied by the colonel's Huey. The Spads are also just about "bingo" on fuel and ammo too (down to just enough gas to get back to *U Tapao*) and disengage. The Air Force, here to save the day for us Army FACs in our raggedy Bird Dogs, has fighter-bombers stacked up overhead and will continue the fight. We have fired all our rockets and will need fuel soon, but we have enough gas to get back to Holloway. *Dak To* is closer than Holloway, but the colonel has gone to *Dak To*. John and I don't want to say hello to that colonel.

It is evening and I am sitting in the "Doghouse," a hangout just for 219th pilots. At the bar I eat a bowl of rice with dehydrated vegetables and shrimp, doused with spicy fish sauce given to me by the woman who cleans my stinking room while holding her nose. A fiery *Nouc Mam,* which is so good, is poured sparingly on the rice. Very sparingly. And a beer. John shows up a little while later and I hand him a beer, which he drinks pretty much all at once. I hand him another. Neither one of us has showered yet. He looks at me and grins.

"You don't smell particularly sweet, Francis."

"You're not exactly a bed of roses yourself. Let's go get cleaned up."

We can't leave. Arlie, with Don Shipp right behind him, walks in, points at the two of us, and announces,

"Just the two idiots I want to see. Who called Colonel Somebody a stupid motherfucker?" John is pointing at me, and I am pointing at him.

"He did."

Arlie gives us his squinty, skeptical, somewhat pissed-off look.

"Do either of you have any idea how much trouble you both are in."

I can tell by the expression on Shipp's face that this is all a big fat act. Apparently, Colonel Somebody called Arlie and gave him a blow-by-blow description of this morning's events, obviously including the "stupid motherfucker" remark, and said that he was recommending us for Silver Stars. Very big-deal medals. Don says we smell so bad his eyes are watering.

When I shower, I start with my flight suit on. As usual. Scrubbing my clothes, my socks, and me. But not underwear. I don't wear any. It chafes and gives me a rash. Who needs an itchy butt? I have enough to worry about. The Doghouse is quiet after my shower. I come back in a clean t-shirt, cut-off jungle camouflage pants and shower shoes. Sitting there by myself with a very big glass of scotch in front of me, I sneak back to specific pictures of the morning. To Huey gunships and A-1 Spads. To familiar battle sounds and colors. The chainsaw, tracer red-bullet stream bursts from the mini-guns and the whump of high explosive bombs. The orange splash of napalm and the green streaks of enemy tracers, the whirling pattern the rotor blades make in the soaking wet air, the grumbling racket of the Skyraiders' big radial engines. And the zipping, popping, cracking noises bullets make as they go by me. Voices on the radio. Some loud and excited, most calm and matter of fact. Engaged in the business of killing.

This morning I watched the sun climb above the mountains that made up the north-south spine of this land. The Annamese Cordillera.

I watched the sky change from the end of night's gray monochrome to dawn's streaks of sunlight. I watched as the sun filled the sky with hot, hazy daylight. I heard the hum of my airplane's engine and saw the red winks from the rotating beacon on John's airplane. Was this the time when I was at my most human? And if I was, then what happened to me as the morning grew towards midday? There were bodies down there, on that battlefield. Crooked and broken, shot down and crumpled, burned and brittle. How many? I didn't know because I didn't count them. I just thought "many."

Have I become ambivalent to killing? Because war gives me permission to not care? Have I become inured to chaos because war gives me permission to not feel? Have I lost touch with who I once was? The me who I was before I got here? Because this steady diet of stress, of bullets, of near dying, has sucked the warm smile out of me? I think about this morning and wonder what I have turned into. How will I ever be able to reassemble the gentle pieces of me? How will I ever be able to make room for that? How will I ever get the good me back? Because I am afraid that all I have seen and all that I have done will take up all the space in me. And leave no place for the good me to go.

A realization began to form on this night in this smelly bar. The realization that I was not a real warrior. I loved the cat and mouse game of combat. I loved the adrenaline rush of combat. I loved the relief that surviving another day brought me. But I didn't love the consequences of combat. I didn't love the bomb craters, the twisted trees, or the burn-blackened jungle that contained the charred bodies of North Vietnamese boys who were not able to get up and walk away when this morning's game was over.

It was early evening a few days later when John Pappas sidled up to me in the Doghouse. I'd flown a SOG mission all morning, doing recon work in northeast Cambodia. An unusual morning because nothing had happened. I didn't see anyone, and that meant that nobody shot at me. Convoy cover this afternoon was a non-event too. And now John sat down next to me, his whole face a big smile.

"You're done, Frank."

I looked at him, trying to figure out where he was going with this.

"I'm done? Done with what?"

"You're done with everything. Today was your last mission. This morning. You're done."

"Is this Deaton's idea? What am I supposed to do during the day?"

"Take a shower twice a day for the rest of your time here. You still smell bad."

I knew I was supposed to go home soon but I had decided not to think about it. I was not even going to look at September on my calendar, on which I had circled the 4 with a red grease pencil. To think about 4 September could jinx the day. My orders could be revoked. The monsoons could come back. The airbase at *Ton Son Nhut* could be overrun. Rockets and mortars could make big holes in the runway so my "Freedom Bird" couldn't leave. I was supposed to go home. And that meant that whatever could go wrong would go wrong. I didn't really believe Pappas anyway about being done. Done? Did that word really exist in the lexicon of Vietnam?

And I was right. It only took most of the next day before John came to find me sunbathing by the swimming pool. Holloway had a swimming pool. I had never been there. I had never even seen it until today. And after my very first chance to swim in this pool John came chugging up to my towel where I was catching rays and dripped sweat on me.

"You gotta get a move on right now. Get dressed and get down to the airplane as fast as you can."

I didn't say anything. There was no point. Something was going on, and somebody was shooting at somebody else. "Done" has been postponed for at least another day. I ran to the hooch, got dressed, grabbed my gear, and tore down the little hill to the airplanes. Yesterday is today again.

At the Seattle Mariners baseball stadium, there is a big Bullseye in straight-away right field, just above the railing that goes around the second deck. Across the Bullseye is the message, "Hit It Here, Junior." Even though Ken Griffey Junior has retired, the sign is still there, celebrating one of the deadliest swings in baseball. Griffey batted left-handed, and that sign in right field was a magnet for his bullet-like line drive home runs. Every time I went to a game at the ballpark, I looked at that sign and thought, "Goddamn Pappas." Because I swore Pappas had a bullseye painted on the fuselage of his Bird Dog with the caption, "Hit it here."

John told me what was going on as we flew toward *Polei Kleng*, the Special Forces camp in the *Plei Trap* Valley. The camp had been taking mortar fire since early morning. Several wounded had been helicopter ed out, and Huey gunships were providing support, but the ARVN (Army of the Republic of Vietnam) Rangers, who had just been given control of *Polei*

*Kleng* from our Special Forces, needed us to find the NVA mortars if we could.

We could. And along with the mortars we found scattered groups of NVA who appeared to be massing for an assault on the camp. The gunships had lots of fuel and started shooting at the North Vietnamese, who were shooting at them. And us. Two A-1s came overhead to give us a hand, loaded with every kind of ordnance imaginable. The only thing missing was the colonel from a few days ago, the colonel who John had called a stupid motherfucker. Not a lot of talking on the radio today thankfully, and what there was, was very perfunctory.

"Yeah, I got that. Got them in sight." The gunship's commander radioed to John.

"Lead, nape on my smoke. AK fire from your left so break right."

And I directed the A-1s.

"Roger, Headhunter. I see white smoke. Break right. Lead's in hot."

And that's how it went. The same colors and sounds that were always part of battle. Oily orange nape-flames, high explosive bomb showers of earth and trees and bodies, minigun scream of bullets arcing red to the ground, green streaked crack of enemy tracer rounds past my ears, the rattly chatter of machine guns, terse yelling over the radio. There were always voices on the radio, the guys on the ground coordinating with me. Sometimes explaining quickly where to have the helicopters aim their miniguns, sometimes requesting ammunition resupply, and sometimes begging for "Dust-off" medevac helicopters to save the lives of the badly wounded.

The essence of conflict never changed. Big fights, little fights, a few boys, a lot of boys. Ours in body bags or swathed in bloody bandages, lifted to hospitals in Hueys marked with red crosses. Their dead and wounded dragged off the battlefield, their presence marked only by blood-trails that disappeared into the jungle. This was my year in summary; war with a small "w," war reduced to its lowest common denominator. How am I supposed to come down from today? From the hurry up of this mission when there wasn't supposed to be another mission. Because that's what John said.

"You're done."

I had been flying over the Trail since the end of November, and now I was almost through August. And in a week or so it will be September. A year here. A year I promised to the Army when I applied for flight school. Since November I have flown every day except for Christmas Eve and Christmas Day. Except for the two days we stood down when Prince Sihanouk was

140

overthrown. Except for the week spent on Kauai, when I was supposed to forget about the war but couldn't, because the surf on the beach sounded like incoming and I rolled under the bed. I managed to keep all the promises I made. Especially my promise to my mother Celestina, to come home in one piece. I was going home in a week or so. Going home to "normal." Is somebody going to tell me how I am supposed to do that?

I parked the Bird Dog, chocked its wheels, and walked up the hill to our hooch. My flight suit sweat-soaked and salt-stained, my ears still ringing from the racket of the gunfire. I wanted a shower, to have a beer or two or ten, and maybe something to eat. And I wanted to think about what was next. I needed to think about what to do with myself in the remaining days here. I left my parachute and my flight helmet and my survival vest in my locker at the flight line. In case John came running to find me. In case John told me to get to the airplane right now because he needed me. So that I could keep doing what I had been doing for almost eleven months. Because I didn't know where the switch was. The switch that shut off the war. The switch that turned me into the boy I was before I got here. The switch that stopped the gunfight being fought inside my head, that dried up the blood, that pointed the AKs and the .51s away from me, away from my airplane. The switch that let sleep come, that chased away the bad dreams. The switch that made it all quiet, finally. The switch that gave me back me.

Meyers and Glashauser and Plaster all knew where that switch was. Their fingers caressed it. They pinched it between their thumbs and index fingers. But they were not able to move it from on to off. Because they didn't want to. I wanted to.

John Pappas wasn't kidding this time. I really was done, whether I wanted to be or not. He didn't come running to find me, to ask me to drop everything, to tell me that I had to help him help some grunts who were probably teenagers live through a firefight. I could finally go for a swim in Holloway's pool. But I was really bored. Trying to just relax was almost impossible. The adrenaline-high of combat was so normal that the motionlessness of not being engaged, of not deciding in rapid-fire, of not living an inch from dying was just so strange. I had to make myself breathe normally.

The last days at Holloway were not remembered because they didn't matter. They didn't mean anything. They didn't count for anything. Because I wasn't over Laos or Cambodia, or over the Trail or VC Valley or the

*Plei Trap*. I wasn't at *Kontum* or *Dak To* or *Plei Djerang* or *Dak Seang*. I wasn't flying. I was going back to normal. Whatever the hell that was.

Arlie let me fly the Beaver to *Qui Nhon*. He was in the right seat. My duffle was in the Beaver's way back, behind the cockpit and the second row of seats. There was a jeep waiting for me when we got to our battalion's parking ramp which would take me across the airfield. Where I would get on a C130 transport for the flight to *Tan Son Nhut*. And then get on Pan American, for the flight to normal.

Arlie and I stood beside the Beaver and exchanged salutes, then handshakes, and then we hugged one another. I heaved my duffle into the jeep, climbed in, and waved goodbye. I couldn't see Arlie. I couldn't see anything. Not like my first night in Vietnam, when mosquitos swelled my eyes shut. This last day I was crying too hard.

Out-processing was the last formality involved when escaping Vietnam. The Army needed to make sure that all my going-home forms were in order. After leaving Arlie in *Qui Nhon* and arriving at *Tan Son Nhut,* I presented myself to another bored-to-death major who handled future assignments. I marveled at the coincidence of majors. On my first full day in Vietnam, when I arrived in *Nha Trang*, I saluted a major so weighted down with the insignificance of his job that he could barely move. Now it was time to go, and I was standing in front of this major who was slightly more animated. But only slightly. Like bookends. Bored majors. Coming and going. Just perfect.

"Well, captain, we need to get you set up back in the world. Any idea where you want to go?"

The different but equally as bored major was smiling. I didn't hesitate with my answer because I knew exactly what I wanted.

"The Sixth Army Flight Detachment at the Presidio of San Francisco, sir." This major laughed loudly, shook his head "no" and asked me again.

"Captains don't get that assignment and you appear to be a captain. So, give me a hint here so that we can get you out from in front of my desk."

"Okay, sir, but be sure you specify that the Presidio is my first choice, please. My second choice would be back to Rucker as a Bird Dog I.P. [instructor pilot]."

The major now looked at me, annoyed at my insistence.

"You are destined for Alabama, captain. Fried catfish, hushpuppies, and sweet tea. Enjoy it."

I hated sweet tea almost as much as I hated Major Smithwick's peanut butter. I ate Smithwick's peanut butter. The sweet tea? Not a chance.

# Chapter 11

# Lloyd Harbor

My mother knew when to expect me. I arrived in Tacoma, Washington, flew to Los Angeles to get my VW, then drove from California to Lloyd Neck, mostly with the top down, in four-and-a-half days so that I could be home for my sister's wedding. Celestina heard the car come up the driveway. I held her in my arms and had to hold her up because she had collapsed in tears. She had always held the "little boy" me. She had always held me, as I was holding her now. I was safe now. I was home

My arrival at our house barely registered a blip on my sister's radar, however. Kathleen was too busy getting ready to be Mrs. Thomas Latham. I was going to be one of the groomsmen. All the groomsmen were supposed to wear tuxedos. The tux somebody had picked out for me could have fit me twice. I wore my Dress Blues instead. No medals. Just my wings. I wore my Blues because I had survived.

I took a short nap in my old room, and when I woke up an hour later, I discovered that all the unit insignias and patches had been stripped from my flight jacket, flight suits, and helmet bag. My two younger brothers, Terry, 16 and Glenn, 12, decided that they could not live without them. My captain's bars, insignias from the 219th Headhunters, from the MACVSOG Green Beret Death's Head Skull with bloody fangs, and from the 1st Aviation Brigade, all suddenly disappeared. If I couldn't have the treasures I brought back with me, I decided to take inventory of the treasures I left behind.

I went into the basement and there were my skis. They looked like they had been run over several times by a road grader. And my collection of HO gauge trains? Not too many still in the cardboard boxes I stored there. Model airplane engines were gone too. My high-school and college letterman's jackets? Do dogs eat coats like they eat homework? I walked around to the back of the garage, to where the little 8 ft hydroplane I designed and built used to live. Not anymore. Somebody sank it. Oh, and the Blue Jay sailboat

I built when I was 15. It was still moored in Lloyd Harbor, but it hadn't seen a sanding or a coat of paint since my airplane lifted off for Fort Knox two-and-a-half years ago. Did my brothers think that I had forgotten about these things? Did they think that since I had gone into the Army everything left behind was fair game? Like one big garage sale, except that all my stuff was free. Or did they think that I was too stupid to survive? I didn't want to start an argument, and I was tired from the cross-country drive. I counted my blessings. Terry and Glenn, just little boys behaving like little brothers, were among the blessings I counted. I was home, I was safe, and nobody was shooting at me. There was a wedding the following day. I was going to see the grandparents, aunts and uncles, cousins, and friends that I hadn't seen since I left for Southeast Asia. I concentrated on the things that really mattered.

Terry and I were standing in the dining room the day before Kathleen's wedding as he described the Christmas dinner scene, when Dad played the "overflight" tape recording. I was looking out of the dining room window as Terry spoke, at the back acre of our property, the oaks and dogwoods that were there since long before I was born. The now matured rhodies, azaleas and laurels Dad and I planted fourteen years ago, on the afternoon he tried to convince me that he was nothing more than a bus driver. I could picture the scene Terry was painting, how everyone sat quietly on Christmas afternoon. Dad pressed the play button on the cassette recorder. My voice filled the room. The emotional Italian side of the table began to cry. First Pop Pop, next Nana, and Celestina, then Uncle Diggie and Auntie Gracie. She was Greek, but that's close enough. It took Pa, Auntie Claire, Uncle Pat, and the rest of the stoic Irish side a little longer.

And the day before my sister's wedding, my father snatched the *New York Times* out of my hands. The *Times* published the names of those killed in action in the first section of the newspaper. I was scanning the names on the list, looking for someone I might have known. I had already seen one, Dick Hostikka, a Green Beret I met for maybe two seconds at *Dong Ha*. This Special Forces camp was so close to the DMZ that Captain Hostikka could have thrown a rock into North Vietnam from where we stood. His family name stayed with me because it had a double k in it. A Finnish name. Like Pakkala and Kakko. Double k. Dad held the first section of the *Times*, closed, and folded up in half the long way and then folded over from the middle, like morning commuters to New York City did on the Long Island Railroad.

"Stop reading the casualty lists, Frankie. You're done with that."

Easier said than done, I thought. I had seen the name of someone I knew in this morning's paper and knew that I wasn't going to be able to stop checking.

The next morning Dad ambushed me as I walked down the driveway to the main road. That's where the *Times* always landed. He let me bend to pick the paper up. If the carrier tossed the paper onto the driveway, it would tear as it skidded across the bluestone. So he always aimed for the pachysandra along the edge. Dad took the paper from me and carried it in his hand that was away from me. Maybe he thought I would make a grab for it, which I would never do. And then he put his free hand on my arm and stopped walking so that I had to stop too.

"You're home now, son."

He said this with softness, and I loved him for that softness. Because softness was going to take some getting used to again. A year of ragged edges had become normal. My father knew that I needed to unlearn that normal. I knew that he had to unlearn it too. But he never talked about that, and so he never told me how. He just said that I needed to.

On the day of my sister's wedding, I wandered out to the end of the dock at the Huntington Yacht Club. The reception was inside, late in the afternoon on a beautiful September Saturday. The women in pearls and the men in suits. Except me. I had to be in my Dress Blues. I had to be in what felt familiar. I had to breathe in the salt smell of the water, the old water-logged smell of the dock pilings, the faint oil smell of marine engines. Smells of my old life, my life before the mountains of the Central Highlands. Carol Smyth, who lived across Fiddlers Green Drive from us, came to stand alongside me. She linked her arm through mine and pulled me close. I had known her since I was little. I babysat her children. Carol's husband Phil fished with Dad and me. My dad's best friend.

"We're so glad you came home, Frankie. Phil and I are so glad you came home."

For a little while I felt better. For a little while.

Survivor's guilt? Was that the name of what I was feeling? Did it even have a name? Was that why I couldn't stop checking the list? Because I wondered how I got out of Vietnam in one piece. Despite Major Smithwick, our idiot SOG operations officer, Edwin C. Guttrobb, our numbskull platoon leader, and the legion of North Vietnamese AK-47s and .51 caliber machine guns that tried to shoot us down. John Meyers and Doug Krout and Charles

Ford and Phil Phillips, my fellow SPAFs, returned home in one piece too. But I remembered the names of seventeen boys I knew, and I found them all years later when I visited our Wall. Their names chiseled into black granite, each one a reminder of my "why me" guilt.

After the wedding reception a few close friends of my parents, along with some family members, went back to our house. I left my VW parked out on the main road. The crowd both inside and on the patio was unavoidable, and so were the questions aimed my way. Mrs. Eckhoff cornered me in our kitchen.

"Is Peter going to be safe?"

How could I possibly know that? I hemmed and hawed and evaded and sidestepped as best I could. Because "of course" would have been a lie that she would have surely seen through. I simply said that our role in the war was winding down and, hopefully, Mrs. Eckhoff's son Peter would not be in the middle of what combat remained.

With a big glass of ice, a half-filled bottle of scotch, and still in my Dress Blues, I escaped in my car to the dock on Lloyd Harbor. There were no questions on the dock. My uncle Diggie, Celestina's younger brother, followed me. He had been a waist gunner in a B-17 that got shot almost to pieces over Holland during the Second World War. I looked at him as he sat down, and I started to laugh. Diggie took off his shoes and socks, rolled up his pant legs, and dangled his feet in the water. I did the same, except that I neatly folded my pant legs instead of scrunching them up like he did. My uncle brought his own glass of ice and his own half bottle of scotch. He wasn't sharing and neither was I.

The harbor was still full of boats. The incoming tide turned them so that their bows pointed toward the head of the harbor, toward Huntington Bay, toward the house where the girl at the top of Richard Lane lived. Some of the sailboats moored here had aluminum masts, and as they rocked with the incoming tide their halyards slapped against the hollow metal, singing the same song they had sung before I left for Asia a year ago. The water was still late-summer warm. I slowly kicked my feet back and forth. Not hard enough to splash my perfectly rolled-up cavalry-blue uniform pants. Just enough to swish the water around my ankles.

"How long will you be on leave before you have to report?"

"I've got three weeks. I've got a cottage booked for a week in Jamaica. Montego Bay. I'm not sure if I want to go. I'm not sure of much right now. I suppose I should go, though. Use the time to slow down."

I looked away from Diggie, out to where my Blue Jay was tied to its mooring buoy. I decided that I would take her out of the water the next day and bring her home. Clean her up, restore her paint and varnish, and get her ready for winter storage. Keep my hands busy, keep me occupied.

Diggie was looking down the harbor, west toward the causeway that connected Lloyd Neck to the mainland, west toward New York City. When he looked back at me, he smiled and almost knocked me into the water with his next few words.

"You'll need to learn how to take your foot off the gas pedal. That happens sometimes when you've been through something like a war. I ran away when I got home from England."

I never knew that he and Aunt Gracie had been apart for a while after his war. But then why should I be told that? Who would tell me anyway?

"You're sitting here on this dock with me and there are bridesmaids back at your parents' house. You haven't been around girls for a year, but you're on this dock with your uncle. Drinking scotch even though all the ice has melted. Instead of screwing your brains out in an empty bedroom. Give yourself a chance to put the war behind you, and I know that's easier said than done, but keep moving forward, one foot in front of the other. It gets better."

Then Diggie laughed, like he didn't believe the last part, his "it gets better" part. Things can't get much worse, I thought.

My half bottle of scotch was now reduced to little more than a sip. I looked at my uncle and smiled. His bottle was too. I loved this man who looked like my mother, who acted like my older brother, who sensed that he needed to spend time with me that day. So, he did.

"How long did it take you?"

"How long did it take me to do what? Get over the war? Ask me tomorrow. Maybe I will have gotten over it by then. This Vietnam thing will always be with you. You'll have it forever. Just remember what I said. One foot in front of you, Frankie. One foot at a time."

"I love you, Uncle Dig."

"I love you too, Frankie."

# Chapter 12

# The Top of Richard Lane

**Huntington Bay, 1970**

That morning, a few hours before my sister's wedding, I stood in Katie Grace's driveway, captain's bars on the gold shoulder boards of my Dress Uniform, but no medals. Only my silver wings on the left breast of my dark blue tunic. I was supposed to run an errand for my father and then drive straight to St. Pats for the ceremony, but I left early and found myself at the top of Richard Lane, staring at Katie's front door. I didn't know if Katie was at her parents' house. I didn't know what I would do if she stepped outside. I was afraid of what she might say if I asked her, "Are you married?" But she didn't come out. Maybe she wasn't there. It had been three years since I had seen her. There would be years to wait before I would be able to tell her how wrong I had been. That I had never stopped loving her. I unglued my feet from her driveway and made myself get back into my car. My eyes were wet.

Six years earlier, New Year's Eve, in 1964. I was a 19-year-old college sophomore, home on Christmas break, my last night before returning to San Francisco. I stood, dateless, in the kitchen, wondering if my father would notice three fingers of Jameson's missing from the bottle in the liquor cabinet. Probably not. There were a lot of bottles in the liquor cabinet. The phone rang. I was saved by the bell from committing grand theft Jameson's, or something like that.

"Get over here right now!"

It was my next-door neighbor Kathie Francis calling. She was having a party and I was invited.

"You're supposed to be here, and I don't care if you don't have a date! This party is really dragging. So, get over here and dance with somebody."

"I need a quick shower."

"Just hurry up!"

It took two minutes to get from our house to Kathie's. I walked in the front door and headed toward the music.

"I'm Katie Grace. Who are you?"

The whole world went out of focus. What color were her eyes? Hazel-gold? Hazel-green? Did they change with different days of the week? Her hair was golden brown, and she had a widow's peak, this Katie Grace who was standing in front of me. She was the most beautiful girl I had ever seen. New Year's Eve. When I was 19 and she was 17.

She smiled.

"I'm Katie Grace. Who are you?"

I knew who I was. I knew my own name. I just couldn't say it. I couldn't say the words because I was afraid that I'd sound like Elmer Fudd. I needed to catch my breath. My composure? Forget it. Gone. Out the window.

"I'm Fwank Dowuddy"

At that instant, and from then on, it was always going to be her. All night, every song was a slow dance, even when it wasn't. At midnight I kissed her, and Katie Grace kissed me back.

Our hooch was stifling at night. Even with Phil's fan blowing a gale, the air it moved was hot and wet. Sometimes shadows from illumination flares danced across our ceiling and the occasional rattle of gunfire kept me on edge. Sometimes my bunk trembled a little from a B52 strike in Laos, a few kilometers to the west. Sometimes the sweep of a searchlight lit up Naked Sandy's curves. Despite the craziness, I could see her. Her maybe hazel-gold or maybe hazel-green eyes, often laughing and always mischievous. Autumn brown hair streaked with light, that widow's peak gracing her forehead. In the sweaty night my thoughtless selfishness buried me. "She's not gone," I kept thinking, "unless I die here."

Over Thanksgiving break, my senior year at USF and her sophomore year at Marymount, I stumbled and marble-mouthed my way through a proposal. I only made it half-way. She didn't say "Maybe." She didn't say that she needed to think about this. Katie said "No." And then there was no air for me to breathe. I asked a few days later if we could talk things over. Katie explained. What she said made me realize then that I never really saw her as anyone other than my girlfriend. She had things she wanted to do, she said.

"I'm going to finish my degree and go to work in New York. I want to have my own apartment and find out who I am and who I can be. I need time to grow up."

She asked me to give her that chance.

"Wait for me and I will wait for you."

I couldn't. I came first. I wanted what I wanted. Flying. The Army. I thought that I was supposed to go forward, and Katie was supposed to tag along. Because that's what I thought girls did. Because that was how I thought our life would be. Me, and then Katie and me. How could I fail to see the ambition in her, the curiosity in her? I trapped myself in my self-absorption.

I stood just outside of her front door. She closed it, disappearing behind it, gone from me. I stood there alone, at her front door, outside of her life.

The very last time I saw her, before Fort Knox, we sat in my driveway for a while. And then I got out of her car. Katie stopped at the end of the drive and turned to look back at me. I stood there, knowing I should run after her, wounded pride and all. I should have dragged my ego down the driveway after her. She wouldn't have driven away. I should have told her that we had time. That she had time for the excitement of New York City, for being employed because of what she knew, not who knew her. And that I had time for the Army and flying and eventually the war.

"Wait for me and I will wait for you."

Katie had promised me the night that I proposed to her. But I didn't wait. My stupid pride held my heart a prisoner. My stupid pride couldn't keep my heart from breaking. And then she was gone.

In the late seventies I married someone who deserved much more than I gave her. We had two little girls. I moved my family from Venice Beach to Spokane to Cincinnati and then back to Washington State, to Port Townsend, always in pursuit of a bigger airplane, or a move from co-pilot to captain. I told myself each time we moved that I was giving my girls a better life, but that was never completely true. Everything I did was always about airplanes, and therefore always about me. All the way back to Katie, it was always about me. I realized way too late that I had put cockpits before children. And it was my fault alone, that over time, because of my selfishness, my family had disintegrated. In a house of my own making, I had been alone for years. When I looked around me, I was the only person I saw.

I had a small photograph of Katie tucked near the back cover of *To Kill a Mockingbird*. The only book I took with me to Vietnam. I still have the book, the pages now yellowed with years. I looked at her picture not every day, but almost every day. I didn't swear that I would survive the war so that

I could find Katie again. But I hoped for that because I knew that I would never stop loving her.

It was not quite noon in New York City on a chilly March morning in 2001. I was looking up. The ceiling in Grand Central Station, recently restored, was just sensational. Painted robin's egg blue, the lights positioned to mimic the stars in all the constellations. When my gaze dropped down, there she was, reading a train schedule and walking toward me. I stood completely still. When she saw me, she stood frozen, as stunned as I was. And then my arms were around her. The space between us disappeared and there were only two people in that wonderful old hall. I believe that I returned from that war so that I could find her again. Years passed; the boy of 19 who fell in love with her became the boy of 55, when I saw her, the girl at the top of Richard Lane.

She began to cry and squeezed herself almost into me. Her gold-brown hair streaked with silver; the widow's peak not hidden by the red beret she was wearing. Her eyes this mid-morning that startling hazel-gold. She was the most beautiful girl I had ever seen on that last night in December, in 1964. She was truly breathtaking now. I kissed her, and she kissed me back. New Year's Eve all over again.

"Tell me you're not married," I pleaded.

"I'm almost not married. I've missed you for years. We were always meant to be together," she whispered.

"It has always been you, Katie Grace."

# Chapter 13

# Alabama Sweet Tea

**September 1970**

There were lists of casualties posted at Rucker too. When I reported to Fixed Wing Training shortly after my sister's wedding, I saw these lists taped to the bulletin board in our orderly room, in the airfield briefing rooms, at the Officers' Club and at the chapel. Not the lists published in the *New York Times*. These were Department of the Army lists. They were lists of the names of the boys killed in action, because this was the Army, and the Army was at war. Names jumped off the pages. Pisacreta, Cinkosky, Wood. From the 219th. Was it ever going to stop?

Instructing from the Bird Dog proved to be a great distraction. I used learning how to instruct from the backseat, and then teaching from the backseat, as a way of hiding from the daydreams, but not the nightmares. There was no way to hide from the nightmares. I filled the day with airplanes and students and maneuver demonstrations, becoming a combination of Arlie Deaton and Mr. Weaver. I taught the way "Arlie Weaver" taught, because everything "Arlie Weaver" taught me got me back home. I filled the night with graduate school courses in Educational Psychology, which never helped me professionally or personally. But studying occupied my brain until it was time to turn out the bedside lamp. Then it was dark, and dark is where the nightmares lived.

Teaching was so much more fun than I had imagined, probably because I was able to make the lessons that I taught my own, using my own words to explain what I wanted my students to do. What I didn't do was tell war stories. I couldn't tell war stories because SOG was still classified. But the blindfolded prisoner on the VC Shuttle, Meyers and the sawed-off M-79, these things I was able to talk about because they were funny. And Phil's poster of Naked Sandy. I had to describe waking up every morning next to Naked Sandy.

Short field landings! My favorite lesson. I loved doing these as a student. I loved doing them on short dirt landing strips in Vietnam. And I loved teaching my students how to do them by demonstrating them from the backseat. Two bamboo poles pointed straight up about 15 ft above the touchdown point on either side of the practice runway. Between the poles a string of little colored flags was stretched. Like the grand opening of a gas station, red, green, yellow, and blue. The pilot had to land just over the string of flags without hitting it, which took a real sense of "feel." Just what Mr. Weaver preached.

"Listen and feel the airplane. It will tell you what to do."

Pure Weaver.

The airplane was lined up with the runway, and the wing flaps were lowered to sixty degrees. We could go very slow. Power was added to keep us flying, but not straight ahead, or climbing, or falling out of the sky. We needed to be descending, and the descent had to be planned so that we came down at about 500 ft per minute (we had a gauge which showed us that). And the airplane had to be listened to, and felt, and nudged, and tweaked, so that we cleared the string of flags and landed in a small section of the runway called the touchdown zone. Too much power and we'd land "long." Not enough power and those little flags would be dangling from our tail-wheeled rear end.

We taught this at night too. If the student couldn't pass the short field night solo landing test, he had to repeat the whole landing lesson until he got it. One student, not mine thank God, whose last name was Goodenough, and who earned the well-deserved nickname "Hardly," cleared the flags on his first night approach. But he yanked the engine power off – no one knew why – as soon as he saw the flags go under his wing. Power off at about 15 ft? The Bird Dog hit the ground in a three-point landing with all the aerodynamics of a stone. And then it bounced back up into the air. "Hardly" jammed the throttle to full power but that was all he did. He should have pulled the stick back a little to climb. He should have added right rudder to counteract the engine torque. But he didn't. He froze. Torque turned the Bird Dog left. It hit the fire truck that was there to save knuckleheads like "Hardly." The fire truck bounced backward with a ruined front end. The Bird Dog bounced backward but landed upright. Nobody was hurt but the fire truck guys were really upset because their truck was a mess. So was the Bird Dog. "Hardly" was chauffeured back to the operations office by jeep, and maybe all the way to the *Mekong Delta*. We never found out. We couldn't ask him because "Hardly" was gone.

Time didn't dawdle over these final months. My remaining two years of active duty went by much faster than I thought they would. Being in the hospital twice certainly made weeks hurry by. My nose's deviated septum was repaired by a surgeon who used a chisel and a hammer. Really! Every time he whacked my nose my head bounced into the padding on the operating gurney, and I could hear the cartilage crunching. I was so loaded up with Novocain that I couldn't feel anything from the neck up. I also developed a cyst on my tailbone from hours and hours in the armored cockpit seat that was the only armored anything on the Bird Dog. If the cyst had shown up while I was in Vietnam, I would have gotten a Purple Heart. Can you imagine that? A Purple Heart awarded for an infected butt blister? I thought the whole thing was very funny even though the cyst surgery hurt like hell.

The casualty lists were still posted but the number of names were dwindling because our involvement in Vietnam was finally ending. One of the instructors in my group, Charlie Finch, flew for Command and Control North, the SOG operation in *Hue*. But he was as closed about it as I was supposed to be, and he left the service shortly after I arrived at Rucker. The commanding officer of fixed wing training, a colonel, asked me for whom I worked when I reported to the training department.

"MACVSOG, sir. CCC out of *Kontum* and CCS out of Holloway."

I had no idea if he even knew what that was. The colonel didn't ask. He didn't respond at all. And I had nowhere to go with the baggage I dragged back from the war.

I was struck by a sense of sadness that replaced the optimism of my first time at Rucker, when I was a flight student in the fall of 1968. That autumn we were told that we were winning this war and that it would be over soon. It didn't end soon, and we didn't win. A feeling of futility had seeped into every nook and cranny of this place. When I recognized another dead friend on another list of lifeless names my fingers curled into fists and my stomach clenched into a knot. Pointless, this waste of a life.

I understood futility when I came back to the bridges I had found in that skinny Laotian valley. Where the Trail had disappeared into a jungle-choked slot in the mountains, so skinny that I wasn't able to turn a little airplane around in it. When I saw the green bamboo of new bridges erected overnight after a flight of F-4s and I obliterated them the day before. When

I told myself as I looked at the green bamboo that we were no match for the tenacity of these people. I knew then that we should pack up and go home. But we didn't. Now, Fort Rucker's lists, more than anything else, hammered home that which I admitted not long ago on a morning over Laos when I saw the green bamboo of bridges rebuilt overnight. I understand now because the lists lend clarity to futility. Names make futility personal. I understand now.

My very last Army event, besides out-processing, was to see a dentist. My teeth seemed okay, but my jaw ached and so did my head. Every morning. An oral surgeon, another major, checked my teeth and jaw, then a hygienist spent two days cleaning up several years' worth of nicotine stains and neglect. Camels, one after another. I was able to fly the airplane, call in an air-strike, and light a cigarette all at the same time. Multitasking!

"Do you have bad dreams at night, captain?"

I answered the oral surgeon's question in a serious tone because this wasn't funny, because I was still flying over Laos in my dreams.

"Sir, I get my ass shot off every night. I've been back for two years and as soon as I close my eyes at night, I get my ass shot off."

"I'm going to give you these rubber bite-guards because you're grinding your teeth at night. That's why your jaw hurts and why you have morning headaches."

The bite guards eventually disappeared but the teeth grinding, and the sore jaw, and headaches, and bad dreams, accompanied me for more than the next few years of my life.

I looked out at the airplanes lined up on the ramp. Bird Dogs waiting for boys to come learn what they needed to learn so that they could go off to a war for no good reason. I looked at the table and chairs where students would soon be sitting. I wished I was able to tell them to go home.

# Chapter 14

# Just Like Dad

July was my last month as an officer and 1972 was my last year as an Army pilot. My uniforms, the Army-green coat, the black-striped pants, the formal Dress Blue almost-tuxedo, my flight jacket, and flight suits, were folded in a neat stack. They were packed in a box that I bungeed to the rack behind the seat on my Yamaha 360cc motorcycle. I parked and went into a little shop just inside Rucker's main gate. The Officers' Wives Club bought and sold uniforms. I put my stack on the counter. A very pretty woman, a lieutenant-colonel's wife she told me, looked at my clothes and said,

"Do you really want to do this, captain?"

It took me a minute to realize that she wasn't talking about my uniforms. Her eyes never left mine. The question she asked was unsettling. I was leaving the first real job I ever had. I was walking away from a structure within which I knew I could excel. I was a good officer. Arlie said so. So did the people for whom I worked when I returned from Vietnam. Teaching from the back seat of the Bird Dog was a joy. A Master's Degree in Psychology looked good on any officer's resume. My medals didn't hurt either. I returned her gaze.

"Do you really want to do this, captain?"

There was a sadness to her words. Because this base was so full of life when I was a student pilot here, when I was a lieutenant on the way to a war. War gave this place a reason to be. War gave this place life. The irony of that was just stunning. Her blue eyes never blinked. She almost whispered, "You'll be sorry if you do this, and you'll be back."

If I said to her right then that I had changed my mind, that I would rescind my resignation, would that mean that there was hope now that life here would begin to return to what it was? Was it the life of Fort Rucker that she was hinting at? Or her own?

"There are other things I want to do."

157

These were the first words I uttered in response to her question and then to her statement. She finally looked away. Then she raised her eyes to mine. Placing her palms flat on the counter she continued,

"I hope you get to do what you want. Good luck to you. Let me figure out what we owe you." I placed my hands opposite hers, middle fingertips just touching. She didn't withdraw her hands and her eyes continued to hold mine.

"Can you give the money from this sale to a charity? Is there one you know of? A church, maybe? Or a family who needs it?"

I took a step backwards and then paused. If I didn't leave, would I ever leave? Or was I imagining all of this?

"You'll be back, captain."

I smiled and opened the door to outside, to California, to the other things I wanted to do. My right foot pushed hard against the kick starter and the engine whined a motorcycle whine. I didn't dare look back to see if she was in the shop window.

Out-processing took the better part of the next day. Paperwork in neat piles, interviews with the paymaster, with a young lieutenant-lawyer, and with a VA doctor who asked me if I had any disabilities that I planned on claiming. Even if I did, I wasn't going to tell him. I wanted an airline to hire me. They wouldn't if I couldn't see. I could. Or couldn't hear. Well, I did have a hearing loss from the cacophony of gunfire and engine noise. But I wasn't letting him put that in my medical records.

I sold the motorcycle and that was that. I was presented with a second Army Commendation Medal, and the rest of my Air Medals for Valor caught up with me the day before I left Rucker. All twenty-four of them, but six short I thought. There were supposed to be two more DFCs, a Silver Star, and a Vietnamese Gallantry Cross, but the paperwork for those was missing in action. John and I never received those Silver Stars the lieutenant colonel from the *Plei Trap Valley* operation requested; the lieutenant colonel John called a "stupid motherfucker." I never really gave much thought. More paperwork that was lost. Years later John made searching for the medal his Last Hurrah when cancer was consuming him. But on that last day, as I left the Army, I let it go. The drive from Alabama to Los Angeles took five days in the July heat. It would have taken two except that Texas was on the itinerary. Texas went on forever. I thought my VW was going to melt.

How long can someone walk around LA with 35 cents in their pocket? My record was ten days. I had no extra money to spend and nowhere to be for four months. There were a few job interviews. I had to go if I wanted to collect unemployment insurance. Every time I drove the San Diego Freeway past LAX, I watched airplanes getting ready to land. And every time I saw them, I thought, I can do that. I didn't want to be a stockbroker. Or sell insurance. I just want to go flying.

While at Rucker I used part of my GI Bill to get a Master's degree in psychology, which did me not one bit of good either professionally or personally. After leaving the service I used the rest to get a Flight Engineer's Rating. Airlines still had three pilots in the cockpit. The third pilot was the flight engineer. I needed that rating. The late summer and fall were spent using colored pencils to color-code the electrical, oil, hydraulics, air conditioning and pressurization, and fire-control systems of a 727. I drew them all on a blackboard, in colored chalk, for the engineer rating's oral exam. I brought my own. The schematics made the systems easier to explain. So that's exactly what I did. The flight check, compared to the oral, was a breeze.

Western and Continental were hiring. I had already been to Continental. So next I sat in Western's employment office with my logbook and licenses. I didn't have an appointment. I arrived at 8:00 in the morning on the first Monday of November and at 4:30 that afternoon the personnel manager finally saw me.

"Don't tell me about all your medals or that you got shot at. I don't care about that."

He stared at me, waiting for a response.

"Okay, I won't. But I do have a couple of medals and I was shot at. I also have an M.S. and I really want to come to work here. My dad flies for TWA, which was originally part of Western. I've always wanted to be a pilot. So here I am."

"What else?"

"Well, my application is in the stack of applications on that table over there. But here's a new one so you don't have to go searching for mine in that stack. Look at this, and if I'm not what you are looking for, put me out of my misery and throw the application away."

The personnel manager laughed, and I received a telegram from Western the next week. Captain Gordon Shields, the Chief Pilot, would like to see me at 8:30 next Tuesday morning. I almost started to cry. The story on Western was that if you got the telegram, you got the job. I wasn't taking any chances. Blazer, slacks, and white dress shirt went to the dry cleaners.

Weejuns were gleaming. Socks where l wouldn't forget them. I even got a haircut. Not an Army haircut. A reasonable haircut.

I was awake at 6:00 in the morning. I showered, shaved without carving my face up, and dressed. I couldn't eat. My MG knew what a big deal today was and started right up, and the car and I were parked at the airport with an hour to spare. Captain Shield's office was easy to find. My logbook provided me with reading material. Numbers and abbreviated place names, almost all Vietnamese, eased me into remembering what happened on the days in the book. And then it was 8:30 and Captain Shields was holding out his hand. He asked me questions and I tried to answer them without swallowing my words, and he held out his hand again.

"Welcome aboard, Francis."

I climbed into my barely running MG Midget, pleading with it to not die on me today. I was convinced that British sports cars were engineered to break down if the owner was Irish. Like me. It was 12 December 1972, and I was headed for the Tishman Building, where orientation would be held. The car managed to get me to the employee parking lot without a lot of complaining.

As I crossed Aviation Boulevard, the entrance to Los Angeles International Airport, I kept looking back over my shoulder at Western's corporate headquarters. I'd just been there two weeks earlier, first in the Personnel Office to have my logbooks checked, and then to be interviewed by Captain Shields. I crossed Aviation in the cross walk because drivers into LAX were known to treat this big boulevard as if it were an extension of the Indy 500.

I kept peeking at Western offices because I was just amazed that a real airline had hired me as a pilot. I was positive that any second a booming voice from over a giant, hidden loudspeaker was going to bellow,

"Not so fast, Doherty. We've changed our minds."

I figured that I must have just made it into the Tishman Building before the Personnel Office realized I had gotten through the door. I had to sign in on a roster, and my name was on it. Captain Shields really meant it when he said that I had everything Western is looking for. When he had said that I was hired I thanked him and shook his hand before he could say, "Hold it, young man." I couldn't help but think that these guys must not have read my resume very closely. The Bird Dog was so little, and I had never flown a jet in my life.

Thirty-three of us, all males, milled around a large conference room filled with chairs with writing tables attached to them, like the desks we all had in college. Several were chatting with people they either knew or had just met. I didn't say a word. I looked around the room and didn't recognize anyone. Then the facilitator, Roger Nelson, came in. We all straightened up at almost attention, and orientation began.

I watched all the other pilots in my new-hire class, struck by how extremely competitive everyone was. Whatever someone flew, some other guy flew something bigger, or faster, or with more engines. Whatever someone did, some other guy did something harder or more dangerous. It was as if I was back at flight school, before Vietnam, where everyone, including me, was jockeying to be first in his pilot class. A "my dog's bigger than your dog" pugnaciousness permeated the atmosphere. The room reeked of testosterone. To me this was very funny, because aside from all of us being a little older and no longer on active military duty, nothing had changed. "My dog's bigger than your dog" was still how the game was played.

After some preliminary remarks we were each given at least 8,432 forms to fill out. My writer's cramp was relieved only by the break for lunch. After an hour we reassembled in the conference room. The stack of forms on my desk and the cramp were waiting for me. Finally, all the paperwork was collected. Time for a break. Some went into the hallway to smoke. Others just chatted. I began talking to Bill Winkler, an Air Force pilot, who was at the same hiring interview I had attended. I think he flew KC-135 refueling tankers during the war. What amazed me about Bill was that he complained about everything, and he looked like he combed his hair with an eggbeater. His whole head was one big cowlick.

After the break the facilitator asked us to introduce ourselves to the person to our right, then stand up and say something about the person you had just met. That was Winkler. I was going to say that, along with being a tanker driver he combed his hair with an eggbeater. I wanted to but I didn't. I wish I had. Because a few moments later Mickey Rivers stood up and introduced Muddy Waters. The names alone had me laughing. Then Rivers pointed both index fingers at Waters and said,

"Muddy Waters is one shit-hot aviator."

The comments got funnier as the teasing slope got steeper. It was like being back in the briefing room, being assigned a combat mission. Put on your best John Wayne, show no fear, and give as good as you got.

The second day of orientation was also the final day. The class was divided into two groups, oldest to youngest. Seniority was predicated on age. The oldest pilot in our class got the lowest seniority number. The higher the seniority number the more junior its owner. I think my number was 938, and there were three other pilots younger than I was. The first seventeen in my class, the more senior group, went to the Boeing 737 as flight engineers. The 737 was designed as a two-pilot aircraft, but the FAA required three pilots in all cockpits, so off they went to the easiest job in aviation history. They figured take-off and landing speeds and flap computations, pushed maybe two or three buttons and switches, conducted pre-flight exterior checks, and otherwise looked outside for traffic. The rest of us, the younger half of the class, went to the Boeing 720 and 707. Nothing was easy about being a flight engineer on these old battleships. Everything was done manually. Trimming generators, balancing fuel, adjusting the air conditioning, pressurizing, and depressurizing. No automatic "set it and forget it" systems. If I didn't know how the systems worked, what would I do if systems were broken? Well, then I'd be trying to sell insurance.

Ground school started on the third morning. So, the rest of that second day was spent being briefed by one of the training department supervisors, Bill Heinbaugh. He talked about the length of training and the number of exams we could expect. He talked about how long we would be third pilots (B-737) or flight engineers (B-720) before moving up to become First Officers. And then he had each one of us stand, reintroduce ourselves to our thirty-two classmates, and tell everyone our branch of service and what we flew.

One by one my classmates delivered their aviation histories. One after another stood and said Air Force, Navy, or Marine Corps. Everybody had flown a jet. Big jets, little jets, bombers, tankers, or fighters. Some had flown fighter-bombers that took off from and landed on aircraft carriers. Some had flown B-52s out of Guam on bombing missions over Vietnam. Others had flown from bases in Vietnam. One of the civilian pilots had flown a B-737 for the FAA. Another had flown cargo throughout the South Pacific in a twin engine, prop driven *De Havilland* C-7 Caribou.

The pilot sitting next to me, a red-headed tree trunk from Louisiana, Hank Causey, had flown S2-F sub chasers while in the Navy. The airplane, called a "Stoof" for reasons known only to other Navy pilots, brought hoots and catcalls from all the Navy pilots in the room. Hank showed me a picture of his "Stoof", and it looked to me like it would be fun to fly. But then, everything looked like fun to fly to me.

I have no idea why I was the last one to stand, but I was. I introduced myself, and said I was an Army pilot. I was the only Army pilot in the class. I couldn't say anything about what I did because the SOG mission was classified and would stay buttoned up for the next twenty-plus years. So, I just said that I had been a reconnaissance pilot. Mr. Heinbaugh interrupted me.

"But you do have some jet time, correct?"

I shook my head, no.

"Okay, what did you fly?"

"Bird Dogs, taildraggers."

A taildragger. A little airplane with an old-fashioned tail wheel rather than a nose wheel. He looked at me and almost grimaced,

"An O-1?"

From somewhere in the conference room I heard, "You gotta be shittin' me," accompanied by a lot of laughter, hoots, raspberries, and boos. I mean, really? Booing my Bird Dog? Heinbaugh squinted at me.

"You flew reconnaissance in a Bird Dog? Where? In Vietnam?"

I didn't respond.

"And you have no jet time?"

"None."

Bill Heinbaugh stood there, quiet, and just looked at me. I stood with my hands in my pockets now, looking back at him. Finally, he smiled a little. Just a little.

"Mr. Doherty, is it? I'm afraid you're going to have a hard time."

I smiled and sat back down, taking Heinbaugh's words in. I memorized them by heart. I let them ring in my ears through every training flight. I called up the things that Arlie told me during his debriefing, after I had failed the check ride Arlie Deaton gave me, in 1968, at Fort Stewart.

"You're going to be a good pilot, Dawtry. Don't let me down."

Not a chance, Arlie. Not a chance.

From that afternoon forward, for every check ride I took over the remaining thirty-two years I flew as an airline pilot, I took Arlie's and Heinbaugh's words with me. Seatbelts and shoulder harnesses on, checklists read, cross-check, cross-check, cross-check, all the flight and engine instruments. I told myself to be a methodical problem solver and fly the jet like you're really good at it, because you are. Never ever let Arlie down. And Heinbaugh?

"Hard time my ass. I'll show you!"

Sometimes, when an event was at its beginning, I found myself wondering about what it's ending might be like. Even though I was standing at the starting line, I wandered for just a moment into the final scene. This was how it was for me with flying. Standing at the threshold of an adventure that would consume over forty years of my life, I found myself wondering about what the final moment of the adventure would feel like. I wanted to take my time getting there though. Because my father, on the day I was hired by Western, said, "It goes by so fast, Frankie. It goes by so fast."

The adventure itself, airline flying? The only denominators common to both the airline and the Army were regimentation and uniforms. Regimentation was at the heart of airline flying. The Army was a little freer. Combat flying was instinctive, reactive, inventive. There was no procedure for evading a .51 trap. A lot of 'now whats'', followed by a lot of 'oh fucks', followed by sincere 'thank you Jesus's.' In airline flying the neck bone was always, somehow, connected to the ankle bone. There was a procedure for everything. And those procedures? I had to know them all.

Touch, smoothness, awareness, all intrinsic skills which were required in both a 767 and a Bird Dog. If I pulled up (on the yoke or the stick) the airplane climbed. If I forgot to add power in a climb, the airplane stopped climbing. If I pushed down, it descended. If I forgot to reduce power, the airplane went down a lot faster, and the ground said hello a lot sooner. Airplanes all work essentially the same way. And for me, the Bird Dog was a lot harder to fly than a 767. The Six-Seven was like flying an oversized sports car. The Bird Dog was like flying a winged skateboard. But flying anything was like flying a magic carpet. After I checked out for the first time as a first officer on the 737, which was the first jet I had ever flown, I would watch planes taking off from LAX. I could see them in the early morning, when I wasn't flying, at the beach, as I paddled my board out to where the waves formed. I could straddle the board and watch, and say to no one in particular, "I get to do that."

I miss everything about flying. Every day I miss everything about flying. Every day. There is a softness to the metal that makes the yoke, the steering wheel, so familiar, so pleasing to my hand. It means flying the airplane. Flying the airplane is what I do. It defines who I am. I have felt the yoke against my palm for thirty-two years. It connects me to the control surfaces, the ailerons, and the elevator, of this big airplane. No, more than that. It connects me to people who have occupied this seat for years and years before me. My father sat in a seat like this. Flying is our connection.

The very first time I stepped into the cockpit at Western Airlines I knew that this final day would come. But I was only 27 years old. Still a boy really, sharing a small space with men who were contemporaries of my father. Veterans of the Second World War. From the Army Air Corps. At least twice my age. Almost 60 years old. Sixty years of age was the end of airline flying. It was the law. Their end of flying was around the corner. Mine was a lifetime away. I knew there would be an end to this. But it was so far in the future that I couldn't see it.

And now that day, 22 November 2004, is here. Western has disappeared, absorbed into Delta in 1986. I have picked this trip to be my last. There's one more trip in my final schedule, but I know I will not be able to fly it. I need to control the time of my leaving, so that I can control myself. I get to Delta's flight operations in Atlanta early on the 22nd, sign in so that crew scheduling knows I'm here, and leave a message for the first officer. It's the same message I've been leaving for as long as I've been a captain.

"If you were in the Marine Corps, don't touch anything in the cockpit until I get there."

Army pilots are required to tease Marines.

In the middle of February, in 1973, I stood in the bowels of Western's terminal in Los Angeles, in a much more primitive Flight Operations. No computers on which to sign in. Clerks with ledgers where I located my name. I found the captain and first officer and managed to introduce myself even though my teeth were chattering. I wasn't cold. I was scared to death. We walked out to the airplane, a Boeing 720B. It looked like a slightly smaller Boeing 707. I was the 3rd pilot, the flight engineer, so I sat sideways, behind the first officer, at a big panel that controlled all the systems that made the airplane work. What could go wrong? Well, everything! I could run this thing out of gas. I could depressurize it, so that everybody passed out. I could mis-handle the air conditioning, so we'd all freeze like popsicles. I prayed a little. "Please God don't let me screw anything up. And if I do screw something up, make it a small thing that doesn't matter too much."

We taxi out this late (and my last) afternoon in the cockpit from Delta's international terminal in Atlanta. The airplane is cleared onto the runway, the thrust levers are pushed forward, and we begin the take-off roll. Pretty soon we're fast enough, and I ease the yoke back to point the nose up a little. We're heavy with fuel and passengers, so the rotation is gentle, the yoke is cradled in my palm and the nose wheel is off the ground. The main wheels break free of the runway. We are flying. I am flying. The airplane and I are dance partners. The same dance I dreamt of dancing as a young boy. A different dance in combat though. Now, a dance I dance for years in safer places. A dance I thought would never end.

The first flight on my first day, when I didn't screw anything up, brought me one day closer to this day. I have thought about this day from time to time, and I have remembered the words my father said to me. "It goes by so fast." When his days came to an end, I saw him really angry. Because he didn't want to stop. Me neither.

Over all the years we only talked about flying twice. The first time was the day I got hired. The day before Thanksgiving, in November, in 1972. I had a big white envelope with an Indian Chief's head, Western Airlines and "Welcome Aboard" emblazoned in red on it. My mother and father were standing in the driveway of my rented house in Los Angeles. I held up the envelope so he and my mother could see it. My father's hands gripped my shoulders, and he said, two times,

"You're following in my footsteps."

I was.

The second time we spoke about flying was more than fifteen years later. Just before my oral exam on the systems of the MD88, my first captain's airplane. My father called me the night before the oral. He said,

"Think before you open your mouth, take your time, and act like you own the joint."

I agreed with him on the first two points, but I wasn't so sure about the third. Arrogance never looked good on me.

On my final trip I fly the jet to Lima, and back to Atlanta. My last jet. I always share the legs with the first officer, but not this time. I apologize as I explain. And ask him not to say anything to anyone. I also ask the head flight attendant, the "A" line in Delta terminology, to please not say anything to the passengers. And that I plan to get off first, once we are at the gate. Otherwise, the passengers will see me crying.

I try to remember all the words I speak and hear during the approach, but I don't. I disconnect the autopilot (I always do this) descending through 18,000 ft. This is against the rules. But I do it anyway. I'm a pilot, not a computer programmer. I forget the words I want to remember. I am too busy dancing this perfect last dance.

Approach Control clears us onto "final." I intercept the "localizer" which points to the end of the runway, and the "glideslope" which takes us down to the touchdown point.

"Fly the jet, Francis."

A little left crosswind. So, a little right rudder keeps the nose aimed at the centerline. And a little twitch of the left aileron drops the left wing down to correct for the drift the crosswind causes. Just enough. The left main gear touches the runway. Contact is almost imperceptible. Then the right main touches, softer than the left. The nose-wheel kisses the runway, right on the centerline. And the dance ends. Thirty-two years, and now the dance ends.

The ground guide motions me forward to the stop point at the terminal gate. He crosses his lighted wands into an "X." We stop, and the parking brake is set. I rub the fat brass button on my uniform coat with my thumb. Could a genie live in there? Could he grant me three wishes? I'd only ask for one.

I think about flying every day. I miss it. Early morning's still air. Dark rainy nights. The engine song of the tiny Bird Dog. The hum of two giant engines on the 767-400. I miss the snow of Montana. And the seduction of Paris. Evening voices echoing across the misty canals of Venice. I miss the tango of flying, the romance of flying.

I miss everything about flying. Every day I miss everything about flying. Every day.

# Chapter 15

# Ask Me No Secrets

When I was a young father, flying for Western, little girl faces looked at mine. My daughters. Did I want them to know who I was in Vietnam? Their eyes asked if I was telling them everything there was to tell. Could I find the right words? I had a few opportunities, but I was just not able to summon the nerve to even try. It wasn't that my whole story was too difficult for two little girls to understand. My whole story was too frightening for me to tell them. Telling all of it would have taken more courage than I had. They were children, my children, and I was their father. I wanted to always be their knight in shining armor.

If they knew the truth of my war year, would they still see me as a good man? Would they still see me as the gentle man that I am now? Or would they see me as a hypocrite, a war-lover, a pretender, a boy-soldier, whose hands remain bloody? I was terrified of that, of their knowing too much of that heartbreak year. Deflect. Deflect to delay for a little while longer. Eventually I would have to explain. My daughters had questions and all the deflection in the world wasn't going to get me off the hook. Young girls were relentlessly persistent. They were like the drip drip drip of some exotic water torture.

How did the questions start? School? TV programs? A phone call from someone with whom I served, maybe? Or maybe old photographs? Or maybe their grandmother said something? Maybe all of these. I was able to tell them some things about the Army and me. I was able to tell them some things about jungles and mountains, about helicopters and airplanes. I just couldn't tell them about death, death I saw or death I caused. Because I was afraid that they wouldn't love me anymore.

I was flying when my friend John Pappas called. My daughter Alanna answered and took his message. John called to tell me that Arlie Deaton had diabetes and was dying. John was contacting all the Headhunters who had served under Arlie, asking them to call their old Company Commander, to give him the same kind of encouragement that he had given us, the boys who flew for the 219th Reconnaissance Airplane Company. Arlie's 219th.

Alanna was probably in tenth grade (1996) at Port Townsend High School when she took John's call. During their brief conversation John mentioned that I was a "real gunslinger" when he and I flew together at the end of my tour in Vietnam. He didn't explain this. Alanna remembered that John laughed when he said it. She didn't question him or the remark. She told her sister Meighan what John had said, and they just held on to "real gunslinger" until I got home the next day. Then they demanded an explanation.

"Gunslinger. Your friend called you a 'gunslinger.' What does that mean, Dad?"

I didn't reply. Having to call Arlie was my excuse, my way of not being a "gunslinger" for a little while longer.

I explained to my girls about Arlie though, about how he saved flight school for me. I talked about love. Ours, the boys of the 219th, for Arlie, and Arlie's for us. About Arlie's common sense, his common touch, his notion of never asking any of us to do anything that he wouldn't do. I told my girls about Arlie's singing *Oh Ruby, Don't Take Your Love to Town,"* about how we had to know all the words and sing along with him at the top of our lungs whenever he sang it.

"Arlie is one of the best people I have ever known."

I didn't tell them about bad missions or bad dreams, the bloody spring of 1970, or how Arlie helped Phil and me through the first few terrible days of April. I did tell them about flunking the check ride, and how Arlie rescued me. And then I called him on the phone.

His answering machine picked up. My message was my name and phone number. The message everybody leaves. And then, a minute later, I called him back.

"Wait a minute, this is Captain Francis Doherty."

Then hung up again. I grabbed the phone one more time.

"Correction. This is Delta 767 Captain Francis Doherty, calling to remind you about that check ride you busted me on. Don't think I have forgotten."

My daughters were laughing and so was I. Since I had just related the check ride story to them the messages were funny. I told them that when Arlie called back, he'd probably fake being angry. Then the phone rang. It was Arlie. He was yelling, he was faking being angry, he was singing *Ruby.*

I chimed in because I knew the rules. Sing the song or be badgered to death. Then he was telling me that I deserved to flunk, and finally how my success as an airline pilot was thanks to him and him alone. I held the phone so that Meighan and Alanna could hear all this. They both thought Arlie was great and wanted to know when they could meet him. I handed them the phone, one at a time. They introduced themselves and said "hello." Arlie did not tell them that I was a "gunslinger." Thank God.

It had always been so much easier to talk to my girls when there was humor involved, when my stories were funny, when Meighan and Alanna were at ease. I am selfish, I think. I never wanted to talk about the bad days. I liked it much better when they were laughing. I think they liked me better when they were laughing. Because they were not threatened by the past, fearful that bad things might repeat themselves.

When we lived in Cincinnati, I took Meighan and Alanna, then little girls in elementary school, to the giant museum at Wright-Patterson Air Force Base. It dwarfed the Smithsonian Air and Space Annex. The museum held thirteen airplanes that their grandfather had flown. One, parked inside and open so that they could go through it, was a B-24, the airplane my father piloted during the Second World War. It was a big, brown shoebox with four huge engines. We entered from the rear and walked forward to the cockpit. If we faced backwards, we could see the tail gunner's turret. We walked past the waist-gunners' stations, the top of the fuselage gunner's turret, the navigator's table, the pilots' seats in the cockpit, and the bombardier's position in the nose. The airplane seemed to go on for days. It didn't really, it was cramped in fact, but seemed bigger than everything else nearby. And, nearby, hanging from the ceiling, was "Daddy's airplane," my Bird Dog. This was the first time either one of them saw "Daddy's airplane." Not even a photograph. Meighan stamped her foot.

"That's not fair."

Alanna began to cry. I put my arms around them and kissed them both.

Tiny compared to the B-24. Insignificant compared to the B-24. Defenseless compared to the B-24. I could have told them that I was able to make that little airplane fly the pants off that B-24, but they'd never believe me. B-24 equaled big. The Bird Dog in comparison was a toy. I knew that I had to be careful about what I said. Only the good stories. I wondered if there would ever be a time when I would be able to tell them who I really was, what I really did with that little airplane. Like the stories I told them about growing up, getting in trouble at school, being in the Army, my stories needed to make them laugh. So many times, the Bird Dog stories were not funny. Not even close.

The war was never a topic of conversation when my daughters were growing up. Meighan and Alanna knew that I was an airline pilot. How I became one was not important. What mattered to them was that they were able to fly from Spokane, Cincinnati, and later Seattle, to visit Grammy in Los Angeles, and Nana and Poppa in Lloyd Neck. Dad was a pilot. He got them free tickets and they got to fly on airplanes. They were busy at school, busy with friends, busy with jazz guitar (Meighan) and classical cello (Alanna), their mom was at home and their dad was gone for a few days working at a job different from their friends' dads. Other dads were home every night. Sometimes I was flying on holidays too. How I got to do this job, this flying job, didn't register with them. It just didn't. A bit of history got lost while they were being kids.

All through my daughters' grade schools, and for most of high school in Port Townsend, Washington, Vietnam was never mentioned. Until Meighan's junior year, when her English teacher assigned the class a book report. Meighan got to choose her own topic. She picked a book on Vietnam because, she said, she knew I was in the Army. No other reason, she said. It was that simple. She wrote her report, and then asked me if I would speak to her class. Her teacher, a woman my age, encouraged Meighan to invite me.

I came to school on a cloudy afternoon. Dressed in slacks and a blue blazer, dress-shirt, tie and penny loafers, I introduced myself to the class and to Meighan's teacher. The look in the teacher's eyes as we shook hands and the quickness with which she snatched her hand from mine alerted me to an impending ambush. I talked about what I did. I talked about the misgivings I had about the war in general. I talked about the futility I felt, about the sorrow I felt, the unnecessary dying, the unnecessary suffering, the loss of friends. It didn't help. The English teacher was not going to be denied her moment to shine, to pontificate at my expense, to condemn me, and to do so in front of Meighan. Her attack was aimed at me, and my child was collateral damage.

"You fought in an unjust war. You bombed and killed innocent people. Doesn't your conscience keep you awake at night?"

I was the stereotypical baby killer, the war lover, the amoral adventurer who supported an immoral and unnecessary conflict. She said these things in front of my daughter. Meighan's face appeared somber, but I was close enough to see the thunder and lightning in her eyes. I couldn't tell if her anger was aimed at me.

I had no intention of interrupting Meighan's English teacher or getting into an argument with her. When she finished speaking, I hugged Meighan, thanked Meighan's classmates for listening to what I had to say, and addressed her teacher directly, my eyes never leaving her as I spoke. I told her that her opinion was her opinion, one to which she was certainly entitled. And that she wasn't faced with the choice of putting on a uniform or running for Canada. She didn't have a draft card to burn.

"There were no consequences attached to your actions. There were to mine."

I left the classroom before the teacher could resume her assault on my character. When Meighan came home later that afternoon, she touched my arm.

"Sorry Dad."

I told Meighan that her "sorry" wasn't necessary, but I kissed her and thanked her for it. I really didn't want her to think that I was a bad person. That's what we really needed to talk about, she and I, because that's what her teacher was telling Meighan's class, that I was a bad person. Sooner or later, we would have to talk about honor, commitment, altruism, selflessness and, more than anything else, acceptance of who I was then, and what I truly believed. It was a conversation we would eventually have. Just not yet. I needed to talk to Arlie first.

It was early evening in Augusta, Georgia, and mid-afternoon in Port Townsend when I called Arlie, after my "presentation" to Meighan's English class. He was so much more familiar with anti-war sentiment than my father would have been. That's not to say that my father wouldn't have been sympathetic. But his war ended so much differently than mine did. Dad's generation got parades, accolades, applause, and kisses. We returned home to silence if we were lucky. I told Arlie that I had been caught off guard. After all these years, my character, my humanity, my worth had been attacked, in front of my daughter, by a woman I had never met. All these years I avoided the insults aimed at veterans of my age, because the airlines I worked for, Western and then Delta, had cockpits comprised almost exclusively of former military pilots. Veterans of the Second World War and Korea filled the cockpits when I first came to work in 1972. Veterans of Vietnam, my contemporaries, arrived when I was hired. Going from a military airplane to a commercial airline sheltered us from the antipathy other returning veterans experienced when they transitioned into civilian life. We merely traded one uniform for another.

I guess there wasn't much Arlie really could say. He let me vent my anger. I did a little, and when I was through, he asked to speak with Meighan. They talked, and then she handed me the phone. I didn't ask Arlie what he said. I simply thanked him for listening, while I studied the expression on Meighan's face. Still somber. Not smiling. Regular Meighan. But the storm clouds had left her eyes. Arlie did for Meighan what he did for Phil and me that April afternoon in 1970, a few weeks after Armstrong and Ridgeway died.

Alanna participated in an Honors English seminar during her freshman year at the University of Cincinnati. The seminar, geared to students enrolled at the Conservatory of Music, looked at music, art, and film about and during Vietnam. Each student drew a topic from out of a hat. Alanna drew "Daughter of a Veteran." She asked me to send her all my photographs, the unit patches and insignia I wore on my uniforms, and any newspaper articles I had saved. Among the things I included was the Christmas card I received from Sister Angela and her orphan children in *Da Nang*, a newspaper article about Alanna's grandmother and her efforts on behalf of the orphanage, my 219th Headhunters patch, and the Green Beret Death's Head with Fangs Dripping Blood patch from the Special Forces Studies and Observations Group. The patch that was given to me by the Green Beret Intelligence officer, who briefed me on the SOG mission on my first day in *Kontum*. The patch that was sure to get me killed if I was ever shot down. The patch that popped up during Alanna's seminar as part of a slide show on art and artifacts.

"Oh, I have one of those."

Alanna laughed as she drew the death's head bloody fangs patch out of the big envelope of memorabilia, I sent her.

Alanna asked me to come and address her class. I agreed to come because my daughter asked me to come. And this time I was ready just in case I had to cross swords with another anti-war activist. I didn't. The professor, a woman my age, could not have been nicer. I talked a little about flying reconnaissance, but only a little. Alanna's classmates knew about *My Lai*, the napalm-burned girl running naked down a road with agony scrunching her face, and not much else. It surprised me how much they didn't know. Even the history books looked away from us. I talked about Sister Angela and the orphanage, about my mother and the trucks loaded with donations, about flying with Luan Hudson, the girl who had been at that orphanage. Alanna's professor had tears in her eyes. Several other students did as well. Because I only talked about the good things, the kind things, the things we did without batting an eyelash. *My Lai* was an aberration, I said. Orphanages and medical clinics and candy bars were every day.

"We were the good guys."

Because we almost always were.

I talked with Arlie at least twice a month for the rest of his life. When they were home from school my daughters always asked for the phone. They never met him. They had only seen his picture. But Arlie's voice on the other end of a phone call made him not just real but mythical. Because Meighan and Alanna both felt the reverence with which I spoke of Arlie. They loved the Arlie check ride story. They loved his Alabama accent. I made all the stories they heard about Arlie good stories. They all were. And then diabetes, the diabetes that John Pappas called to tell me about, killed him. He died on 22 November 2011. Arlie was 71 years old. I still talk to him. Just not on the phone.

I was stuck in Seoul, Korea, working as a flight instructor and check pilot for Boeing, on the morning that I received emails from Phil Phillips and Charles Ford and John Meyers and Clarence Duckworth and Don Shipp and Ben Brown and Doug Krout and Bob Jackson and George Savani and Bernie Bernhardsen and Chuck Slimowicz and Richie Kane and Joe Kurley and Bob Segal and John Pappas, telling me that our friend had died.

So many boys who knew Arlie, who served with Arlie, who worked for Arlie, who loved Arlie, stood up to salute. Four of them were able to gather in Augusta, where Arlie lived. They attended his funeral, they hugged his widow, they shook hands with his children. They honored him.

The words to *Ruby* were printed and passed around. Everybody in the church sang.

# Chapter 16

# Now Dad Knows

It was December 1992, a week or so before our last Christmas in Cincinnati. I had been commuting from Spokane to Dallas so that I could fly as a captain. We moved east to Cincinnati in 1990, where we could live, and I could fly out of the same city. My parents came from New York for a long, pre-Christmas visit. My father had his "I think we should have this" menu all ready to go. He would start with "I would like you to make…" and the rest of my day was spent over the stove. Not just any stove either. A 1924 white porcelain Magic Chef six burner gas restaurant range. It weighed a ton. I loved that battleship. Oh yes, dinner was a stuffed, boneless leg of lamb, wrapped in an herbed pastry dough. Kind of like a Beef Wellington. Only Greek. That was his first requested entree on this trip.

"You know Frankie, the Army Air Corps taught me just enough about flying to keep me from killing myself."

We were back at the big airplane museum at Dayton's Wright Patterson, standing in front of a contraption called a Vultee BT-13. A basic trainer that my father flew as an Aviation Cadet during the Second World War. As Dad talked about the Vultee I couldn't help thinking that this looked an awful lot like the Cambodian plane that chased me, shooting at my Bird Dog and missing, all the way to the border with Vietnam. But no side tracking to Vietnam right now. I needed to make sense of his remark, regarding what he did or didn't learn about flying as an Aviation Cadet. I had to decide if I wanted to ask him to explain or wait until later. Later was better, I decided. After Wright-Patterson.

As we walked through the museum it was more important for me to hear everything he had to say about his flying, his airplanes, his war. He pointed at a Boeing Stearman, a fabric-covered, open-cockpit biplane that he also flew as a cadet.

"That Stearman was a real pain in the ass to fly compared to this."

175

He meant the Vultee.

"Look at how narrow the landing gear is on the Stearman. It was hard to control because the main wheels were so close together. Hard as hell to land, and miserable to manage on the ground. The Vultee had a much wider track. More stable on landing, and after, when taxiing. Much easier."

I decided that there was no reason to interject anything about Vietnam here because Dad was finally talking about his time in the Army, and I really wanted him to do exactly that. The more he talked, the slower we walked among so many airplanes.

We strolled past a Spad, a French fighter flown during the First World War by Eddie Rickenbacker and the "Hat in the Ring Squadron," the *Lafayette Escadrille*. Beautiful. If I had to pick only one airplane that I was allowed to fly, it would have been a Spad. Pilots who flew Spads were knights, heroes galloping into battle on horses with wood and cloth wings. That would have been me in a flash. We had to stop in front of an Italian twin-engine Caproni, a First World War bomber with a varnished fuselage that reminded me of a wooden Gatsby-era speedboat. The bombardier stood on a platform that looked like the fantail on a yacht. I looked at this airplane and laughed, expecting nothing less from the gang that gave us the Ferrari, Alfa Romeo, and Lamborghini. I was hard pressed to call this warplane anything other than what it was, a DaVinci-inspired work of art.

Dad spotted the B-24 and picked up his pace as we approached it. He was becoming much more animated, punctuating his words with waves of his hands and bobs of his head. And he was talking faster. Getting to see this "brick with wings" bomber with Dad, someone who really flew it, was going to be special. We made our way into the fuselage, past the gunners' stations to the cockpit. Dad stood near the pilot's seat, and I stood alongside what must have been the navigator's table. Dad looked forward, scanning the instrument panel, the steering yoke and the throttle quadrant. Time for him was rolling backward, from this early spring day in 1992 to 1942 in a single beat of his heart.

"A guy in my squadron toggled his bomb-load on takeoff."

"What? You're kidding!"

"Yup. A pilot named 'Two-gun McCoy.' Dumped them on takeoff. Scared the hell out of me."

I looked at my father and laughed.

"Two-gun McCoy? Holy smokes!"

Dad smiled.

"We called him Two-gun because he wore a gun belt with two pistols. I was the "airfield officer" on the morning McCoy tried to bomb us, so I wasn't flying. I had to run the takeoff and then the recovery, when the airplanes came back from the mission."

The mission, the one he flew almost every day, was bombing Japanese cargo ships in Rangoon Harbor.

"Everybody was running for the bunkers. I think I got there first."

I asked the obvious question.

"Did any bombs explode?"

"No. They didn't drop long enough to arm, thank God."

This was the one and only war story my father had ever told me. He gave me three single spaced, type-written pages of "memoirs" years later, in which he repeated the "Two-gun McCoy" story. Everything else he wrote dealt with smuggling my mother on a troop-train from New York to Tucson. Except for a few sentences about towing targets behind a B-25, targets which Chinese anti-aircraft gunners shot at for practice. Dad said this was far more dangerous than any bombing mission he ever flew.

After looking at airplanes for several hours we discovered a topographical display of the China / Burma / India theater of operations. The "CBI," my father's little corner of the Second World War. The whole display appeared to be sheets of plywood, side by side, taking up about a hundred square feet. Calcutta, mountains, Rangoon and its harbor, more mountains, China, a river or two, and more mountains. Dad talked for about an hour. Not about what he did. No personal anecdotes. Instead, a wonderfully detailed overview of events fifty years in the past.

My father was still deflecting, staying away from anything that revealed fear, pride, elation, or regret. He probably didn't even know he was doing that. Because that was what he had always done: stayed away from things he couldn't bear to remember. And I knew by now that I wasn't going to get answers to questions that went to the places he didn't want to visit.

When Dad finished his history lesson, he remained looking at the CBI display. Saying nothing now, just standing and looking. Surely reliving. The colors of the jungles, the shapes of the mountains, the number of cargo ships crowding Rangoon Harbor, the pounding sounds of the wing-mounted cannons aimed at him by Japanese fighters diving at his B-24 from out of the sun. I didn't interrupt. Then my father turned to me, put his hands on my shoulders, and softly spoke unforgettable words.

"We survived, Frankie. We survived."

My father and I had a great day at Wright-Patterson. At the museum, at dinner and afterwards, Dad had talked more about the war than ever before. Then he and Mom said goodnight and climbed the stairs to the second-floor guest room in our turn of the century Cincinnati house. Everyone else had gone to bed as well. I poured a final glass of wine and wandered back to Dad's admission. The one about the Army teaching him just enough about flying to not kill himself. I never did ask him to elaborate when he first made the statement. I needed to think about his words a little more. There was no way I could compare his Army Air Corps training to what I was taught in Army Flight School. I didn't know who taught him what, he never mentioned an instructor's name, and he apparently didn't have an Arlie Deaton or a Mr. Weaver like I did. Dad didn't revisit that sentence in the car on the way home from the museum, or during the evening. Not at dinner or after. I never brought the "keep me from killing myself" remark up again.

What I found so amazing was how he took the "just enough" part of what he said he learned and turned that little bit of knowledge into a giant success. What I saw in the museum's B-24 was an airplane not that much more technically advanced than the Italian Caproni. And not nearly as pretty. Dad's airplane was a weapons platform. All it needed to do was drop bombs on a target. Was it heated? No. Was it pressurized? No. It was a point-to-point, bombs-away, nothing more, nothing less, airplane.

From the war he went to Trans World Airlines and a little Martin 404 cargo plane, flying into municipal airports up and down the Ohio Valley. In the summer the corridor from New Orleans to Minneapolis was one thunderstorm after another and his Martin had no weather radar. Oh my God! In the next few years came a flood of innovations. Radars, instrument landing systems, bigger engines, jet engines, rudimentary computers. The Lockheed Constellation, then a Boeing 707, and finally a 747. One airplane smarter than the last. City to city, coast to coast, continent to continent. What the Army Air Corps didn't show him the airline showed him. That was a lot to learn. My father learned it all.

I never bought into his statement that he was "nothing more than a bus driver." But I did agree with him, for the most part, on his "just enough to keep me from killing myself" remark. I knew that his training was as short as possible. The Army Air Corps needed bomber crews, so they taught Dad just enough to get him airborne, but that was it. Don't crash on takeoff or landing. Everything else he figured out for himself. I couldn't compare his military flight training with mine. I was so lucky with Arlie Deaton and

Sheldon Hanneman and Mr. Weaver. And I knew better than anyone what he accomplished in transforming himself from the barely adequate pilot he thought himself to be into a 747 captain. Because I traveled the same self-taught path.

I moved my family from Cincinnati after two years. I was never going to be a Midwest guy. There was no ocean in Ohio. East coast or West coast would be fine, but I was not going to stay in the middle with no ocean. We bought property on the northeast tip of Washington's Olympic Peninsula, in Port Townsend. And just as my father did in Lloyd Harbor, on Long Island, I also built a house, on a bluff above the Strait of Juan de Fuca, looking out at Victoria, on Vancouver Island, in Canada. I went flying because my father went flying. My father seldom talked about his war, and it took me a very long time to talk about mine.

We never shared a lot of words, my father and me. But we did share airplanes and boats and building houses and fishing. We always went fishing. My grandfather, Pa, in his tie and bowler hat went fishing with us. My brother Terry went fishing with Dad and me, but not Pa. Pa had died before Terry was old enough to tag along. And when I started flying, we shared Alaska fishing. The first time I flew into Anchorage I knew I had to come here and bring Dad. We started going together in 1980. Fly fishing for salmon every first week of July. Dad and Terry, sometimes one of my children, my friend Neil, and me.

Dad, because he was who he was, always had a recipe suggestion. It didn't matter that the dinner had to be cooked over a wood fire using an old refrigerator shelf for a grate. Sometimes it rained and we had to rig a tarp over the fire pit so that the fire stayed lit. The chef de cuisine, in a flannel shirt and a fleece and a wool sweater and a rain jacket, sat on a log stump under the tarp, tending to one of Dad's elaborate dinner recommendations. Some fishermen have burgers or franks and beans when they camp. Not Francis John Doherty Himself. Grilled mustard and garlic and rosemary and olive oil crusted boneless leg of lamb suited him just fine. Zinfandel. Two bottles please. I even had a fold-up oven that fit on top of my camp stove. We had hot, (bought pre-baked, then baked) baguettes. I swear. And one year he gave me a recipe for salmon with a basil-cream sauce. The sauce required a food processor to make it. I wasn't lugging a Cuisinart to Shrode Lake, and besides, there was no place to plug it in. He survived. I don't know how.

Time didn't stand still for Dad, even though he did everything he could to slow time down. Our trip to Shrode Lake in the summer of 1995, when he was 76 years old, would be my father's last. Celestina said he couldn't go anymore. My father said that Mom was trying to make him old.

The rain played against the metal roof of the A-frame cabin like a snare drum. Its staccato rattle increased with the intensity of the downpour. Alaska rain. All-day rain. Our fly rods were outside, leaning against the cabin's slanted roof. A normal day at Shrode. I was sitting at the long table centered in the cabin's one room, tying orange and white marabou to number two size salmon hooks, making flies I knew the salmon would chase. The stubby oil stove chugged like a small train, making the room drowsy warm, and a Coleman lantern hissed as it put out just enough light to work by. Rain or no rain, as soon as I had tied a few more of these I was going down river, below the falls, to where the fish were. Where they strained my fly rod to nearly breaking. Where I released them back into their natal creek to spawn.

Terry was dozing on and off, reading and snoring in equal parts. Dad was watching me, probably counting the flies I was trying to make sure he got what he considered his fair share.

Then his question shattered the silence. Out of nowhere my father asked, "What was it like?"

I knew right away that he was asking about my Vietnam of twenty-five years ago. He hadn't asked three years ago, on that day we spent together at Wright Patterson, or any other day before today. He asked here, in this little cabin, on this dreary, pelting-rain morning. I had no idea what prompted him to ask. He just did. For the first time, and for what turned out to be the only time. About what I really did. And so, I told him. I didn't hold back. I just kept the words quick and tight. No war stories.

I told him about MACVSOG, the Studies and Observations Group, about Laos and Cambodia, about recon teams along the Trail. About the incredible bravery I witnessed. About how many Bird Dogs were shot down (more than half), about how many pilots died (more than half) flying the airplane that I flew, and about not being able to explain why I survived while others didn't. I told him about seeing men killed. Our guys being shot out of helicopters' doors, or from ropes thrown out of helicopters, while they were trying to scramble up them, trying to escape from being overrun. Their guys, trapped in open terrain, chewed up by miniguns, burned to death by napalm, vaporized by bombs.

I told him that I killed some people, and that I saw them as I killed them. I told him about the friends I had lost, the faces I remember. I told him about the fear, the adrenaline screaming through me like a freight train, about how sick-scared I was all the time. I told him that my Vietnam was a million shades of green: green leaves, green elephant grass, green NVA tracer rounds. And that my Vietnam was hot-bright orange too. Splashes of orange from tumbling canisters of napalm. Flashes of orange, from the whump of exploding bombs, dropped from the F-4s and A-1s that sometimes I directed. Vapor trails of Agent Orange, sprayed from C130 tankers, that I stayed far away from. I told him about the nights. About sitting on top of a bunker, looking at the kaleidoscope of stars, thinking about a girl who wouldn't marry me. I told him that I prayed that God would save me from tomorrow and tomorrow and tomorrow, because I didn't want to die here. Not here.

I didn't tell my father about later contemplating suicide, about almost driving my Jeep off the Menock Bridge into the Spokane River. That I couldn't say. I couldn't tell him how close I came to that, an act that I eventually considered cowardly, and I didn't see myself as a coward. I made myself say all that I could stand to say that early summer day in rainy Alaska. And when my words stopped my brother Terry removed his glasses and rubbed his eyes. Dad put on his rain jacket and walked out to the river.

# Chapter 17

# Ashes

The top was down on the car because the sun was hot, and it was Florida. Spring, 2009. A zip-lock baggie, hiding from the sun under a towel, rested on the front passenger seat. It took almost two hours down I-95 from Edgewater to Vero Beach. The Interstate was a straight road for the most part, and I kept the cruise control on because this little car was a rocket ship on wheels. I didn't need a ticket.

I couldn't stand it anymore. I lifted the towel, glanced down at the baggie, and smiled.

"So, Dad. How do you like riding in a convertible?"

I imagined that I heard him groaning, then reprimanding me for my addiction to cars.

I was looking down at the baggie of ashes that used to be my 91-year-old father, Francis John Doherty. Just after Christmas 2008, I stared at his pale body, his chest rising and falling to the rhythm of the breathing machine. Dad looked like an empty shell, like a dried-up corn husk. There were no feeding tubes connected to him. My father would die when he ran out of gas, when his engine sputtered and quit. I knew how that worked when I flew over the pitched battle that was *Dak Seang* for what seemed like hours and then barely made it back to *Dak To* on fuel vapors as my Bird Dog's engine, starved of avgas, stopped just before I landed. That's how my father would die, with no fuel remaining, only vapors of air from the breathing machine. We pushed my airplane off the runway. His removal from the pallet upon which he was laying would be more dignified I hoped. I kissed him and told him it was okay to call it a day. Later that evening he surrendered. My brother Glenn called me to tell me that Dad had died. I didn't cry, I thanked him for letting me know and hung up. Katie held me close that night. The next morning, I cried. Later in the day I called Arlie because I needed to tell someone else that my father was killed by a brain that had disintegrated, that had short circuited. Death had left his body behind and had run off with his heart.

I called Dad just before his final Christmas. I knew he was in the hospital. He had another stroke. When he answered the phone, I could tell by the slurring of his voice that this was no small stroke. But he was able to tell me that he'd be home on the 23rd. I let him struggle through our conversation because I could tell that he wanted to talk. That his searching for words wasn't going to deter him. But this was wearing him out and comprehension was slipping.

"Goodbye."

His last words to me. Ever.

After Dad died, I thought about how few times we talked. About anything. We never had the "sex talk." He never talked very much about flying a B-24 during his war. There were no stories about India. No long conversations about his life or mine. Lectures sometimes, one-sided monologues, punctuated by a rare question or two. But not much about the guts of things, the aches and pains of his life or mine. When I sat next to him as he lay dying on that pallet, I took his hand in mine. It was warm but stiffening and I knew that the Gaels and Druids and Leprechauns would be coming for him soon. I told him how I tried to be him and that I hoped he knew that. I thanked him for a great life. The following summer, with my back to the breeze, I spread his ashes in Long Island Sound. And on that summer afternoon, I said the words said maybe never by either of us. I told him how much I loved him.

Celestina lived for only a few years longer. After Dad's death I would sit with Mom on the porch of her assisted-living home in Daytona Beach and she would talk, mostly about my father. She told me one afternoon how upset she was that she hadn't caught the flu this last winter.

"I don't want to be here anymore. Your father's not here. Why do I have to hang around?"

Sometimes we would sit in her room and look at old photographs. Celestina had favorite albums. Photographs of her with Dad. Of her as a young woman. Dad just returned home from the war in his Army khakis, Dad in his TWA captain's uniform. Some pictures of me as a little boy, of me with a fly rod in my hand, of me as a new first officer. But not one of me as a soldier. Not one. One afternoon Celestina closed the album we were looking at and whispered through her teeth.

"I hated that you did that."

That surprised me. Her words reminded me of the one and only time she ever slapped me, when I told her that I had joined the Army. On the drive home, after I left her, I considered what she had said. Celestina saw her two brothers go off to war. She saw childhood friends go off to war. She saw my father go off to war. None of those departures came with a guarantee of a happy homecoming. And then years later her oldest son announced that he too was going off to war. Understanding her slap was easy.

The boat-bag that stored my Garmin GPS and a few other bits and pieces of my Whaler's paraphernalia was in front of my *Rose*'s steering console. I had tied the boat bag to one of the four rod-tubes I can't use. Fly-rods don't fit in rod-tubes made for spinning-rods. But they made good tie-down points for boat-bags, so they're not blown overboard on windy mornings like this.

I looked into the bag and saw the small brown box I had since my mother died. Since Dolly died; her father, Antonio, called her *Bambolina*. Dolly. Since Celestina died; that was her given name. I have always loved to refer to my mother by her beautiful name. The box contained my mother's ashes. I kept it in my closet, then after a while, I put it in the boat bag. For the last few years her ashes had been here. I didn't do anything with them because I couldn't. I guess I wasn't ready to say goodbye to my mother yet. I took the little box to and from the *Rose*. Intending to deposit the ashes into the same Long Island Sound that I put Dad's, so that their ashes would be together. But not yet. Just back and forth, to and from the boat, until this spectacular morning. Today's bright blue sky said that today was the day. It was.

I took the *Rose* close to Fiddler's Green beach. Maybe the ashes should go here? Or maybe not here. Because I remembered how there used to be swimming races at this beach around the Fourth of July when we were little. Races not just for kids. A race for moms too. Celestina loved the beach, but she really hated those swimming races. Dad insisted. I wish I knew why. So off she went, complaining about the rocky beach, complaining about the slippery, seaweedy, horseshoe crabby water. That one and only time she swam in the "Mom's Race," when she had to be rescued by the lifeguard, when that Fourth of July night at our house was not much fun. Hot dogs and corn on the cob, lobster, and clams, but fun? Not that Fourth of July.

Or maybe not here was the right decision. Celestina would not have wanted to be eternally reminded of the swimming races. I continued around the eastern end of Lloyd Neck. Past Target Rock. During the American Revolution, Admiral Richard (Black Dick) Howe was said to have anchored his fleet in Huntington Bay while the battle of Long Island was being fought. The story goes that Howe used Target Rock to correct the aim of his ships' cannons. People claimed to have seen scars on the rock from cannonballs. I looked for the cannonball scars but never could see any. I loved this sliver of local lore nonetheless and didn't care if it was true or not.

As I headed into Lloyd Harbor, I wished I had saved Dad's ashes. My father and mother could have gone into the Sound together. It occurred to me that I could have put their ashes into an empty wine bottle and pushed a cork in tight. Then flung the wine bottle into the current. Kind of like going on their first cruise. I entertained that for only a moment. It struck me as funny. And then it didn't.

The water was calm and still in the harbor. The breeze had picked up, but it was out of the north. Lloyd Harbor runs east-west; it was protected from a wind that was gusting upwards of twenty knots. The calm would have pleased Celestina. No white caps to frighten her. A safer place for my mother's ashes. This harbor that sheltered our first boat. This harbor was at the entrance to Fiddlers Green, and the home my parents built. The home where I grew up. There are lots of houses there now. When we came to Fiddlers Green, there were only five. We were one of the first families. Celestina was one of the first moms.

The *Rose* was slowed to idle, positioned to drift a little. Looking west toward the causeway that allowed cars to come from the mainland to Lloyd Neck, I could see the salt marsh that occupied that shallow end. It turned gold in the fall. Mom loved it then. In the fall. When the red-gold leaf-colors crowded the water's edge. When the days were as crisp as New York apples. When I brought home flounder from this harbor and Mom broiled them for dinner. When she was happy. A safe place, a calm place, a loved place. This was where her ashes belonged. This little harbor.

Words came later. I had no words when I released my mother from her zip-locked bag. The ashes made a gray streak in the water as the Rose bobbed slowly west. I took a match from my pocket and lit the mailer box. Her baggie was inside it. The box went into the water when I could no longer hold it. The *Rose* and I drifted for a minute or two more, and then the engine came out of idle, and we turned back east, heading for the mouth of the harbor, for the Sound, for Connecticut, to where I live now, which will never be home. I looked over my shoulder, to where I was a little boy. To where I grew up and kissed Katie, the girl whom I have always loved. To where I started flying, and flew through my mother's tears into war, and again through her tears when I flew back. This place to which I flew and flew and flew until flying ended. To my mother's heart-place. This harbor, which has always been our home.

Words are here now. These words. About Celestina, my mother. She will always be a Pandora's box of contradictions to me. No matter how hard I try to bring order to someone who is like a million unanswered questions, flying everywhere, and I reach up to grab just one before another crashes into the one I hold in my hand. The one I think I understand. I don't. What I finally figured out is that I am never going to understand my mother. All I ever needed to do was just love her.

"Love me," Celestina asked.

I did. All she asked of me was to love her. I did. She needed me to love her. I did.

Every time I bring the *Rose* out of Rowayton, as I ease her into the Sound, I look south, across the water to the three stacks at Asharoken. I always look. The Long Island coast. To the west, a few miles along the beach, are the bluffs that mark the old Field estate. Just east of those bluffs is Fiddlers Green. Where I grew up. Where Mom and Dad and our home will always be. Where I returned with Mom, with Dolly, with Celestina. So that I could finally let her go.

My friend Darwin Kellogg had a "gentleman's farm" in Enumclaw, just southeast of Seattle. And on this farm, he had a rooster (E I E I O). Darwin was convinced the rooster was the anti-Christ. The bird guarded the henhouse with unmatched malevolence and was ready to attack any, and all, intruders. Darwin watched from his front porch as his young son and some of his son's friends, absorbed in a game of tag, blundered into the domain of that miserable creature. The knot of little boys tore around the backside of that henhouse and then reversed their direction because the rooster, intent on defending his territory, was in hot pursuit, running and then jumping, spurs flailing, at the fanny of the last kid in the pack.

"Help. Dad! Help," Darwin's son hollered at the top of his lungs. Darwin, who had repeatedly warned them to stay away from the rooster, just laughed. And then yelled back, "You're on your own, Ward."

Karma never forgets. Darwin, unable to run because of a sore back, opened the gate to the fence that surrounded the henhouse to collect eggs, and the rooster appeared out of nowhere. Darwin had his large housecat in his arms. The rooster levitated on outstretched wings, spurs bared, and began to slash away at Darwin's pajama pants. The house cat clawed its way to high ground, which happened to be the top of Darwin's bald head. Blood was trickling down his nose. And he heard laughter from the porch. It was his son, Ward, laughing.

"Help, Ward. Help."

"You're on your own Dad."

This was how I felt when both of my parents had died. On my own. There was no one between me and the abyss, between me and the promise of a heaven made by a God I still wanted to believe in.

I know that my children are on the "porch" watching as I grow older, grow nearer to the edge of eternity. What I regretted when my mother and father died was that there were so many things left unsaid between us. I regretted that I had so many words left over that I should have used.

I need to be sure that, for the people I love, who come after me, I use all the words.

# Chapter 18

# My Old Heart

"Maybe she'll marry again. Maybe she won't. But whatever happens, bury me near her. Please, please, let me be her favorite ghost."

Sherman Alexie

It was so early. I woke up on 20 September 2017 at 4am, unable to catch my breath. I lay still and tried to go back to sleep. But I couldn't. I felt like I had an elephant sitting on my chest, sitting on my heart. Something was wrong. My old heart was not working the way it was supposed to work. At 6am I got up, let the dogs out and brought in the *New York Times*. The pooches raced back into the house, into the kitchen, and began their morning "give me my carrot" dance. The dogs in and out, the carrot dance, the *New York Times*, all of this was normal morning stuff. Except for the way I struggled to breathe. This was not normal morning stuff.

I called my cardiologist to explain to her how I felt. Dr. Cusack said that I was to go to the emergency room at Stamford Hospital "right now." Katie took me. She was calm but riveted on her driving. I teased her about her aggressiveness, and how she learned to drive in Pakistan. From a turbaned cabbie. Who was a maniac. In the emergency room I was hooked up to blood pressure and heart rate monitors and was given an EKG. The diagnosis was congestive heart failure, and atrial fibrillation. I had never been sick.

At Stamford I was wheeled up to the ninth floor, the cardiac floor. How did this happen? I had been a six-days a week gym rat. I was a runner until I tore my Achilles tendon four years ago. Now I was waiting for the staff cardiologists to tell me what they planned to do to me. To my heart.

It was Wednesday, about two o'clock. My window faced south, toward Long Island Sound. The afternoon sun turned the whitecaps to golden bursts of water. The sunlight didn't shimmer; it ricocheted off the waves. I had to squint into it to make out defined shapes. I smiled, realizing that definition wasn't necessary. The sunlight was enough.

The view was beautiful, and comforting, because it was familiar. From here Stamford drifted toward Shippan Point. I was able to see across the Sound to Long Island, to Lloyd Neck. To where I grew up. The sand bluffs above the stretch of beach announced the Field Estate were easy to pick out. They marked Diamond Point, a natural jetty that created a rip tide that Striped Bass loved. I fished here for years with my father.

I was able to see the entrance to Cold Spring Harbor. Just out of sight was West Neck Beach, where I spent my college summers being a lifeguard and perfecting my cool moves on all the 14-year-old girls who parked their beach towels around the white guard stands. At the east end of Lloyd Neck was the entrance to Huntington Bay, to Katie Grace Land, where Katie grew up, where my debutante waltzed through her perfect childhood. And where a not-so-perfect boy, who was me, loved her madly. Nothing has changed.

The day nurse took my blood pressure. The IV in my right arm was for drugs only. The vampires that lived in the basement only accepted blood from the crook of my left arm.

"You have great veins."

Day Nurse Stephanie drew another half a gallon. I am so glad.

As the afternoon wandered into night, I ordered dinner. The hospital called it room service. I had my own menu. So, I ordered a Caesar Salad which I was told I could not have, and a decaf iced tea which I was told I could not have. I was allowed to have a shredded carrot salad with raspberry vinaigrette and water though. The sodium / caffeine police had organized my menu for me. Lots of stuff on the menu I had was now crossed off.

It was time for Katie to go home. She had been with me since early in the morning and the pooches had been baby-gated off in the kitchen all day.

"Should I come back?"

No. Her day had been as long as mine, and worry showed heavily in her eyes. Katie had to be as tired as I was.

"Go home and rest."

She would come back in the morning to be here for doctors' rounds. We should see the cardiologists then. Katie knew the questions to ask.

"I'm practically a nurse, you know."

She told me this often, a line she used which always made me laugh. She has always been brilliant.

189

The day was gone. The lights of Stamford stopped at the black void of the Sound. Only a few lights shone from Lloyd Neck. The red lights from the smokestacks at Asharoken flashed to the east. There was no warmth through my window. And just to intensify my gloomy mood I turned on PBS because I couldn't help it. Ken Burns's Vietnam documentary. Profound sorrow. More heartache for a heart that already ached.

There's this sound that rotor blades make. Every time I hear this sound, I go straight back to 1969, straight back to Vietnam. The sound of the rotor blades is always the same. Except when they are shot up or chewed up. Then they don't go "whupwhupwhupwhupwhup" anymore. Sometimes they are like tattered sails that have been shredded by bursts of ground fire. Sometimes they are mangled by treetops which the blades have struck trying to get close enough to the jungle floor to lift our troopers out. Sometimes rope ladders are lowered through the leafy canopy. Sometimes just ropes. Our recon teams scramble up into the Hueys. Sometimes they are shot before they make it. I see them fall. Mangled rotor blades always sound like "kawhupwhup kawhupwhup kawhupwhup."

Night Nurse Stephanie arrived. It was nine o'clock and the floor was very quiet. I glanced at the cart that she wheeled in and automatically stuck out my left arm. She automatically drew another half-gallon of blood. How many vampires were hiding out in the basement anyway? A "pulse-ox" was clothes pinned to my finger.

"Oh, that's a pulse-ox," Katie said when the emergency-room nurse had used it earlier in the day. How the hell does she know this stuff?

The faces in the Vietnam documentary are the faces of boys. Not grizzled tough guys. Boys. Even Army Lieutenant Matt Harrison, who is old at 24 is just a boy. He is a West Point graduate, class of 1966. We call West Point grads "ring knockers." Lieutenant Harrison is inserted by a Huey onto Hill 875, southwest of *Dak To*. So many boys on both sides give their lives in a pointless fight for a pointless piece of ground. And then this shattered, treeless hilltop is abandoned by us and by the North Vietnamese. The carnage is unspeakable. I can see that Harrison's heart aches still. Like Matt Harrison, I am a 24-year-old lieutenant then too. I am a boy then too. Back then I am a boy too.

Night Nurse Stephanie wrapped the blood-pressure cuff around my bicep and pressed the machine to "on." I couldn't see the read out; the monitor was turned away from me. But I was able to see the numbers, systolic over diastolic, register in her eyes, which grew big. She made a hurried phone call. I needed my blood pressure medication adjusted. A lot. The new dosage was pushed through the IV in my right arm and into my vein. Stephanie took another reading a half-hour later. Frowning, she was on the phone again. More stuff through my IV. She waited another half-hour and then my blood pressure was retaken. Stephanie's eyes relaxed. She smiled now.

"That's better."

I don't want to watch TV, but I can't help myself. Maybe I'm looking for Fritz. I know he's dead. Charles tells me he is. Charles sees Fritz fall face-first from the Huey onto matted-down elephant grass. Ground fire is too intense to try to gather his body back into the helicopter. Maybe I'm looking for Donald. I know he's dead. I see his faceless head held in place by his flight helmet. Maybe I'm looking for…

"Stop looking," I tell myself. This can go on for hours. One name after another. One name after another.

Two cardiologists saw me on this bright Thursday morning. They came because Katie demanded that they come.

"Where have you been?" Katie asked. She and I have been here since yesterday and this was the first time someone from cardiology had seen us. Despite their belated arrival the doctors were gentle and reassuring and informing. They explained that I wasn't "critical." Yesterday they had patients whose hearts were in more danger than mine was. And maybe the procedures I needed could be performed today! So, no lunch for me. Not until later, when it was determined that there wasn't enough time for surgery today. Katie stretched out next to me on my bed. The Sound in my window glinted with the afternoon sun. We looked to the south, toward our childhood. I held her hand.

"We were always meant to be together," she said.

"Always," I said, and kissed her.

Thursday had slipped into evening. My window was cold again, and so was I. Katie, weary from the stress of this day, was cold too. She went home. Night Nurse Christina came to draw more blood. Midnight snack for the vampires I guessed. She took my blood pressure, which was better than last night, and then glanced up at the TV. PBS and the war.

"Were you there?"

I think I will be there forever. Christina squeezed the diuretic into my IV. I was started on this stuff last night and I've been like the Trevi Fountain ever since. We talked a little more and she told me to get some rest.

"Oh sure! I'll just take a pillow into the bathroom," I laughed.

I couldn't sleep because memories I'd rather not revisit showed up anyway. I tried to change the subject. I tried to picture the small of Katie's back and the way my fingertips felt when I traced circles across her shoulders. Tonight, it wasn't working. Thinking about tomorrow's surgery didn't relax me either. I worried about what the surgeon might find. I lost Katie once, years ago. I was not ready to lose her again.

A "Loach," an OH-6, has to make an emergency landing on *Dak Seang's* already cratered runway. The little scout helicopter crosses over the Special Forces camp at about 50 ft, with his partner, a Huey Cobra gunship, in trail behind him. Despite the Cobra blazing away with his miniguns, the Loach takes enough ground fire from the NVA to cripple it. The pilot and the observer jump out of the Loach the minute its skids touch the ground and race for a bunker not far from the side of the runway. About half-way there they are passed by five Vietnamese troops going in the opposite direction. The aircrew dives into the bunker. The five ARVNs dive into the two-man Loach.

I am flying at about 100 ft above the camp, directing helicopter gunships on targets, mostly heavy weapons that I find, while staying as close to the compound as I can. The disabled helicopter and its new occupants are right under my nose. And because the NVA are right on top of the barbed wire perimeter they can see the Loach as well, so they start walking mortar rounds toward it. When a round impacts about a 100 meters from the downed Loach one of the ARVNs sticks his head out of the observer's open door. When the next round lands 50 meters closer, the other four almost trample him trying to get away. Even though the run-over ARVN is the last guy out of the helicopter he beats his buddies to the same bunker the Loach's crew made a beeline to.

At the outset of this battle, I think that this must be Armageddon. I think for certain that this rage of combat is going to rend the earth open and expose hell itself. The dead are everywhere. This is what carnage really means. And then a lunatic Keystone Kops, run for the bunker, run for the Loach, routine takes place. And I can't help but smile. I am not laughing because I can see the dead sapper that I killed, still tangled in the perimeter's concertina wire. But I know I am smiling because I see my reflection in the

Bird Dog's little rear-view mirror. I am smiling a smile that lasts until a .51 sends rounds whipping by my cockpit. These fuckers.

At 4 am Nurse's Aide Shawnte wheeled in a scale to weigh me. Didn't everyone get weighed at 4 am? I extended my left arm without her asking and she poked it with a new IV that was to be used for surgery. Shawnte taped the IV in place and then swabbed my left arm again. She seemed half-awake as she wrapped the rubber band around my bicep. But she was painless when draining my blood, and I could hear Dracula leading cheers in the basement. Breakfast was on the way. Shawnte asked me if she could get me anything. Like what? I'm not allowed to have anything. I'm supposed to be in surgery in five hours. I can't even have a sip of water. Water? The very suggestion had me heading for the bathroom. Again.

"You could go back to sleep?"

Oh. please!

I was in pre-op by 9.30 Friday morning, and Katie was with me until the nurse told her that she couldn't be. The plan was to snake a catheter up my right arm and into my heart, entering from my wrist. If the snarl of veins at my elbow couldn't be navigated, then plan B was to enter through my groin. A very efficient nurse in purple scrubs, a Harley pin on her tunic, with tattoo-covered arms, and very short blond hair shaved my forearm. She announced that she also had to prep for plan B. Now equipped with an electric razor and a little vacuum she man-scaped my crotch. My pubic hair was trimmed into a "landing strip." Almost a bikini wax for boys. I was laughing, but not out loud.

I closed my eyes and scenes of wounded soldiers crowded my brain. Dirty compression bandages over bloody wounds, eyes scrunched up from pain, shredded leaves on splintered trees, raw earth churned up by artillery fire. But I was in Stamford and there was a buffer of decades protecting me from the profound agony of remembered combat. Compared to combat this was easy. This was like R&R, Rest and Relaxation, a vacation from the war.

I sensed the catheter crawling up my arm even though I couldn't really feel it because I couldn't move. I was immobilized by drugs, but I was able to hear all the conversations in the operating theater. The surgeon had found two blockages and asked for number sixteen stents. They were going to reopen the arteries with stents. Except one of the attending nurses advised the surgeon that she wasn't sure if there were any number sixteen stents available.

"Let me look."

I pictured her rummaging around in the storage room, digging through bins of gizmos and other assorted bits of hardware.

"Don't think there are any," she said.

"Okay, how about a number fifteen?"

"Not sure about them either."

I joined the conversation.

"How about you call Home Depot?"

The surgeon burst out laughing and then told me to shut up. Propofol was injected into my IV and my lights went out.

I was forbidden to move my right arm. There was a hole near my wrist that was covered by a compression bandage. Katie fed me Italian Wedding Soup she brought from home. I loved the funny irony of this. She constantly reminded me of my mixed heritage, my Irish and Italian ancestry. But this straight-up Irish princess made a great Italian Wedding Soup.

We were both glad this day was done. I felt so much better, and so did Katie. The stents brought all parts of my heart, except for the Atrium, back into rhythm. We would get the atrial fibrillation fixed in a few weeks. And I'd probably get to go home tomorrow morning (I do). It had been a very long day. I took Katie's hand and kissed it. I kissed her cheek. I kissed her lips. I held her as close as I could. It was almost dark outside. We said goodnight. We said, "I love you."

Sleep wouldn't come. The diuretic injected into my IV every night had me peeing every ten minutes all night long. I turned on the TV and scanned the guide to see what was on. Who am I kidding? I went to PBS. I went back to that war again. I went back to that war that I was once a part of again. I went back. It was like a magnet. I could not stay away. How did I ever do that, I wondered?

"How did anyone do any of that."

I think in Burns's documentary that it was Marine Lieutenant Karl Marlantes who said that, with his company pinned down by automatic weapons fire, he just stood up. He just stood up! Lieutenant Marlantes advanced up Hill 484, on the machine guns that were chewing up his soldiers. He thought he was alone. But after the North Vietnamese guns were knocked out, he looked around and saw the faces of 19-year-old kids who stood up with him. Wasn't that what we all did? Those of us who volunteered. We all stood up.

I dream again.

I am over Cambodia, flying south toward the *Ia Drang Valley* to check out possible landing zones, hanging out the left window, looking for trucks, or troops. And for no reason an eerie sense of uneasiness causes me to pull my head and shoulders back into the airplane and to straighten up. I look behind me. I have company, flying formation with me, just behind my right wing. So close we can pass lunches or hand grenades to one another. Where has this guy come from? A Cambodian Air Force T-28. A propeller-driven airplane that is much bigger than my Bird Dog. And I think I see machine guns mounted to "hard points," to attachment brackets, under his wings. His landing gear is down so that he can fly as slow as I fly at normal cruise. His wing flaps are also down, the universal signal to surrender. Cambodia is still a neutral country, and I'm not supposed to be in Cambodia or be flying around over it. Except that I am. I am violating their neutrality, which is nothing new. Everybody here has been ignoring Cambodia's neutrality for years.

The pilot points at me and then points at the ground. He again points at me which means that I am supposed to follow him. Fat chance of that. I can't outrun him, but I think I can "out-juke" him. Sweat is dripping off the tip of my nose. I flip the Bird Dog upside-down and then dive straight at the ground. I hear a few rounds snap by my cockpit window. I am ever grateful for lousy shots. I don't pull out of my dive until I am on the treetops. The engine is "red lined," at haul-ass power, my Bird Dog going as fast as it can go. I am heading east, twisting, turning, running back into Vietnam. More bullets from the Cambodian, which all miss, because there are no straight lines of flying from me. As I cross the border – I know exactly where I am – I turn around to look. The T-28 has broken off and doesn't follow me into Vietnam. I am home free. The rest of the war in a Cambodian prison? Not a chance in hell.

How do I do any of this? Because I say I will. I volunteer, I give my word. Scared to death? Of course. But I am even more frightened by the idea that I may be perceived as a coward, especially by me. I put one foot in front of the other. And no matter how hard it is to get them to move, I make them move. I am terrified, and that is allowed. But failing to do what I say I'll do? No, no. That never enters my mind. I wake up. The vampires want breakfast.

We were home from the hospital before lunch on Saturday. I didn't want lunch. I wanted a shower. That tiny little hole in my wrist where the catheter was inserted was covered with a clear plastic adhesive that was like super-glue multiplied by fifty.

"Don't get it wet," Saturday's Day Nurse Jessica warned me. No problem there. I was going to have to melt this stuff off with Katie's hair dryer. If she'd let me borrow it, that is. She's always protective of her beauty accessories, and she's always skeptical of my commitment to my feminine side. I'd get the bandage off tomorrow while "Almost a Nurse" was at work. She'd never know so long as I put the hair dryer back exactly as I found it. Because she was also "Almost Sherlock Holmes" too. Right now, it was shower time.

I was allowed to drive on Monday, so I went down to Rowayton. It was quiet on the dock. I pulled the cover off the Whaler and perched myself on the big seat in the bow. I christened my old boat *Wild Irish Rose* after this girl I know. Every year on my birthday I gave Katie a gift and a mushy card, with the same note each time.

"Thank you for saving me from myself."

From now on I could add,

"Thank you for saving my heart. Thank you for being so much of what's good in my life."

I have never forgotten how close I had come to losing her.

# Last Words

No amount of explanation can do justice to the selfless message this expanse of black granite, this V-shaped Memorial, this compilation of names and dates, delivers. This symbol of anguish, of the war in Vietnam. It tabulates the cost of our misadventure. A sacrifice of youth. A collage of the faces of those I know here. I have been here before, although it has been a while. I am glad to be back, because I can visit friends, speak the chiseled names of those I know, honor the gift of their lives, and bear witness to their courage. I know I will cry. I always do. I will try to describe this place to Katie. I can't. She needs to see it. That's why we come here. It is our first trip after my heart surgery. Seven months after my heart surgery. I am strong enough now. The two stents in my arteries have seen to that.

It is a bright and sunny Friday morning, this 20 April 2018 morning. I steady the ladder while the docent makes a pencil rubbing of the name I point out. I ask for five rubbings of that name. He is happy to oblige me. And after he completes each rubbing, he hands it to Katie. He gives my wife an envelope in which to put the rubbings so that they don't smear. So that they don't wrinkle. She is careful with them.

The docent asks me if I am a veteran and was I in Vietnam. I tell him I was a FAC, a Forward Air Controller in the Central Highlands. He tells me he was a Marine on the DMZ.

Katie holds the rubbings and I steady the ladder as the docent climbs down. While I fold the ladder the docent retrieves a button from his bag. It says "Vietnam War Veteran" on its face, an eagle in the center. On the back, "A Grateful Nation Thanks You." It's about time, I think. But I would never say that. Not to this man. He hugs me. I am barely containing my tears.

The day I write this, 27 April, marks the anniversary of Major Frederick Krupa's death. Forty-seven years ago, today. Shot out of the doorway of the helicopter that inserted Fritz and his "Hatchet Force" reconnaissance company into the *Plei Trap* Valley. Fritz fell from the UH-1 Huey helicopter onto the elephant grass of the Landing Zone. He is still there. The rubbings are of his name. For men who knew him. Four pilots. Captains John Meyers, Phil Phillips, Charles Ford, and me. And a Green Beret, Sergeant Michael Buckland, who I believe is the bravest of us all.

The rubbings, in protective sleeves that say "Vietnam Memorial" are mailed in puffy envelopes to John, Phil, Charles, and Michael. No note. Only the rubbings. I hope they arrive today. We all remember this day. No half a century of cobwebs obscuring the memory. Phil and I were home from the war when Fritz died. John too, I think. Charles was flying, and Michael was at the Special Forces camp in *Kontum*. Waiting. Fritz never came back. On a layover in Mobile, while flying for Delta, Charles and I had breakfast together. He told me about how Frederick Krupa died. Charles Ford, born and raised in Mobile, still lives there.

Katie and I walk beside the black granite panels. I tell her that these panels, so many etched names, tally the price of this pointless war. She is fierce in her protection of me. I am finally opening the door to my terrible year. She opens her heart to protect mine. Katie takes my hand, holds me together, cradles my grief, caresses my sorrow. I need her. Her eyes tell me that she knows how much.

Katie and I pass the statues of the nurses; I remember Faye as we walk. I saw her, my college friend, at the big Evac Hospital in *Qui Nhon*. She became an Army nurse, to pay for her education. The Army sent her to nursing school, and then it sent her to the war. My unit's big headquarters was in *Qui Nhon*. I delivered an airplane to HQ, borrowed a jeep, and found Faye. She had a golden aura. She had angel's wings. She had a halo. Because she tried to give life every chance she could. And in her face, I saw the sleepless nights. I also saw the blood, the trauma, the amputations, the screaming, and the nightmares. I wondered then if, when she returned home, her nightmares were going to be worse than mine.

The rest of the day is spent at the National Gallery. There is an exhibition of Cezanne. Katie and I visited, a decade ago, his atelier in *Aix*. Today's display of paintings is clearly brighter than the dark weight of the morning's black granite. I feel better. We find the Da Vinci on special exhibit. Then Cassatt, Rembrandt, Van Gogh, and, my favorite, Vermeer. They celebrate life. I feel much better.

A bright and sunny Saturday morning, this 21 April morning. Katie drives past Marymount, a two-year college when she went there, a university now. We're headed to Dulles Airport, to the big Smithsonian Air and Space Museum annex. A hangar filled with airplanes. One airplane I can hardly wait to show her.

Hanging from the ceiling is a Bird Dog, a Cessna O-1, the airplane I flew over the Ho Chi Minh Trail. The airplane I flew so low one day a North Vietnamese soldier threw a rock at me. He had either run out of ammunition or run out of respect. I'm not sure which. Or if it even mattered.

Katie has seen pictures of my Bird Dog, old photos from the war. Of me flying it. She now can see how small it was, how vulnerable we were. The O-1 hanging there in front of us, dwarfed by almost everything else. The museum has an elevated walkway that goes around the building so all the airplanes that are suspended by wires are at eye level. An airplane little girls saw as insignificant, inadequate, almost unworthy compared to their grandfather's B-24. Katie takes a picture of an aging pilot standing in front of a little airplane that somehow kept him safe, that somehow delivered him home in one piece.

We look at all the other airplanes gathered in the Smithsonian annex. There are helicopters used for recon team insertions, fighter-bombers used for protecting those teams if they got in trouble. They always did in the spring of 1970.

I recognize planes I worked with flying the mission over the border. They recall sounds, sounds merge into a jumbled cacophony. The collective sounds of firefights, of Special Forces camps being overrun, of hand-to-hand combat, of inevitable death. Rotor blades beating the air, jet engines roaring, voices yelling over radios, rockets whooshing at the ground, bullets snapping by my cockpit's open windows. I look around the museum every few minutes, looking back at the Bird Dog hanging from the ceiling.

"Thank you for saving my life."

I think now that Katie understands why composure is so hard to maintain. How difficult that year was, 4 September 1969 – 4 September 1970. How personal it was. Because my death was a possibility every day. Because I knew the names of too many friends, Fritz included, etched on black granite. Because my ride home, my Bird Dog, was so small, its thin sheet metal skin no protection at all, really. Because my Bird Dog and I had to survive together. That was the only way to avoid the black granite. Because, when all was said and done, this beautiful, gallant, tough as nails Bird Dog saved me. It brought me home. It delivered me. To this moment. To this person. To my Katie. I will never let go of her hand.

These are all the words I have.

# Acknowledgements

On the first night of my first creative writing class the instructor, Rifke Krummel, said that all good writing was about love and death. I wrote that in my notebook. Her words were my compass. They always will be.

My friend Michael Buckland and I spent hours together in a Bird Dog over the Ho Chi Minh Trail. He was on his third tour with the Studies and Observation Group in the Central Highlands of Vietnam, a Special Forces sergeant. When I first met him, Bucky ran the photo shop at Forward Observation Base Two, in *Kontum*. He went on to become a professor of Aviation Science at the University of Alaska. Dr. Buckland spent hours on the phone with me, helping me to understand the part I played in a very secret war. I could not have asked for a better resource, or a better friend.

Captains Claude Phillips, John Meyers, Douglas Krout, and Charles Ford, my fellow SPAFs, I'm alive today because of you. Thank you for flying above me and below me and on my wing. We survived because of our devotion to one another. I'd call that love.

I met my agent, Ann Tanenbaum, in a bar. Well, sort of in a bar. She was having lunch at Caffe Grazie, on 84th Street, close to the Metropolitan Museum of Art, sitting at the bar and having a salad bigger than she is. Katie and I were having lunch with Katie's sister Sharon. Sitting in a nearby banquette. Sharon asked me how a reading I gave at Fordham-Westchester went. Katie responded first, telling her sister that I mumbled too much. And Ann was eavesdropping. Of course she was. As we were leaving Ann asked if any of us were writers. Katie and Sharon pointed at me, and Ann asked me if I would like to submit some of my work to her. I didn't submit some work. I submitted all my work. A pile of essays. I had no manuscript. Just a pile of essays. She liked what I had done, she liked me, and I liked her. We signed each other up. Lucky me. Ann recently brought on Kate Ellsworth as her assistant. Brilliant move. Brilliant Kate.

At the Westport Writers Workshop in Westport, Connecticut I encountered two magical, inspirational women. Outstanding mentors. Lyrical, beautiful writers. Christine Pakkala and Julie Sarkissian. For six years they listened and critiqued my work. And for six years they encouraged me, pushed me, and became my friends. Allison Dickens, also at the Workshop, was a senior editor at Penguin and Random House. Allison's classes gave order to my work. She took a very raw manuscript and made it flow smoothly. I would have been lost without her help. I would have been lost without help from all of them.

Five writers from the Workshop meet weekly to critique one another's work. Alfred G. Vanderbilt named the group the "Renegades." Only he knows why. We have been together for two years, teasing, criticizing, suggesting, and praising one another's efforts. Rebecca Martin, Deborah Kasden, Holly Mensching, and Alfred have been generous with their time and suggestions, as well as unsparing in their criticism of my writing and my occasional, pointed sarcasm. I love this group.

Jean Williamson Carter has read and corrected every word I have written. Every word. She is the younger sister of a childhood friend and volunteered to be my reader. I know there were several times when she wished she had never spoken up. Like when I sent her about a hundred pages of work without telling her how many pages I sent or that I forgot to number them. She automatically hit the print button on her phone, which fired up her printer and turned her den into a cluttered, unnumbered, mess. But she stuck with me, and had it not been for her help I'd still be stuck on my first chapter. There is no way to repay Jean for her loyalty, her generosity, her encouragement, and her experience as an English teacher. Because grammatically, I was hopeless. Thank you, Jean. For every corrected tense, for every corrected punctuation. More importantly, thank you for the questions. The "where are you going with this" questions that made me rethink direction, content, continuity. Without you, dear Jean, there would be no book. Thank you, thank you, thank you.

Finally, my wife Katie. The girl at the top of Richard Lane. My usually-but-not-always patient wife, who kept me on task, who encouraged me and cajoled me and pushed me to stay with this project. It was you, who stood by my side and held my hand at the West Point gravesite of my friend John Pappas, a very special man with whom I flew at the end of my tour in

# ACKNOWLEDGEMENTS

Vietnam. I cried that day, and you asked me to tell you what the tears were about. You asked me to tell you what prompted tears you'd never seen. And that opened the door to writing about a year in my life I thought I would never revisit. You gave me the time, the space, the encouragement I needed. Thank you, my Katie. For insisting that I see this work through. I will never let go of your hand.

# References

Burns, Ken, *The Vietnam War* (Documentary) 2017, WETA/Florentine Films

Caputo, Phillip, *A Rumor of War* 1977, Holt, Rinehart and Winston

Cowee, Bruce, *Vietnam to Western Airlines Volume 1* 2013, Alive Publishing Group

Cowee, Bruce, *Vietnam to Western Airlines Volume 2* 2017, Alive Publishing Group

Cowee, Bruce, *Vietnam to Western Airlines Volume 3* 2018, Alive Publishing Group

Cowee, Bruce, *Vietnam to Western Airlines Volume 4* 2021, Alive Publishing Group

Creedence Clearwater Revival, *Susie Q* 1968 Fantasy Records. Written by Dale Hawkins, Eleanor Broadwater, and Stan Lewis

Duncan, David Douglas, *War Without Heroes* 1970, Harper and Row

Edelman, Bernard, *Dear America: Letters Home from Vietnam* 1985, W.W. Norton

Gole, Henry G., *Legacy Of Lies: Over the Fence in Laos* 2019, SOG Publishing

Hersey, John, *A Bell for Adano*, 1944, Alfred Knopf

Hooper, Jim, *One Hundred Feet Over Hell* 2009, Zenith Press

Karnow, Stanley, *Vietnam: A History* 1983, The Viking Press

Mahony, Phillip (ed.), *From Both Sides Now: The poetry of the Vietnam War and Its Aftermath* 1998, Scribner

Marlantes, Karl, *Matterhorn: A Novel of the Vietnam War* 2010, Atlantic Monthly Press

Marlantes, Karl, *What It Is Like to Go to War* 2011, Atlantic Monthly Press

McAfee, John P., *Slow Walk in a Sad Rain* 1993, Warner Books

# REFERENCES

Meyer, John Stryker *Across the Fence: The Secret War in Vietnam* 2003, SOG Publishing

O'Brien, Tim, *Going After Cacciato* 1978, Random House

O'Brien, Tim, *The Things They Carried* 1990, Broadway Books

Plaster, John, *SOG: Secret Wars of America's Commandos in Vietnam* 1998, NAL Publishing

Plaster, John, *Secret Commandos: Behind Enemy Lines with the Elite Warriors of SOG* 2005, Dutton Caliber

Plaster, John, SOG: *A Photo History of the Secret War* 2022, Casemate Publishers

Robbins, Christopher, *The Ravens: The Men Who Flew in America's Secret War in Laos* 1987, Crown Publishers

Sullivan, Leo, *The Columbia Eagle Incident* 2021, Edith Lane Publishers

Veterans Writing Workshop, *Afterwords: Who Can Forget* 2018, Fordham Westchester Campus

West, Francis, *The Village* 1972, University of Wisconsin Press

Wolff, Tobias, *In Pharaoh's Army: Memoirs of the Lost War* 1994, Alfred Knopf

# Index

Abt, Frederick, 57, 99
Aiken, George, 4
Annamese Cordillera, 137
Anti-aircraft weapon;
  Chinese .51caliber machine gun,
    52, 72, 146, 164, 193
  Chinese 12.7-millimeter
    machine gun, 91
Ao Dai, 11
Armalite Assault Rifle;
  AR-15, 127, 134
Armstrong, Donald, 4–5, 106,
  109–12, 114–16, 191
Armstrong, Kenji, 106, 111–12
Army Republic of Vietnam
  (ARVN), 76, 119, 139, 192
Avtomat Kalashnikov,
  AK-47, 52, 56, 59, 72, 78–9,
    102–103, 109, 111, 141, 146

Bac Si, 7, 87
Ban Me Thout;
  185th Pterodactyls, 50
Barber, Ted, 10
Bell Huey Cobra, 192
Ben Het, 2
Bernhardsen, Bernie, 174
Bessor, Bruce, 4

Betel Nut, 11
Binh Dinh, 22
Bird Dog, 1, 3–4, 6, 14, 32, 50–2,
  62–4, 71, 73–4, 76–8, 80–3,
  86–7, 91–4, 99, 103, 106,
  109–11, 113, 118, 120, 127,
  129–30, 133–4, 136, 139,
  141–2, 153–5, 157, 163–4, 170,
  193, 195, 199–200
  O-1, 20, 163, 199
  Operation Ford Drum, 96
Boeing 707-720B, 39, 165
Boeing 737, 164
Boeing 767, 164
Bomb Damage Assessment
  (BDA), 99
Brown, Ben, 73, 114, 174
Buckland, Michael, 61, 93–7,
  115, 198
Bu Doi, 15
Burns, Ken, 190, 194
  Documentary, 190, 194

Cambodia, 14, 22–4, 30, 96, 98,
  105, 113, 117, 126, 138, 141,
  180, 195
  Cambodian T-28, 195
  Salem House, 58

Caproni Bomber, 176, 178

Causey, Hank, 163

Celestina, 6, 16–17, 34, 41, 44–5, 55–6, 58, 141, 146, 183–6

Central Highlands, 5, 14, 22, 34, 63, 93, 101, 146

Chaminade High School, 39

China Burma India Theater (CBI), 177

Chu Lai, 6

Cincosky, David, 153

Combat Rations, 15, 90, 96, 118, 126

Command and Control Central (CCC), 57–9, 82, 93, 99–100, 106, 113, 155
Hatchet Force, 93, 198

Consolidated Liberator Bomber;
B-24, 39, 170, 176, 183, 199
Rangoon Harbor, 177

Continental Airlines, 159–60

Covey, 77, 82
Covey Rider, 77
U.S. Air Force FAC, 77

Cozart, Robert, 4

Creedence Clearwater Revival;
Susie Q, 70

Cusack, Dr. Evelyn, 188–9

Da Nang, 6, 9–10, 21, 23, 173

Dak Bla River, 73, 83

Dak Seang, 2, 102–104, 108, 114, 142, 182, 192

Dak To, 2, 85, 90, 95, 103, 108–109, 111, 116–18, 120, 136, 142, 182

Deaton, Arlie, 47–9, 55, 63, 87, 113–16, 118, 126–8, 137, 139, 142, 153–4, 163–4, 168–9, 178

DeGuira, Anthony "Diggie", 145, 147–8

DeHavilland;
Beaver, 113–4, 142
Otter, 9, 20–1

Delta Airlines, 165–6, 169, 172, 198

Deuce and a half, 17

Direct Air Support Center (DASC), 135

Doherty, Alanna, 88, 105, 169–74

Doherty, Francis John (Dad), 29–31, 33–41, 44–5, 50, 70-1, 145–6, 165–6, 175–83

Doherty, Glenn, 144–5

Doherty, Meighan, 105, 169–74

Doherty, Terry, 35, 144–5, 180

Dong Ha, 6

Douglas A-1 Skyraider, 28, 100, 135, 137, 140, 181
Spad, 137, 140

Demilitarized Zone (DMZ), 9, 145, 197

Du Co, 23, 58, 128

Duckworth, Clarence, 174

Dutch Roll, 3

Fiddlers Green, 34, 185–6

Finch, Charles, 155

Flying Tigers, 83

Ford, Charles, 125, 127, 147, 174, 191, 198
"Jerry", 125, 127

Forward Observation Base 2 (FOB2), 57, 64, 77, 115
Fort Knox, Kentucky, viii, 6, 42, 55, 60, 68, 99, 145, 151
  Armor Officer Basic School, 42, 61, 151
Fort Ord, California, 71
  DeHavilland Otter School, 71
Fort Rucker, Alabama, 20, 70, 142, 156–7, 159
  Army Aviation Center 70
Fort Stewart, Georgia, 44, 114, 163
  Primary Flight School, 44, 46
Forward Air Controller, 66
  FAC, 56, 66, 136, 197

Gabriel, Faye, 198
Glashauser, Gregory, 61, 78–84, 86–7, 141
Goodenough, Phillip, 154
  Hardly, 154
Grace, Katie, 83, 101, 104, 107, 149–52, 188–9, 191–2, 194, 196, 197–200
  Richard Lane, 35, 101, 152
Green Berets, 96, 98
Grenade Launcher;
  M79, 86
Gole, Henry, 52
Guttrobb, Edwin C., 123, 130, 132, 146
  Gutz, 123–8, 131

Headhunter Four-Five, 26
Heinbaugh, William, 163–4
Hey Blue, 101, 112

Ho Chi Minh Trail, 2, 5, 24, 27, 50–2, 56, 59, 77, 82, 98, 110–11, 113, 180, 197
Holloway, 22–3, 30, 34, 77, 79, 81, 84–5, 98, 113, 118, 133, 129–30, 136, 141, 155
  219th Aviation Company, 22–3, 30, 120, 168, 173
Hue Citadel, 6, 10–11, 23
Hue Phu Bai;
  220th Catkillers, 50
Huey, 10–11, 90, 100, 129–30, 135–6, 140, 198
  UH1-C Gunship, 103
Hughes OH-6 Loach, 192

Ia Drang Valley, 58, 88, 195
Idlewild Airport, 36
  John F. Kennedy Airport, 40

Jackson, Robert, 128–30, 174
Jaynettes, 78
  Sally Go Round the Roses, 78

Kane, Richard, 174
Kellogg, Darwin, 186–7
Kontum, 1, 22–3, 54, 69, 70, 73–4, 76, 87, 92, 104, 111, 113, 116, 118, 120, 122, 124, 129, 142, 155
Krout, Doug, 61, 76–7, 79, 93, 146, 174
Krupa, Frederick, 4, 6, 80, 191, 197, 199
Kung, 64-6
Kurley, Joseph, 174

La Guardia Airport, 37, 42
Lafayette Escadrille, 83, 176
 Spad, France, 176
Landing Zone (LZ), 59, 77, 80, 100
Laos, 30, 77, 79, 80–3, 86, 88–91,
 95, 96, 98, 105, 114, 117–19,
 141, 180
 Daniel Boone, 58
Levittown, 36
Lloyd Harbor, 69, 185
Lloyd Neck, 8, 144, 185, 188–90
 Battle of Long Island, 185
 Target Rock, 185
Lockheed Constellation;
 C-130 Hercules, 8, 73–4, 142, 181
 Connie, 37
 Hillsboro, 95
Long Islander, 16
Los Angeles International Airport
 (LAX), 159–60, 164

Mag Drop;
 Magnetos 75-6
Marble Mountain, 9, 12
Marlantes, Karl, 194
Marymount, 150
McDonnell Douglas;
 F-4 Phantom, 4, 181
 MD88, 166
Mekong River, 117
Meyers, John, 28, 61, 79, 84, 87,
 141, 146, 174, 198
Military Advisory Command
 Vietnam (MACV), 8, 76, 80
 MACVSOG, 106, 106, 108,
  144, 155, 180
 MACV Compound, 115-16,
  122, 125

Military Auxiliary Radio
 Station, 68
 MARS, 68
Montagnards, 73, 92, 100, 102
 Rhade Tribe, 57

Naked Sandy, 61, 79, 122,
 150, 153
Naumann, David, 22, 30–2, 84–5
New York City, 152
 Grand Central Station, 152
New York Times, 145–6,
 153, 188
Nha Trang, 6, 72, 142
Nguyen Dynasty, 10
North Vietnamese Army (NVA),
 2, 24, 29, 78, 89–90, 92, 94–5,
 106, 119, 129
 Charlie, 56, 74–5
Nouc Mam, 137
Nung Mercenaries;
 Ethnic Chinese, 70, 102

Pappas, John, 101, 107,
 128–9, 133–6, 141, 158,
 168–9, 174
 West Point, 101, 108, 134
Pathet Lao, 119–22
Phillips, Phil, 59–61, 76–7, 79, 93,
 107, 109–12, 114–16, 122–6,
 150, 153, 169, 172–4, 198
Pho, 72
 Pho Ga, 85
Pisacreta, George, 4, 6, 153
Plaster, John, 61, 88–90, 99, 141
 Recon Team California, 92
Plei Djerang, 76, 142
Pleiku, 22–3, 29, 30–3, 58

Plei Trap Valley, 134, 139, 142, 158, 198
Polei Kleng, 134, 139
Poole, Jerry, 4, 99–101, 112
    Recon Team Pennsylvania, 100
Prairie Fire, 26
Promotion to captain, 99

Quang Ngai, 6, 9, 23
Qui Nhon, 6, 9, 20–1, 23, 113–14, 142,
    Evac Hospital, 198

Reserve Officer Training Corps (ROTC), 40
Ridgeway, Willie, 114, 116
Rivers, Mickey, 161

Saigon, 6
Saigon Cowboys, 12
Saint Patrick's School, 16–18, 149
Satchel Charge, 102–103
    Sapper, 102–103
Savani, George, 174
Segal, Robert, 174
Shelly, James, 130
Shields, Gordon, 159
    Western Airlines Chief Pilot, 159–60
Shipp, Donald, 23, 129, 174
Shrode Lake, 179
Sihanouk, Norodom, 98–9, 115, 140
Sister Angela, 15–19, 50, 173
Slimowicz, Charles, 174
Smithsonian Annex, 199

Smithwick, K., 114–17, 124, 143, 146
    SOG Operations Officer, S-3, 114–7, 122
Sneaky Pete Air Force (SPAF), 2, 60, 77, 92, 96, 109, 123–6
    SPAF Jeep, 124–5
Stearman, 175
    Boeing PT-17, 175
Studies and Observations Group (SOG), 2, 30, 62–3, 77, 83–4, 91, 94–5, 96, 98, 101, 118, 122, 128, 131, 138

Tai Chi, 82
Tan Son Nhut, 139, 142
Tay Loc Airfield, 10
Tet Offensive, 10
To Kill a Mockingbird, 151
Trans World Airlines (TWA), 29, 31, 36, 44, 70, 183

University of San Francisco (USF), 39–40, 69, 150

Viet Cong (VC), 9, 12
VC Valley, 128, 141
Vietnam Memorial, 197–8
Vietnamese Air Force (VNAF), 10
Vultee, BT-13, 175

Waters, Muddy, 161
Weaver, Mister, 48–50, 66–7, 178

Western Airlines ('Western'),
    104, 159–60, 164–6, 168, 172
Whaler;
    Boston Whaler, 184
    Wild Irish Rose, 184

Winkler, Bill, 161
Wood, Victor, 4, 153
Wright-Patterson Air Force
    Museum, 170, 175, 178

—